PENTAGON PRESS

COMMITTED TO SERVE THE ARMED FORCES

MONGOLIA TODAY

Internal Changes and External Linkages

MONGOLIA TODAY

Internal Changes and External Linkages

Edited by

Sharad K Soni

Under the auspices of

Area Studies Programme

UGC-CENTRE FOR INNER ASIAN STUDIES

School of International Studies, Jawaharlal Nehru University, New Delhi

PENTAGON PRESS

Mongolia Today: Internal Changes and External Linkages
***Editor*: Sharad K Soni**

ISBN 978-81-8274-858-3

First Published in 2016

Published by
PENTAGON PRESS
206, Peacock Lane, Shahpur Jat,
New Delhi-110049
Phones: 011-64706243, 26491568
Telefax: 011-26490600
email: rajan@pentagonpress.in
website: www.pentagonpress.in

Branch
Flat No.213, Athena-2,
Clover Acropolis,
Viman Nagar,
Pune-411014
Email: pentagonpresspune@gmail.com

Printed at Avantika Printers Private Limited.

CONTENTS

PREFACE

Mongolia, formerly known as the Mongolian People's Republic and also referred to as Outer Mongolia to distinguish it from Inner Mongolia, an autonomous region of China, has the locational disadvantage of being directly associated with countries other than Russia and China. Bordered by Russia to the north, Inner Mongolia Autonomous Region (IMAR) of China to the south, Xinjiang Uighur Autonomous Region (XUAR) of China to the west and rest of China to the east, Mongolia is a landlocked country with a peculiar geostrategic situation. After centuries of being cut off from the international mainstream first because of its remote location and then by Chinese and Russian domination, Mongolia has now come a long way, especially after it staged a democratic revolution of its own in 1989-90. Its democratic evolution has been so successful that one wonders if the Mongolians ever imagined that Mongolia which is Asia's first and the world's second communist state will become the Asian model of democratization in the post-Soviet era. Mongolia's international profile became impressive in July 2011 when it took over as Chair of the Community of Democracies, an intergovernmental organization established in 2000 with a commitment to strengthening and deepening democratic norms and practices within emerging democracies worldwide.

However, Mongolia's transition to a democratic state structure has not been an easy task since it remained isolated from the outside world except the erstwhile Soviet Union for almost seven decades. With the emergence of a new Mongolia following the Soviet collapse in 1991 and subsequently the end of the Cold War, the geostrategic situation surrounding this tiny populated country underwent a change. This has had a significant impact on Mongolia that brought internal changes in political, social, economic and security fields. Having discarded the Soviet style communism and state controlled economy,

Mongolia of today is a young democratic country with free market economy. It seeks to ensure security by strictly observing the policy of not allowing the use of the country's territory against other States. This ensures its Nuclear-Weapon-Free-Zone status at the international level and making it an important element of strengthening the country's security-both strategic and economic-by political means. Thus, safeguarding the country's national interests both internal as well as external has become the main goal of Mongolia. No wonder then that in the democratic era the previously made commitments to strengthen international communist order went into oblivion and instead the pursuit of fundamental national interests described as "pragmatic realism" came into focus.

Mongolia's external linkages today are based on 'third neighbour' foreign policy. In other words, this new foreign policy approach has guided Mongolia to adopt a spirited posture of gracious defiance, rejecting dependency on Russia or China and reaching out to countries that can counterbalance the inclinations and serve as a check on the economic, political, and strategic ambitions of Moscow and Beijing. Even an updated Concept of National Security approved in July 2010 and a revised Concept of Foreign Policy ratified in February 2011 continued giving much emphasis on the 'third neighbour' approach of Mongolia's diplomacy of external relations. From the Mongolian perspective, 'diverse foreign and trade relations are an element of broader stability'. This is relevant given that Mongolia of today possesses abundant natural resources, including Asia's largest copper mine and massive uranium deposits, which points to a promising future in terms of economic growth. The country registered a record of 17.5 per cent growth in 2011 and has since been continuing to maintain a double-digit growth as against 6.4 per cent in 2010 due to an enormous coal and copper mining boom in addition to thriving resources of rare earth minerals, uranium, gold and silver that brought the attention of some quarters to call it as the 'Asian Wolf'.

The central focus of Mongolia's 'third neighbour' policy is on developing a strategic partnership with the US, Germany, India, Japan, the Republic of Korea and Turkey, and an expanded partnership with Canada and Australia. It is more so because they are geographically distant and do not present the same jeopardies that its immediate neighbours can potentially do. Nonetheless, one crucial challenge faced by the Mongolian leadership is to achieve a balance of influence between the two immediate neighbours-Russia and China by building on the strong economic and political competition in which they engage in Mongolia.

With regard to India and Mongolia, both countries have had civilisational links traversing over a period of 2,500 years despite being geographically far-off. The two countries are the southern and northern ends of a Buddhist arch which provides the cultural foundation of a political and cosy strategic relationship. It is this cultural compatibility that defines the strategic interests of India and Mongolia, which has been observed recently during the first ever visit of Indian Prime Minister Narendra Modi to Mongolia on 17 May 2015. The two countries have the potential to work together in regional and sub-regional groupings as India's 'Act East' policy and Mongolia's 'third neighbour' policy are compatible enough to realise this in the true spirit of a strategic partnership. In the past twenty five years, Mongolia's internal developments and its activities in external linkages demonstrate how democratic principles bind the like-minded countries together and let them take advantage of new economic and political opportunities.

It is against this background that a Student-Faculty Seminar was organized on 26 March 2012 on the theme MONGOLIA TODAY to discuss relevant issues relating to internal changes and external linkages of Mongolia from the historical, cultural, geopolitical, geo-economic and geostrategic perspectives. The Seminar was organised by the UGC's Central Asian Area Studies Programme, Centre for South, Central, Southeast Asian and Southwest Pacific Studies, School of International Studies, Jawaharlal Nehru University, New Delhi. The UGC's Area Studies Programme is now a part of the Centre for Inner Asian Studies.

This book is an outcome of the above mentioned seminar consisting of academics and PhD scholars who are exclusively engrossed in research activities on Mongolia. The book, however, is also a humble attempt to highlight the viewpoints of young research scholars on issues concerning Mongolia today. The whole idea is to provide another addition to the slender collection of literature on Mongolian studies in particular and Inner Asian studies in general which will be an asset for the researchers, students, think-tanks and policy makers. For a proper understanding of the issues concerned the book has been divided into three thematic components: 'Linking Past to Present', 'Connotations of Internal Changes' and 'Assessing External Linkages'. These three components consist of 20 articles discussing various facets of Mongolia's internal changes and also its external linkages.

New Delhi **Sharad K Soni**

LIST OF CONTRIBUTORS

Alok Kumar is a PhD Scholar at Centre for Inner Asian Studies, School of International Studies, Jawaharlal Nehru University, New Delhi.

Anurag Tripathi (PhD) is Assistant Professor at Christ University, Bengaluru.

Guntash Kaur is a PhD Scholar at Centre for Inner Asian Studies, School of International Studies, Jawaharlal Nehru University, New Delhi.

Jitendra Uttam (PhD) is Assistant Professor, Korean Studies Division, Centre for East Asian Studies, School of International Studies, School of International Studies, Jawaharlal Nehru University, New Delhi.

Jyoti Pandey is a PhD Scholar at Centre for Inner Asian Studies, School of International Studies, Jawaharlal Nehru University, New Delhi.

Kundan Kumar is a PhD Scholar at Centre for Inner Asian Studies, School of International Studies, Jawaharlal Nehru University, New Delhi.

Madan Yadav is a PhD Scholar at Centre for Inner Asian Studies, School of International Studies, Jawaharlal Nehru University, New Delhi.

Mahesh Ranjan Debata (PhD) is Assistant Professor at Centre for Inner Asian Studies, School of International Studies, Jawaharlal Nehru University, New Delhi.

Mukesh Kumar Mishra (PhD) is Research Associate at Centre for Inner Asian Studies, School of International Studies, Jawaharlal Nehru University, New Delhi.

Pooja Pingua is a PhD Scholar at Centre for Inner Asian Studies, School of International Studies, Jawaharlal Nehru University, New Delhi.

Raj Deep is a PhD Scholar at Centre for Inner Asian Studies, School of International Studies, Jawaharlal Nehru University, New Delhi.

Rajeev Kumar Raju is a PhD Scholar at Centre for Inner Asian Studies, School of International Studies, Jawaharlal Nehru University, New Delhi.

Renu Sainis a PhD Scholar at Centre for Russian and Central Asian Studies, School of International Studies, Jawaharlal Nehru University, New Delhi.

Ritesh Rai is a PhD Scholar at Centre for Inner Asian Studies, School of International Studies, Jawaharlal Nehru University, New Delhi.

Ritu Jha is a PhD Scholar at Centre for Inner Asian Studies, School of International Studies, Jawaharlal Nehru University, New Delhi.

Santosh Kumar Jha is a PhD Scholar at Centre for Inner Asian Studies, School of International Studies, Jawaharlal Nehru University, New Delhi.

Sharad K Soni (PhD) is Director, UGC Area Studies Programme, Centre for Inner Asian Studies, School of International Studies, Jawaharlal Nehru University, New Delhi.

Subhash Kumar Baitha is a PhD Scholar at Centre for Inner Asian Studies, School of International Studies, Jawaharlal Nehru University, New Delhi.

Vaishali Krishna (PhD) holds her Doctorate in Mongolian Studies from Centre for Inner Asian Studies, School of International Studies, Jawaharlal Nehru University, New Delhi.Currently, she teaches at Ramanujan College, Delhi University.

PART I

Linking Past to Present

CHAPTER 1

Mongolia in Historical Perspective

Kundan Kumar

Modern Mongolia, also known as "Outer Mongolia" before its independence in 1921 and afterwards as the "Mongolian People's Republic (MPR)" until 1992, occupies a distinctive place in the geographical heartland of Asia. Having a rich past and historical tradition it has been placed in the league of great civilizations. As a region it has been the home of nomads for centuries before the Mongols became popular and established one of the largest land empires in the world. In addition, being a landlocked country and surrounded by two powerful neighbours—China and Russia, Mongolia has always been an entity having a peculiar geo-strategic importance, though it is one of the smallest countries of the world in terms of population. Its significance, therefore, lies in the territory rather than in population, which contributed much to the shaping of its distinct nomadic civilization and history.[1] From early times, due to its geographic setting Mongolia was at the crossroads of world communications. Two great highways, the Great Silk Route and the Eurasian steppe corridor, also known as the Silk Route of the Steppes, linked Mongolia with the centres of civilization of East and West. The birth of nomadic civilization was an appropriate response to the physical challenges in that specific part of Central Asia.[2]

Written descriptions of the Mongolians date back as far as 5000 B.C., courtesy of China, Mongolia's southern neighbour. They foretold the ensuing 7,000 years of history as well as describing the present. They suggest the mutual enmity, suspicion, and slander that have characterized the Mongolian-Chinese relationship at many times in their history.[3] Mongols first appear under that name, e.g., in Chinese transcription, *Menggu*, in the Chinese sources of the Tang Dynasty (618-906). During the Sung Dynasty which came to power in 960, the name becomes a fairly common referent. These early sources seem to suggest that the *Menggu* of the T'ang and Sung were located somewhat to the north of the present Mongols.[4] During the Manchu reign, Mongols were known by more specific term as the Manchus made distinction between northern and southern Mongols who came to be called as *Wei Meng-ku* (Outer Mongols) and *Nei Meng-ku* (Inner Mongols) respectively.[5] After the fall of Manchu and establishment of a Republic in China in 1912, the term Mongolia or Mongols began to be applied mainly to Outer Mongolia.[6]

The Mongols of today are descendants, however, of those who remained in East Asia during the Mongols' Yuan dynasty. After 1368 those Mongols who had remained nomads in the heartland were joined by those expelled from China. Over the following centuries these Mongols created a unique culture of Buddhist nomads, receiving influences from Tibet, China, and the hunting peoples of Siberia and Manchuria and synthesizing them with their own pastoral nomadic traditions. For the Mongols of today, the culture of the empire period is only the beginning of their national history, one that continues in succeeding dynasties and confederations: the Northern Yuan, the Oirats, Zünghars, Khalkha, and others.[7]

Prehistory of Mongols

The history of Mongolia goes far back into the remote ages—to the era of the primitive commune system. The land now called Mongolia has been inhabited for a long time. Evidence of human activity 500,000 years ago has been found in the country—axes made of river pebbles, sharp-pointed implements, disc-shaped flints. The people who used these were predecessors of the Neanderthal people. The climate of Mongolia was milder in this period than it is now. The mountains were covered with deciduous as well as coniferous forest. Where the land is now dry, there were well-watered meadows frequented by antelopes, ostriches, Tartar foxes, and mammoths. Forty thousand to 50,000 years ago, the climate cooled, and glaciers grew and shaped valleys and depressions. Around this time, primitive Mongolians also developed finer tools—knives, spearheads, and scrapers for processing animal skins and wood. They also learned to make fire, build shelter, and wear clothing.[8]

Mongolia before Mongolians proper was inhabited by various nations since the ancient times. The earliest known governmental entity in what is nowadays Mongolia is the Xiongnu, or Hun state. Historians still argue whether the Huns were a proto-Mongolian tribe, or a proto-Turkic ethnic group. Nevertheless, the Huns formed a highly elaborate state in Central Asia. The Mongols see the Huns as their ancestors, on the basis that they were nomadic and some Hun words (recorded in Chinese) suggest that their language was related to Mongol. According to Chinese sources, Huns were called Xiongnu. The first Emperor (Shi Huangdi) of the Qin dynasty (221-207 BC) linked together fortifications constructed by the rulers of earlier states in the northern China to build the original Great Wall as the barrier against these "barbarians". The Han dynasty (206 BC to AD 5) tried to appease Xiongnu chieftains by buying them off with gold and silk or by arranging marriages with Chinese princesses. The Xiongnu split in 54 BC and split again in 91 AD, into northern and southern alliance, then migrating westwards. These Xiongnu may have been ancestors of Huns who ravaged Europe in the fourth and fifth centuries.[9]

Around 155 AD, the northern Xiongnu in central Mongolia were attacked by the Xianbei (Hsien-pi), who came from the Hinggan area (Inner Mongolia). The Xianbei were Mongol-Turkic people who quickly expanded their territory but were unsuccessful in their attacks on the Chinese cities. The Xiongnu remnants allied themselves with the Chinese and moved south of the Great Wall. In 308 their chief, Liu Yuan, proclaimed himself emperor of the northern Han (Pei Han dynasty) in Taiyuan. His son Liu Ts'ung seized the western Jin dynasty capital Luoyang in 311 and captured the Jin emperor. After 349, the Xiongnu leaders fell out with one another, and their power declined.[10] The Xiongnu who were a confederation of tribal peoples are important particularly because they created the first empire on the steppes. It has been widely held that the Xiongnu, or at least their ruling clans, had or were acquiring a Turkic identity, or at least an Altaic one. Furthermore, the earliest Turkic peoples appeared on the peripheries of the late Xiongnu Empire. Peoples associated with it also spread far to the west, if, as often thought, what Europeans called the Huns were an extension of the Xiongnu. If not their ethnic progenitors, then, the Xiongnu had manifold ties to the later Turks.[11]

The Tabgatch or Toba, Northern Wei dynasty (386-528), established by the Tuoba clan of the Xianbei, had its capital from 493 at Luoyang. Buddhism flourished greatly in northern China at this time. The Tabgatch came under attack by the Jujuan (Nurun or Juan-Juan), who dominated the Gobi border. They seem to have been Mongols from Orkhon. Their capital was at Muma, an old Xiongnu site on the river Tamir. They used the title *khan* rather than Xiongnu *shanyu.* In the fourth and fifth centuries, there were raids and counter raids across the Gobi,[12] which later cleared the way for the Turks coming to power.

The Advent of Turks

The greatest power before the Mongols to rule the steppes was the Turkish dominion in its various forms during the sixth and seventh centuries AD, which faced the great T'ang dynasty on nearly equal terms but without prolonged warfare. The centre of the Turkish power was usually north of the Gobi in the Orkhon basin, a tributary of Selenga, the same region which the Mongols chose when they established their capital at Karakorum. It had the same organization of the army, and its Khans regarded themselves as chosen by Heaven to rule all the nomads, as early inscription in the Orkhon valley show. Much of the Mongol vocabulary of rule of social organization, and of military command was taken from the Turks, for they once ruled the Mongols. These are *ordu, tumen, khan, darkhan* and *ulus.*[13]

Among the vassals of Juan-Juan were the T'u-chueh, the Chinese name for the Turkut or Turks, whose totem was the wolf. Around 546, the T'u-chueh chief, Bumin (T'u-men) form an alliance with the now sinicized Toba to defeat the Juan-Juan, who fled to China and abandoned Mongolia to the T'u-chueh. When Bumin died in 553, his brother with the lessor title of yabghu, received the western T'u-chueh Khanate (Jungaria, Yssyk Kol, and the Ili and Chu basins). The yabghu of the western khanate stopped paying homage to the khans of the eastern khanate. The Chinese Sui dynasty (581-618), which had reunited China, supported the western T'u-chueh khanate against the eastern khanate, and in subsequent strife, feuding, and conspiracy managed to bring to power khans who accepted Chinese control. However, the khan of the eastern khanate revolted, and in 615, the Sui Emperor Yang Ti himself was besieged at Yenmen on the Great Wall.[14]

In 624, the new khan of the eastern T'u-chueh marched on Chang'an, the capital of the Tang dynasty (618-907). He was defeated in a surprise attack by the Tang prince and took his remnant forces back to Mongolia, only to return in 626 and again in 630, when he was finally defeated. The western Turkish khanate also collapsed in 630 but from 665 was in revolt against rulers appointed by the Chinese. The eastern khanate was resurrected in the Orkhon area under Qutlugh Khan and his adviser Tonyukuk, and they raided Chinese territory around Beijing. Qutlugh was succeeded in 691 by his brother

Mocho, who in brief alliance with China in 697 helped destroy the power of the Qidan (Khitan), then returned to his campaigns against northern Chinese cities. Mocho also slew the rebel leaders, reunited the factions of the western khanate, and recorded a successful expedition across the Tannu Ola against the Yenisey Kirghiz. After Mocho's death, Qutlugh's son Kultegin killed off Mocho's family and installed his elder brother as *bilgakhan*, the "wise khan," in 716. After the khan was poisoned (734), rivalries and revolt finally brought down the eastern khanate, and the royal clan fled to China in 743.[15]

Between the dissolution of the first empire of the Turks and the rise of Chinggis Khan lies an interval of four and half centuries, during which no one tribe or confederacy attained supremacy over the steppes. The interval was filled with the local and temporary dominance of Uighurs in Mongolia.[16] The Uighurs, whose name is said to mean adhering to, uniting, coming together, replaced the Eastern Turks in Mongolia in 744.

With the approval of the Tang, Qutlugh Bilga installed himself in 744 as the Uighur Khan on the former territory of the eastern khanate. The Uighur were also a Turkish people, and their capital Karabalgasun was built at what is now called Khotont in the Orkhon valley, the area favoured by the Xiongnu and T'u-chueh chiefs before them. The Uighurs became allies of the Tang China, and Kolo Khan helped defend Luoyang against rebels in 757-63. During this period, he was converted by missionaries to Manichaeism, and this faith flourished in the Uighur khanate and in China. The Uighur adopted the Sogdian alphabet to write their own language, displacing the old Turkic runic script.[17]

The Uighur Empire lasted until 840, when Karabalgasun was destroyed and the Uighur Khan killed by the Yenisey Kirghiz. The Uighurs dispersed to Turfan and Kucha (in Xinjiang) and to Gansu. The Kirghiz people were also Turks but were nomadic barbarians with little use of towns or farms. Their control over the Orkhon heartland lasted until around 920, when they were forced to back to their Yenisey homeland by the invading Qidan. The Qidan, a Sinicized Mongol tribe originally from Jehol and Liaoning, established the Liao dynasty (947-1125) with their capital at Yanjing (Beijing). The Liao dynasty was brought to the end by the Jurchen (Nuzhen), a Tungisic people, related to the later Manchu, who established the Jin (golden) dynasty in northern and northeastern China.[18]

The Mongols and Chinggis Khan

The rise of Mongol Empire in the 13th century was an important event in history. The Mongol Empire of the thirteenth and fourteenth century was extended what is today Korea to Hungary, encompassed the entire Asian continent up to India, South-east Asia and Eastern Europe. It existed in this size for more than hundred years and in some regions for even longer as partial of successive empire. The main difference between Mongols and earlier conquerors is that no other previous nomad empire had controlled the Asian inner steppe and vast regions of settled people.[19] The tribes of Mongolia in the twelfth century have to be described as 'Turko-Mongol', since it is by no means clear who were the Turkish and who were the Mongols. Even this would mean no more than they spoke Turkish or Mongolian respectively. In any case, the tribes intermarried freely, in accordance with exogamous customs. The most important of the tribes were perhaps the Tatars,[20] living like Mongols in the eastern Mongolia; the Keraits[21] in the centre; the Merkits[22] to the north of them; and Naimans[23] to the west.

The beginnings of the Mongol Empire are to be found in the intertribal politics and warfare on the Eastern Steppe following the overthrow of the Khitan by the Jurchen. The Tungusic speaking Jurchen were not a steppe people like the Khitan and did not maintain a military presence in the steppe. Instead, they supported the strongest single people there, the Tatars. The peoples of the Eastern Steppe were divided, and none of them could establish dominance over the others in the face of the powerful Tatars. When Khabul Khan, head of the Borjigin lineage, managed to put together a Mongol confederation, and the Jurchen were unable to dislodge him by force, they recognized his position as paramount ruler of the Mongols (in 1146/1147), though they also officially considered him their vassal. After his death, his successor, his cousin Ambaghai, was captured by the Tatars and sent to the Chin court, where the Jurchen killed him. The Mongols then selected Khabul Khan's third son Khutula to succeed as Khan, giving rise to enmity against him and his descendants by the descendants of Ambaghai. Khutula attacked the Tatars, largely unsuccessfully and his end is unknown. After him the early movement toward a unified Mongol realm disintegrated into internecine warfare, which dominated the Eastern Steppe when Khabul Khan's grandson Yesügei (d. 1175/1176), who had begun to reconstitute a Borjigin confederation, was murdered by the Tatars and his people and flocks were taken away by a pretender to the succession, leaving Yesügei's wife and children alone in the steppe.[24]

The threats from outsiders might have been one of the reasons for the Mongols to unite and become powerful in order to give blow to their enemies. For this purpose they needed a mutually acknowledged leader whom they found in the person like Temuchin.[25] Chinggis Khan's father, Yesugei, was a minor chieftain of the noble descent. He named his son, the future Chinggis Khan, Temuchin, after he had defeated a Tatar shortly before his son's birth. Temuchin's rise to power still had its marked ups and downs, but he was eventually recognised as Khan of the Mongols, and it may have been at this time rather than later that he assumed the title of Chinggis ('Oceanic' = universal?) Khan. In the years before 1206, the tribes of Mongolia were one by one brought under Mongol rule, though the process was not one of unbroken Mongol success. In some cases, a large number of defeated tribesmen was massacred. The Tatars could expect no mercy, and Temuchin had a score to settle with the Merkits. They had kidnapped his chief wife Bortei just nine months before the birth of Jochi, his eldest son, and the uncertainty over Jochi's true parentage remained to trouble the Mongol royal house. But for the most part the tribes, once defeated were neither killed nor driven out: their manpower was potentially far too useful for that. They were incorporated into the new Mongol military machine.[26]

In 1204, Genghis Khan set off against the Naiman and fought a great battle in the Orkhon valley, in which the Naiman tayang (king) was mortally wounded. The Naiman were pursued into the Altai Mountains. The Kirghiz surrendered to Genghis Khan without a fight. The traitor Jamuqa was handed over to Genghis Khan and at his own request was killed (but without the spilling of blood). The Naiman submitted to Genghis Khan. (Sanders, 2010: 10) The unification of the Mongol tribes now more or less completed, paved the way for The Mongolian Great Assembly first convened in 1206; at it, the Mongols elected Temüchin as Great Qahan. Temuchin was proclaimed the supreme Khan of all the Turko-Mongol tribes of the area at a great quriltai on the bank of Onon held in 1206, from which his imperial rule is commonly dated. The authority of Chinggis Khan was based on his personal prowess in war, his hereditary descent from the ancient Khans of Mongolia, and an invincible success which indicated to the people the benign approval of the heaven.[27]

The Mongol Empire

The years immediately after 1206 were spent in tying up loose ends. Through the process of detribalization, Chinggis Khan wanted to create a system of centralization with himself as the supreme authority on the Steppe and beyond with the creation of a Mongol World Empire. Having settled their internal affairs, the Mongols began to incorporate all other nomadic peoples living outside Mongolia in their state. Thus a huge empire built up, perhaps the largest land empire in the human history came into being which could not have been possible without the establishment of what is called in a more specific term "the Pax Mongolica". Such an empire not only produced an advanced socio-political system in Mongolia but also offered a good opportunity to those who aspired to power and glory in the steppe.[28]

Chinggis Khan divided his empire among his four sons of his principal wife. Eventually, after his numerous grandsons had helped to expand it, the empire was composed of four Khanates. On the geographical basis, the Mongol empire may be divided into five parts: (a) Mongolia itself as the centre of empire, beginning with the rise of Chinggis Khan and ending with the death of Mongke Khan in 1259 AD (b) the Yuan dynasty in China, beginning with the enthronement of Kubilai Khan (1264-1294 AD) (c) the Il-Khans of Persia (d) the Golden Horde in Russia and (e) the Chaghatai Khanate in Middle Asia. Though the Mongol empire witnessed itself a conglomeration of various peoples and countries and their socio-economic structure, it also had many common features and similarities that turned it into a "coherent entity" for almost the whole period of its existence. But what contributed greatly to the rapid extension of the boundaries of the Mongol empire was its military supremacy which also resulted in the political domination of the mighty Khans.[29] Chinggis Khan opened up new fields of conquest in northern China with a campaign in 1207 against the Tangut (Xi Xia) state in the Ningxia/Gansu area. In 1215, he defeated the Jin and seized their capital and in 1218 defeated the Qidan. Turning next to Central Asia, Chinggis Khan attacked Khwarazm in 1219 and in 1221 took Samarkand. By 1223, Mongol troops under Jebei were probing the defences of the Russian princes. He was back in Mongolia by 1225 and prepared a new campaign against the Tangut. This time he succeeded in capturing the Xi Xia capital and killing the ruler in 1227, but on the way back to Mongolia, he died.[30]

When Borte's first son, Jochi, was born, his paternity was not questioned, but in 1218, Genghis Khan had favored his third son, Ogodei, to succeed him. Jochi died in 1227, shortly before Genghis Khan, and Ogodei became the new Great Khan in 1229. Ogodei built the walls and palaces of Karakorum, the Mongol capital, in 1235. During his reign, the Mongols invaded Korea (1231) and expanded farther into northern China and Russia, capturing Kiev in 1240. Batu Khan. Jochi's sonstyled his Russian territory "the Golden Horde" in 1243.[31] The death of Ogedei in 1241 led to a long interregnum. After him, Guyuk, his son, managed to secure election as a Great Khan, but it did not occur until 1246. After the death of Möngke Khan in 1259, internecine disputes broke out among the Toluyids themselves. In 1260 the two sons of Möngke, Arig-böke and Qubilai, simultaneously had a quriltai convened and each declared himself Khan. In the Mongol traditionalist view, Qubilai's rise to power was illegal and a four-year fratricidal war between the two brothers ensued, with Ariq-böke wishing to retain the centre of the empire in Mongolia. After his defeat, the struggle was continued by Qaidu until his death in 1303.[32]

Less than two decades later the Mongol Empire, the first truly world empire in history, uniting much of the territory of Eurasia and a substantial part of the Old World's population under its control, was gone, replaced by four successor Khanates based in China, Turkistan, Russia, and Iran, known respectively as the Yuan Dynasty, the Patrimony of Chaghatai *ulus*, the Golden Horde, and the Ilkhanate. Within less than a century these too were started declining, although various Golden Horde successor states persisted into the 16th century, and, in one case, into the 18th.[33]

The Yuan Dynasty

During the reign of Qubilai Khan (1260–94), the Mongol empire underwent a great transformation. The transference of the empire's capital from Karakorum to Khanbalïk (or Dai-du) in northern China, and the adoption of the Chinese title Yüan (The Origin) for the Mongol reign in China, meant a change in the traditional policy of Qubilai's predecessors. Theoretically, Qubilai Khan was the ruler of the whole empire and tried to avail himself of his rights in all the subjugated countries. But in reality, in his time and particularly in the reign of his successors, the component parts of the Mongol empire progressively achieved such a degree of independence that it was difficult for the Khan to claim the status of universal ruler. It is probable that Qubilai Khan realized this and regarded himself more as a Mongol-Chinese emperor than as a universal sovereign. Despite having settled in China, Qubilai did not forget that he was a Mongol emperor and did his best to make the Mongols an elite group in the conquered country. Having thus secured Mongol rule in China, it became possible for a small, non-Chinese ethnic group to govern the huge Chinese sedentary society for almost a century.[34]

The new Chinese-style Yuan Dynasty officially began on Chinese New

Year's Day, January 18, 1272. Despite the orthodox procedures followed in the establishment of the dynasty, and in much of the structure of the administration, the new government was very clearly Mongol. Unlike their Jurchen predecessors in North China, the Mongols generally did not trust the Chinese. Qubilai himself did have many important Chinese advisers, but his successors put Mongols, Central Asian Muslims, Tibetans, Tanguts, or other non-Chinese in all key administrative positions. The Great Khanate continued to exist, and included Mongolia and Tibet as major constituent parts that were recognized as not being Chinese. While in many respects Yuan China was integrated into the Mongol Empire, the Great Khanate continued to be the larger unit. The two were not equated with each other.[35]

When Qubilai decided he wanted to have a unified "Mongol" script for all the languages of the Mongol Empire, he appointed to the commission the Tibetan Buddhist leader 'Phagspa, who was his National Preceptor and the viceroy of Tibet. The new script, based on the Tibetan alphabet (but written vertically like Chinese script and Uighur-Mongol script), was promulgated as the official writing system in 1269. Known today as 'Phagspa Script, it is in effect the world's first multilingual transcription system. Examples of it are preserved in several languages from around the Mongol Empire, including Chinese, and it is thought that the script influenced the later creation of the Korean Han'gul writing system. 'Phagspa was also in charge of other intellectual projects, including the compilation of a great comparative catalogue of the Chinese and Tibetan Buddhist canons, the respective compendia of translations of sacred texts from Sanskrit.[36]

In 1294, Kublai's grandson Tomor-Olziit succeeded to the Yuan throne. The following period was one of great turbulence. Ten Yuan khans were enthroned, killed, or plotted against; came to the throne as children; or died young—in 1328, three in one year. In 1368, the Chinese brought down the Yuan dynasty, drove Togoon Tomor Khan out of Beijing, and established the Ming dynasty. Togoon Tomor, the last Yuan emperor, died in Inner Mongolia in 1370, and his son Ayuushridar was enthroned in Karakorum. In 1380, invading Ming troops destroyed Karakorum.[37]

Mongolia during Manchu Rule

When the Ming dynasty was overthrown in 1368 and expelled from China, many Mongols remained behind, but the fleeing emperor managed to gather several *tumen* or ten thousands together and lead them back towards his new headquarters on the Kerulen river. The imperial Mongol dynasty did not die out then, but was continued under the name of northern Yuan until the death of last emperor, Ligdan Khan, in 1634. But most of this period the actual emperors failed to exercise supreme authority. The years were filled with internecine quarrels and later with wars with the Oirats or western Mongols whose power was not broken till Altan Khan of Tumet (1507-82), recaptured Karakorum, the former imperial capital, from them.[38]

In the middle of the 16th century, a significant figure stepped on the stage—Altan Khan of the Tumet, an eastern Mongol tribe. In the 1550s, Altan Khanagreed on peace and border trade with the Ming, fought the Oirat, and foundedhis capital of Hohhot (blue town, from the glazed tiles on the city wall). In 1559, he set off on a campaign against the Kokonor (Qjnghai) Mongols. In 1578, Altan Khan invited the Tibetan religious leader Sonam Gyatso to meet him in Kokonor. He was converted to Sonam Gyatso's Gelugpa (yellow hat) school of Tibetan Buddhism and gave Sonam Gyatso the title "Dalai Lama." Later, when the matter of reincarnation was looked into, it was decided that Sonam Gyatso was in fact the third Dalai Lama. The first Dalai Lama was declared to have been Gedun Truppa, a disciple of Tsongkhapa, founder of the Gelugpas.[39] In 1639, Zanabazar, the son of the Tusheet Khan Gombodorj of the Khalkh, was recognized as an incarnation of the Tibetan scholar Taranatha and through him of the line of Tibetan Javzandambas. Zanabazar assumed the title of Ondor Gegeen or "high enlightened one" beginning his own line of incarnated Mongolian "living Buddhas," who take third place in the Lamaist hierarchy headed by the Dalai Lamas and Panchen Lamas.[40]

Meanwhile, important events were taking place on Mongolia's northern border. Russia's conquest of Siberia had begun in 1582 with the Cossack chief Yermak's capture of Kuchum Khan's capital, Kashlyk. Traveling the great rivers of Siberia, the Russians founded the towns of Tobolsk in 1587, Krasnoyarsk in 1627, and Irkutsk in 1661 and demanded tribute {*yasak*) in furs from the local native peoples. Russian exploration of Siberia extended as far as the Pacific coast, and Russian fortified settlements (Nerchinsk, Albazin) were built in the no-man's land between Russia and China.[41] In northeastern China, the Manchu, a growing power, asserted themselves against Russian expansion on the river Heilongjiang (Amur). Their border with Russia was agreed in 1689. Southern Mongolia came under Manchu control. The Khalkh people of northern Mongolia were increasingly pressed from the west by the Jungarian khanate. Having railed to form an alliance with the Khalkh against the Manchu, in 1687, the Jungarian Khan Galdan Boghist attacked the Khalkha.

The Ondor Gegeen Zanabazar recommended seeking the protection of the Manchu. The Manchu (Qing) emperor Kang Xi accepted the Mongols' oath of allegiance at Dolonnor (Duolon) in 1691. Subsequently, southern Mongolia became known as "Inner" Mongolia, and northern Mongolia as "Outer" Mongolia.[42]

The Qing control of Khalkha Mongolia certainly enriched a few Chinese merchants but it impoverished much of the Mongol population. Seeking to prevent foreign influence and to preserve the existing political and economic system in Mongolia, the Manchu court hindered the economic development of northern country. It delayed the modernization of Mongolia and bred anti-Chinese feelings among the Mongols. The Qing, in fact, attempted to reduce the role and functions of the Khans. In ennobled almost seventy other Mongols and awarded them powers equivalent to those of the Khans.[43] One of the principal Qing goals was to isolate Mongolia and to keep the Russians out of the land of the Khalkha as a defense measure. The Chinese merchant viewed it as a means of limiting competition and of ensuring a monopoly of the Mongol trade. Qing negotiators attempted to elicit a Russian pledge of non-interference in Mongol affairs. By the treaty of Kiakhta of 1728, the Russian agreed, in return for commercial concessions, to abandon contact with the Mongols and they kept their promise till the nineteenth century.[44]

The Manchu rulers promoted Buddhism in Mongolia, built monasteries and temples, and encouraged the translation, copying, and, later, the xylographic printing of religious works. When Zanabazar died in 1723, the Qing emperor ordered the construction of Amarbayasgalant monastery in his memory (1737). The nomadic palace (orgoo) of the Ondor Gegeen was replaced in 1706 by a new great monastery (Ikh Khuree), which, in 1778, finally took root in the valley of the river Tuul. In 1837, the first permanent temple buildings were built there, marking the foundation of Mongolia's capital city.[45] The monasteries grew rich and powerful, but this could not conceal the growing weakness and corruption of the Qing. The Mongols were oppressed by the cruelty of Manchu administrators and impoverished by the greed of their princes and the rapaciousness of the Chinese traders. Rebellions at home (the Taipings in 1851 and the Boxers in 1900) and disadvantageous treaties with Russia and other foreign powers undermined the Qing regime. There was an anti-Manchu mutiny in Uliastai garrison in 1900. An anti-Manchu liberation movement was formed in Outer Mongolia in 1903. There was an uprising in Inner Mongolia in 1905. The situation was made worse by the decision in 1906 to permit Chinese settlers into Mongolia. In 1910, a clash between Mongols and Manchu troops in Ikh Khuree led to the departure of the Manchu *amban* (Governor) Sanduo.[46]

The Mongolian Revolution and Proclamation of the MPR

The departure of the Manchu governor of Urga from Outer Mongolia in December 1911 marked Mongolia's restoration as independent state. It was encouraged by the revolution in China and by expression of support from the Tsarist government in Russia, independence was declared by princes and lamas. On 16 December 1911, the Bogd Gegeen Jetsundamba Khutgat was proclaimed Khan in Urga and a government was formed. The Chinese government refused to recognize the separation of Mongolia, but, in November 1912, a Mongolian-Russian agreement was concluded, 'legalizing' the existence of Mongolia's autonomy.[47]

It is to be noted that Mongolia was one of the first nations in modern times, outside Europe, to escape successfully from subjugation to an alien power. Mongolia leaders were inexperienced, and to a very great extent naïve in their approach to international realities. The immediate aim before Mongolia was to incorporate within her boundaries of huge areas, hitherto subject to the Manchus, where happened to dwell. But this aim was limited by her neighbours, Russia and China, and they had their own interests to pursue in Mongolia. In this regard, Russia's freedom of action was circumscribed by secret treaties with Japan. Mongolia failed to achieve any effective international recognition for her independence, and this was scaled down by Sino-Russian Accord of 1913 and the three-power Treaty of Kiakhta of 1915, to mere autonomy under Chinese suzerainty. The turmoil of the Soviet revolution gave China the opportunity to re-assert her control for a while and in 1919 autonomy was cancelled, ostensibly at the request of the Mongolian government, though not at that of the Khutgat himself. For a time Mongolia was incorporated in the state structure of the Republic of China, an advance of the Chinese imperialism over what had been claimed by the Manchu Emperors.[48]

In early 1921, there followed a brief restoration of the monarchy under the brutal, though historically irrelevant, regime of the white Russian leader Baron Ungern-Sternberg. Simultaneously, a 'popular' revolution was being prepared by a few conspirators, for most part inside Soviet territory, and a provisional government was being organized just inside Russia at Kiakhta. This provisional government took upon itself to invite the Soviet army into Mongolia in April 1921. It occupied Urga and overthrew the existing government and establishing what on the surface was a constitutional monarchy which was presided over by the Khutuktu, until his death in 1924.[49] In 1924, when the Bogd Khan died, Mongolia's religious leaders were forbidden to search for a new incarnation. A Congress of the MPP proclaimed the Leninist "non-capitalist path of development," and the party was named as the Mongolian People's Revolutionary Party (MPRP). Under the first constitution, the Mongolian People's Republic was proclaimed in November 1924, with its capital renamed as Ulan Bator or Ulaanbaatar (red hero).[50]

In conclusion one finds that Mongolia went through several ups and downs in its history but finally events unfolded in the early 20th century gave birth to a new independent Mongolia. However, Mongolia went through two distinct revolutions in the decade between 1911 and 1921. The first one, which resulted in the declaration of independence, was "essentially" a national movement and was aimed mainly at the removal of Manchu authority. The second, inspired by the Bolshevik revolution, was carried out under Russian guidance and control, and was the run up to a period of profound change. The trend of Mongolia's history over the past century since the revolution has rightly been described by Bawden who says that it has been, first, the transformation of what had been a backward, feudalistic dependency of China into a 'People's Republic to a liberal democracy' and secondly, the search for international recognition, both by individual states and by the United Nations, of Mongolia's independent nationhood and these both aspirations have been fully realized in fact.[51]

Notes and References

1. K. Warikoo and Sharad K Soni (2010), *Mongolia in the 21st Century: Society, Culture and International Relations*, New Delhi and London: Pentagon Press, p. v.
2. Sh. Bira (1998), 'The Mongols and their State in the Twelfth to the Thirteenth Century', in M.S, Asimov and C. E. Bosworth (eds), *History of Civilizations of Central Asia*, vol.4, Paris: UNESCO Publishing, p. 248.
3. Jennifer L. Hanson (2004), *Nations in Transition: Mongolia*, New York: Facts on File, p.4.
4. Paul. D. Buell (2003), *Historical Dictionary of the Mongol World Empire*, Maryland, Scarecrow Press, p.2.
5. Sharad K. Soni (2006), *Mongolia-China Relations: Modern and Contemporary Times*, New Delhi: Pentagon Press, p. 2.
6. Ibid.
7. Christopher P. Atwood (2004), *Encyclopedia of Mongolia and the Mongol Empire*, New York: Facts of File, p.viii.
8. Hanson, *Nations in Transition*, p. 3.
9. Alan J. K. Sanders (2010), *Historical Dictionary of Mongolia*, Maryland: Scarecrow Press, p.6.

10. Ibid, p.6.
11. Carter Findley (2005), *Turks in World History*, New York: Oxford University Press, pp.28-29.
12. Sanders, *Historical Dictionary of Mongolia*, p.7.
13. E.D. Phillips (1969), *The Mongols*, London: Thames and Hudson, p. 24.
14. Sanders, *Historical Dictionary of Mongolia*, p.7.
15. Ibid, p.8.
16. J.J. Saunders (1971), *The History of the Mongol Conquests*, London: Routledge, p. 31.
17. Sanders, *Historical Dictionary of Mongolia*, p.8.
18. Ibid, p. 8.
19. G.D. Gulati (2010), *Central Asia under the Mongols*, Delhi: Dev Books, p.19.
20. Turkic-speaking peoples living primarily in Russia, Ukraine, and Uzbekistan. Generic name for various nomadic communities who inhabited Mongolia in the later first and early second millennia BC which is also applied to early historic groups found in Siberia and eastern Russia.
21. The Keraits were located on the upper Onon. They were converts to Nestorianism since the year 1000 and were almost certainly Turks. Their titles are Turkish.
22. The Merkits, a Turco-Mongol people, had their pastures in the valleys of the Selenga Basin, east of Lake Baikal. They were partially Christianised.
23. Naiman in Mongolian language means "eight", because Naimans were direct descendants of the Segiz Ogyz people, "segiz" means "eight" in the Kazakh language. They were a Mongolian name given to a group of Turkic tribes dwelling on the steppe of Central Asia, having diplomatic relations with the Kara-Khitan, and subservient to them until 1177. The Naimans are most often classified as a Turkic people.
24. Christopher Beckwith (2009), *Empires of the Silk Road: A History of Central Eurasia from the Bronze Age to the Present*, Princeton: Princeton University Press, p. 184.
25. Soni, *Mongolia-China Relations*, p. 4.
26. David Morgan (1986), *The Mongols*, Oxford: Basic Blackwell, pp. 57-61.
27. Saunders, *The History of the Mongol Conquests*, p. 52.
28. Sharad K. Soni (2002), *Mongolia-Russia Relations: Kiakhta to Vladivostok*, Delhi: Shipra Publication, pp. 13-14.
29. Ibid, pp. 14-15.
30. Sanders, *Historical Dictionary of Mongolia*, p.10.
31. Ibid, p.11.
32. Morgan, *The Mongols*, pp. 114-15.
33. Buell, *Historical Dictionary of the Mongol World Empire*, p.viii.
34. Bira, "The Mongols and their State", p. 264.
35. Beckwith, *Empires of the Silk Road*, pp. 193-94.
36. Ibid, p.194.
37. Sanders, *Historical Dictionary of Mongolia*, p. 12.
38. C.R. Bawden (1968), *The Modern History of Mongolia*, London: Weidenfield and Nicolson, pp. 23-24.
39. Sanders, *Historical Dictionary of Mongolia*, p. 13.
40. Ibid, p.13.
41. Ibid.
42. Ibid, p.14.

43. Morris Rossabi (1975), *China and inner Asia from 1368 to present day*, London: Thames & Hudson, pp. 150-51.
44. Ibid, p.150.
45. Sanders, *Historical Dictionary of Mongolia*, p. 14.
46. Ibid, p.14.
47. Alan J. K. Sanders (1987), *Mongolia: Politics, Economics and Society*, London: Frances Pinter, p.15.
48. Bawden, *The Modern History of Mongolia*, pp. 187-88.
49. Ibid, p.188.
50. Sanders, *Historical Dictionary of Mongolia*, p. 16.
51. Bawden, *The Modern History of Mongolia*, p. 189.

CHAPTER 2

Shamanism and its Influence on Mongolian Society

Rajeev Kumar Raju

Shamanism is all pervading phenomenon, though its locus classicus is north Asia. It is like so because of its dramatic nature and its religious dominance in such a vast area.[1] For a long period of time Shamanism has been a complicated religious development as in long historical journey it has acquired many elements and given some of its own features to others. These various patterns are known as classic Shamanism with great Shamans or Shamaness as its performers. Various local manifestations of Shamanism, particularly in Inner Asia which appear in the ethnographic descriptions, were effete because either several elements of the classic pattern were absent or external elements were present.[2] Thus, classic Shamanism is a construct held by Inner Asian people who believe that it existed in the past and exemplified by the practitioners known as Shamans.

Shamanic Traditions, Rituals and Practices

Since the age of the recorded history Shamanism has been practiced in Mongolia and its neighbourhood. In the primordial phase, it was connected to the other aspect of life and to the tribal society of Mongolia. Later on, it was also "influenced by and mingled with Buddhism."[3] While during the socialist period in the twentieth century it was brutally suppressed, it has made a strong return afterwards. Shamanism is a system of belief that includes medicines, religion, and a belief in ancestor worship. At the heart of the system are the actions of male and female conduits who act between the human world and world of spirits. Shamans are also known as *boge* and Shamaness as *idugan* respectively.[4] There is a belief that a person does not take the occupation as Shaman rather he is chosen for the profession by the conveyer from the spirit world. The arrival of this representative is usually announced by the chosen person's falling seriously ill or experiencing hallucinations.[5] A Shaman called in to cure the sick person, would pronounce the patient possessed by the spirit, indicating that he or she had been chosen to be Shaman or Shamaness.

Traditionally, the chosen person would be initiated by an older person of the same tribe into the lore of magic formulas and the songs and dance, which the Shamans used to combat the supernatural sources of evil. During the initiation the newly chosen Shaman was given a staff. Its finial was carved in the shape of the horses head and its lower end in the shape of a hoof. When the new Shaman has practiced rituals for years, the staffs were replaced with a drum. Other paraphernalia of the Shaman were successively added to his arsenal.[6] If, a misfortune like hunger, sickness or natural disasters came it was considered to be a devilish mischief by malicious demons. Timely offerings, virtuous conduct and observance of taboos were to ensure the benevolent nature of ancestral spirit. However, peace and harmony were disturbed by evil spirits and Shaman assistance was needed.

The Shamans were assisted by the army of auxiliary spirits to face adversaries from the spirit world. Numbers and might of helpful spirits determined the magic and healing powers of Shamans. Alcohol—induced trance and smoking of herbs helped Shamans to take his voyage to the realms of demons. It would help them to subdue the evil spirit. The shaman could bring back the spirit of dead people. The Shamans and Shamaness were protected against supernatural evil forces by the magical properties of the tools of his trade. The headgear was decorated with antlers of deer, which gave the shamans speed and versatility. A headdress decorated with eagle feather provided them strength, while owl feather empowered them to see at night.[7] Metal objects symbolizing armour such as arrow heads, bells and mirrors were attached to the Shaman's upper garments. Feathers were attached to the sleeves of his dress symbolizing wings. The horse's head or drum was crowned with Shamans staff the handle of which was carved in the shape of a horse head symbolizing his mode of transportations.

Later on, since the sixteenth century onwards prohibition of Shamanism, its persecution and suppression by lamaist missionaries came into the sight. Stimulus for them came from third Dalai Lama himself. The Shamanist idols were replaced by lamaist idols, in place of the forbidden Shamanic magical songs and hymns, *dharni* formula and exorcist prayers were taught. Copies of these were also spread among the people. Tantric magic and miraculous healings of lamaism appealed to the princely class and they were agreed to forbid Shamanism. But situation in the last two decades have changed and concepts and theories related to Shamanism have gained more and more popularity. Besides, the revival of genuine Shamanic traditions, Mongolian neo-Shamanism came into force in the 1990s.[8] A number of Shamans have had their own offices and staff in the prominent towns in the country. These are known as centre of Shamanic activities (*Böögínn zan üiliin töw*). The centre is headed by a Shaman himself in most of the cases. In the Mongolian culture region there are a number of Shamanic traditions, which greatly vary from each other, though the path of becoming a Shaman is similar in all cases. Shamanism is mainly practiced by minority community such as Darkhat, Buryat and the Uriankhai.[9] These people are blessed with superhuman knowledge and spiritual power. Shamanic traditions of different ethnic groups are regarded as different ways of practicing Mongolian Shamanism. In reality none of these have Mongol roots. The Shamanism of Darkhat and Uriankhai is clearly related to the neighbouring Tuvan Shamans. The Shamanic practices of Buryats resemble with Ewenk and Daur.[10]

Sociologically, Mongolian Shamanism had a close correlation to the social and societal organization. Mongolian society was complex and the formative principle of society rested on patrilineal descent from a common ancestor and the hierarchical order of descent lines and agnatic relations.[11] Next to the nomadic village, the clan was central social organization. The clan was the basic social, political and territorial unit and a ritual community. The clan had Shaman and Shamaness descent lines which had a particular position and function in Mongolian society. Based on descent lines Shamanism has influenced Mongolian society in many ways. In Mongolia bone setting has been regarded as an indigenous skill practiced especially by the Shamans. They are heirs to the oldest religious traditions of the Mongols. Bone setting in Mongolia has been one of the traditional medical repertoires of the Shamans. They also use singing, music and dance to cure a wide variety of ailments caused by the spirits. Nowadays, other forms of Shamanic practices can also be seen which are confined to rural regions, though bone setting has become a respectable and even profitable practice.[12]

Shamanism response to market economy gives us an interesting picture to look into. Contrary to the Buryat expectation that Shamanism would solve the uncertainties brought about by the market economy, it has created additional spiritual uncertainties. The sceptical Buryats repeatedly propitiate their angry spirits to "alleviate the causes of their misfortunes".[13] They also reconstruct their history, which was suppressed by the state socialism in which Buryats make their current calamities meaningful by placing them within shifting history of their tragic past. The sense of uncertainties, fear and disillusionment experienced by the Buryats also characterizes daily life in Mongolia.[14] If we examine the revival of religious feeling, we find that it corresponds with resurgence which claims a specific Mongolian identity. Under communism, Mongolian culture was pushed to a folklorist level as an old tradition not compatible with the new Soviet age of progress. Nowadays, the liberal market and religion allow the Mongol people to regain their culture. Shamanism is instrumental in this process of rebuilding the national identity.

Mongolian Shamanism goes far back into the history. The sources of the 13th century (the time of the formation of Mongolian empire) give only a few direct and systematic accounts of the religious ideas and Shamanic traditions.[15] Folk-religious beliefs and sources from 17th century onwards are far richer in context. These are used to understand the references from the records of earlier history. The folk religious texts have been inferred by Heissig (1953 and 1970) as well as Passim and Bawden (1958) in their various articles on Mongol religion which hint clearly on an older Shamanic tradition.[16] Several early Buddhist missionaries in the 16th and 17th century widely used old Shamanist scripture to formulate lamaist religious text, though the former fell victim to arguably the lamaist atrocity.

Mongolian Shamanism can be defined in general as a belief system, a world view, though anthropologically it is a folk medicine and a religious magic cult of nature, especially a particular form of ancestral cult. Here functionaries and protagonist were the Shamans and the Shamaness who communicated with spirits and cured sickness and diseases.[17] They were considered to be divine weather magicians as well as bards, mimics and poets. The Shamans, male and female, called the spirits for blessings, support and protection against evil. Shamans also had important functions in the clan-life in the communal hunts and in times of war; they asked for prosperity and health of the members of their social units and herds, cared for the sacred fire of the clan and so on. Mongolian terminology for the Shamans and their works are many. Usually, as mentioned earlier, Shamans are known as *boge* and the Shamaness as *Idugan*. The Mongolian specialist considers *boge* and *idugan* as small (white and black) Shaman and Shamaness and the great Shamans and Shamaness as *jigarin* and *abiya* respectively..

Mongolian Shamanism had 99 *tngri*/deities-55 white or benevolent and 44 black or terrifying; besides these there was the conception of 77 earth movers. The highest entity was *Koke Mongketngri,* the eternal Blue Sky. These 99 *tngri* or deities were common to all Mongols. Apart from the white and black *tngri* there was a large number of minor *ginni*; the spirits of the ancestors divided in white and black and hierarchically differentiated groups. According to Bawden (1970), these ancestors had special idols (*Onghhot*) which were subject to veneration and had special position in the Shamanic ritual.[18] Everybody could appeal to the lord spirits of the clan, worship and sacrifice to them by the intermediary Shaman to increase the material and spiritual welfare of the members of clan. Another kind of Shamanism known as Yellow Shamanism is the term used to designate the particular version of Shamanism which incorporates rituals and traditions from Buddhism. Yellow indicates Buddhism in Mongolia since most Buddhists there belong to what is called a *gelug* or yellow sect of Tibetan Buddhism, whose members wear yellow hats during services.[19]

The soul of the great Shamans and Shamaness were the "protector spirits" and that of simple and small Shamans and Shamaness were the "guardian spirits" of locality of clan territory.[20] The soul of the famous long deceased Shamans becomes the spirits of mountains and river valley, forests and so on. According to Heese (1982), the lord spirits, protector spirits and the guardian spirits occupied a central position in the culture of the ancestors of Mongol.[21] The other three clans were the spirits of nobles (white) spirits of the commoner (black) and in the third category were the evil spirits of non-human or goblins. The great (black) Shamans called upon the black and terrifying *tngri* and high spirit against evil from outside and for securing victory in wars.[22] In this regard, a thesis have been put forward that the nobles and leaders of Mongols who participated in the state formation from 10th to 13th century were Shamans. However, the earliest records of Mongolian Shamanism are traced during Hunnu dynasty in 209 B.C., when Shamans played a crucial role in diplomatic matters and treaties with the neighbouring countries.[23] The Hunnu emperors constructed Shrines and Shamans were encouraged to synthesize diverse practices into a national religion. Thus, Shamanism became the organizational basis for governance and military activity. This continued for nearly 400 years. Kevin Turner opines that, Shamanism was greatly respected in the era of Great

Khans.[24] In the era of Chinggis Khan; Shamanism was primary religiosity of Mongolia. Shamans' views were important on all state matters and no military endeavour was taken without the consent of Shamans. Deceased Khans were considered as spirits to be honoured, worshipped and invoked for Shamanic practices.

State of Shamanism after Advent of Buddhism

While writing on Mongols' conversion to Buddhism Walther Heissig (1980) says that prohibition, persecution and suppression of Shamanism by Lama Missionaries are the features of the second conversion of Mongols. From the sixteenth century onwards anti-Shamanic resolution of Dzasktu Khan (1558-82/83) and edicts of Altan Khan of Tumet (1557/58), punished those who possessed *onghhot* figures and worshiped them through bloody sacrifices.[25] This followed the replacement of Shamanist idols by Buddhist representation and six armed *Mahakal.* In the place of Shamanist songs and hymns, *dharni* formulae and exorcist prayers were taught. Princes of Khorchin was won over by the healing power of Neyièi Toyin, a Lama who promoted Buddhism towards 1636. Tusiyetu Khan of Khorchin promised to give horses and cows to those who learn and recite the Buddhist doctrine and *dharni.*[26] Heissig, on the basis of biography of Neyièi Toyin, says that after hearing the Toyin's address, the ruler and nobility sent their messengers accompanied by one of his monks to collect the idols, after collecting it they took it to Neyièi Toyin who piled the idols and set fire to them.[27] The 25 cm high confiscated *onghhot* can still be found today. Thus, the number of *onghhot* collected in the territory of the Khorchin alone must have consisted of several thousands.[28]

Mongolian biography of Caya Pandita says that around 1650, Rab byams Pa took similar measures in Ili territory. He said to his monks and disciples, "whoever among the people whom you see worshipping *onghhot,* burn their onghhot and take their horses and ship. Let the Shamans and Shamaness perform fumigations, takes horses. Fumigate the Shamans and Shamaness, however, with dog dung.[29] Poppe and Kudryavatsev are of the view that same kind of lamaist procedure against Shamanism and *onghhot* worship happened in the last decades of the eighteen century among Buryats. He further says that though lamaist tradition was present among the Khori Buryats as early as the first third of seventeenth century, however lamaism did not flourish among the Buryats before 1712.[30]

Lamaism consists of a theological, systematization of the old magical practices of Indian and Tibetan folk religion which helped missionaries to replace the existing functions with similar practices. Max Weber (1923) explained this phenomenon by arguing that, it had to happen because the small urban householders and peasants could hardly get very far with the products of the "soteriology of the educated aristocracy".[31] Buddhism in Tibet incorporated traits and deities from the Bon Po demonology into its system. In confrontation, Indigenous Bon religion was forced by more highly developed theological systems that is Buddhism to camouflage itself with Lamaist traits. Thus, Lamaism had the example of the confrontation of Buddhism with Bon religion. Magical formulae were taught to the Mongols by the missionaries to destroy evil, misfortune and demons to protect and increase cattle, keep away horse plague, remove and drive out liver ailments.[32] Neyièi Toyin, propagated *dharni* of the system of *Yamanthka* and *uniomystica* to gain the attention of Mongols.[33]

The Dyanèi Lama, who cultivated meditation, enjoyed particular veneration here, cut off from all profane things he lived for 404 days in complete isolation and prayer. During the fasting ritual he went through hallucinations and delusions and had to make various ritual implements out of bones from the corpses, a rosary made out of human bones, a trumphet from young girl's tibia and eating bowl from a human skull. Further, more elevated form of substitute for the exorcizing Shaman was provided by the Gurtum Lama. This name was given to a Lama who possessed the ability of placing himself into ecstacy and trance or to drive out demons. Nebesky and Wojkowitz (1956) draw a similarity of physical strength between Shamans and Lamas. They say that the Lamaist prototype for the Gurtum was certainly provided by Chos Skyong in Lhasa who went into trance and ecstasy several times each year manifesting the supernatural power. Thus wearing an Iron hat without assistance from others which normally could not be held by several men, like this a 76 year old Shamaness who had to spend all day in bed from weakness of age, but during her exorcist activity would maximize in ecstasy through a whole night in heavy clothes.[34]

According to Heissig (1966) and Sodnam (1962), despite all its persecutions Shamanism continues as a form of religion, though incarnation of pure mixed and completely lamaized form can be recorded in all parts of Mongolia up to the present day.[35] It is to be noted that in 1940, one of the east Mongolian regions had thirty Shamans and Shamaness. In 1960, Shaman songs were noted down in northern Mongolia, in Barga territory and in southern Mongolia.

Shamanic Influences on Mongolian Society

Influences of Shamanism are both positive and negative. Positive influence of Shamanism can be observed in the healing powers of Shamanism having therapeutic arsenal. Entheogen, which is used as morphine in western medicine, has been the discovery of Shamanism. This act of borrowing can be seen as an acknowledgement of Shamanic practices over the time. Landy (1977) describes that Shamans often possess formidable pharmaceutical expertise, which combined with ritual acts and intense human interaction may achieve remarkable causes.[36] In his article "The effectiveness of symbols in structural anthropology", Claude-Levi-Strauss (1963) suggests that Shamanic healers like western psychotherapists assist their patients in constructing a reading of their illness. Narrative and symbolic understanding which serves to alleviate or even resolve the patients' problem have become a part of western psychotherapy today.[37] Mongolian bone setting is seen as part of Shamanic healing because best bonesetters, especially from eastern part of Mongolia have been descendants of a powerful female Shaman, Naran Abai. She inherited the traditional Shamanic healing rituals that had been practiced by her ancestors and developed them further. Her abilities were then inherited by her son and grandson.[38] According to Tax (1937) and Fabrega (1973), there are two kinds of bone setters in Mongolia: Practice based bone setters and Shamanic-inheritance bone setters. Thus, one group of bone setters obtained their knowledge from their family via inheritance and mystical transmigration, while the other obtained their knowledge from practical experiences considered less powerful and professional than the former.[39]

Negative influence of Shamanism can be witnessed while dealing with anxiety brought out by uncertainties of capitalism. Buyandegeriyan (2007) is of the view that Shamanic practices have proliferated among ethnic Buryats at least in part as dealing with the anxieties and uncertainties brought about by the collapse of socialism in incipient market economy. The Buryats attribute their current misfortunes to their original spirits who have returned to seek their revenge against their descendants for abandoning them during the socialist state suppression of religion.[40] Kendall (1996) observes scepticism of clients and common people towards Shamans. He says that clients are anxious to figure out whether Shamans are business-driven actors or real (not out for profits). Among the Buryat Mongols, a Shaman who is either too rich or too poor may provoke doubts about his or her credibility. On the one hand too much wealth creates too much doubt about the Shaman's motivation (profit is connected with a lack of morality) and on the other hand, poverty indicates the incompetence of the spirits especially if the Shaman has been practicing for years. Overall, the prolonged disruption and secularization by the state and the greed that has been bred by the market economy have increased the suspicion about Shamans.[41] Suspicion has led Buryat Mongols to search for more authentic Shamans and spirits. As Adam Ashforth (2001) argues that in addition to dealing with poverty, people in the African city of Soweto have to wrestle with spiritual insecurity and suppressing witchcraft. The same is true for Mongolia where most people who have gone to Shamans have found themselves experiencing ever greater anxiety and are suspicious of Shamans. A desire to find out the truth drives people to seek out additional Shamans and to appropriate origin spirits.[42]

While writing on contemporary Shamanism in Mongolia, Maytas Balog (2010) opines that in the Mongolian cultural region there are a number of Shamanic traditions which can greatly differ from each other, but the ways of becoming a Shaman are very similar in all of them. Shamanism here is chiefly practiced by minority groups such as the Darkhats, the Buryats, and the Uriankhais; though none of these have Mongol roots. Here, Shamanism of ethnic groups is regarded as different ways and traditions of practicing Mongolian Shamanism. The Shamanism of the Darkhats is closely related to that of the neighbouring Tuvans, and many of the contemporary Darkhat Shamans are descendants of famous Tuvans.[43] According to X. Nyambuu (1992), the Darkhat ethnic groups comprise a number of clans of Tuvan origin. The Shamanic practices of the Buryats resemble to those of Ewenk and Daur. Most Buryat Shamanic tools, accessories and rituals have their Ewenk and Daur equivalents which are alien to the Darkhats and Uriankhais.[44] While taking an interview of a Shamaness, G. Gantogtox (1997) found that she performed various kinds of rituals except for curses and anything that she might have considered harmful. She further said that Buryat Shamans have to take ninety nine oaths during their first initiation, which prevent them from causing any kind of harm. It is prohibited to endanger human life but they have to help all the living creatures.[45] White Shamans in Buryats are not regarded as real Shamans but as bone setters. They are able to set broken bones with skilful measures and have familiarity with minor illness. Further, Balog (2010) says that Darkhats who live in north-west Mongolia are often regarded as dangerous people, endowed with special ability of calling down curse to those who treat them badly. This area is regarded by many Mongolians as an exotic and remote region where the purest form of Mongolian Shamanism managed to survive. Another ethnic group Tsaatan—remembering

1000 individuals—is regarded as having the most powerful Shamans. Darkhat and Tsaatan Shamanism are often regarded as pure black Shamanism.[46]

Conclusion

The earliest records of Mongolian Shamanism have been traced back to the period of Hunnus when Shamans played a vital role in diplomatic matters with the neighbouring countries. The Hunnu emperors constructed shrines and Shamans were encouraged to combine diverse practices into a national religion. However, it was the period of Great Khans that Shamanism received great respect so much so that under Chinggis Khan Shamanism became the primary religiosity of Mongolia. The views of Shamans were important on all state matters and no military endeavour was taken without the consent of Shamans. Although Shamanism received a set back with the advent of Buddhism in Mongolia, today one can find the coexistence of both Shamanism and Buddhism. But the distinction between the black, yellow and white Shamans clearly exists in the contemporary Mongol world. Yellow Shamans are religious practitioner employing a mixture of Buddhist and Shamanists methods in his/her practices. White Shamans are those who communicate with the spirit of heaven and do not use his/her power to harm any living being. It is widely believed that only yellow Shamans are beneficial for the people as they can serve the latter in a righteous way, i.e., yellow Shamans heal the sick whose sickness is caused by the curses of black Shamans.

Notes and References

1. Cited in M. Eliade (1961), "Recent work on shamanism", *History of Religions,* vol.1, p.153.
2. For more details see John T. Hitchcock (1967), "A Nepalese shamanism and the classic Inner Asian Tradition," *History of Religions,* vol. 7, no. 2, pp 149-158
3. "Mongolian Shamanism", at http://en.wikipedia.org/wiki/Mongolian_shamanism (accessed on 15 May 2014).
4. Klaus Hesse (1986), "A Note on the Transformation of White, Black and Yellow Shamanism in The History of the Mongols", *Studies in History,* vol. 2, no.1, pp.17–30.
5. "Dancing Demons—Ceremonial Masks of Mongolia–Asia", at http://sites.asiasociety.org/arts/mongolia/shaman.html (accessed on 22 March 2014).
6. *Ibid.*
7. *Ibid.*
8. For more details see Matyas Balog (2010), "Contemporary Shamanism in Mongolia," *Asian Ethnicity,* vol.11, no. 2, p. 229.
9. *Ibid,* p. 230
10. *Ibid.*
11. To know more about social organization of Mongolia see Klaus Hesse (1987), "On the

History of Mongolian Shamanism in Anthropological Perspective", *Anthropos,* vol.82,p. 404.

12. L. Narangoa, and L. Altanjula (2006), "From Shamanist Healing to Scientific Medicine: Bonesetters in Inner Mongolia", in Ole Bruun and Li Narangoa (ed.), *Mongols from Country to City: Floating Boundaries, Pastoralism and City Life in the Mongol Lands,* Denmark: NIAS Press, pp. 237-252.
13. For more details see Buyandelgeriyn, Manduhai "Dealing with Uncertainty: Shamans, Marginal Capitalism, and the Remaking of History in Post socialist Mongolia", *American Ethnologist,* vol.34, no.1, 2007, pp.127-147.
14. *Ibid.*
15. Hesse, "A Note on the Transformation of White, Black and Yellow Shamanism", pp.17–30.
16. Cited in Heese, "On the History of Mongolian Shamanism in Anthropological Perspective", p. 404.
17. *Ibid.*
18. Charles Bawden (1970) "Notes on the Worship of Local Deities in Mongolia," in L. Ligeti (ed.), *Mongolian Studies,* Amsterdam, pp.239-247.
19. Ippei Shimamura (2004), "Yellow Shamans (Mongolia)," in Walter, Mariko Namba, Neumann Fridman, Eva Jane. *Shamanism: An Encyclopedia of World Beliefs, Practices, and Culture,* pp. 649-650.
20. Walther Heissig (1953), "A Mongolian Source to the Lamaist Suppression Shamanism in the 17th Century," *Anthropos,* vol. 48,pp.504-505
21. Cited in Heese, "On the History of Mongolian Shamanism in Anthropological Perspective", p. 405.
22. *Ibid.* p. 406.
23. Purev (2008) *Mongolian Shamanism,* Ulaanbaatar Press, pp. 30-34.
24. For detail accounts of historical understanding see Kevin Turner (2011), "A Revival of Mongolian Shamanism," *Shamanism Annual,* vol. 24, p. 4.
25. Walther Heissig (1980),*The Religions of Mongolia,* London: Routledge & Kegan Paul, p. 37.
26. *Ibid.*
27. *Ibid.*
28. Cited in *Ibid.* p.39.
29. *Ibid.*
30. *Ibid.*
31. Cited in *Ibid.*
32. *Ibid.*
33. *Ibid.*
34. R. de Nebesky & Wozkowitz (1956), *Oracles and Demons of Tibet,* Œ-Gravenhage, p.411.
35. Cited in Heissig, *The Religions of Mongolia,* p.45.
36. David Landy (1977), "Role Adaptation: traditional curers under the impact of western medicine", in David Landy (ed.),*Culture, Disease and Healing: Studies in Medical Anthropology,* New York: Macmillan, p.469
37. Claude-Levi-Strauss (1963), "The Effectiveness of Symbol in Structural Anthropology", USA: Basic Books, pp. 186-205.
38. Narangoa & Alatnjula, "From Shamanist Healing to Scientific Medicine", p. 239.
39. Cited in *Ibid,* p 240.

40. Buyandelgeriyn Manduhai (2007), "Dealing with Uncertainty: Shamans, Marginal Capitalism, and the Remaking of History in Post-socialist Mongolia", *American Ethnologist,* vol.34, no.1, p.127.
41. Cited in *Ibid*, p. 127.
42. *Ibid*, p. 142.
43. Balog, "Contemporary Shamanisms in Mongolia", p. 230.
44. Cited in *Ibid.*
45. *Ibid,* p. 233.
46. *Ibid,* p. 231.

CHAPTER 3

Revival of Traditional Culture in Mongolia

Pooja Pingua

Mongolia is a landlocked country sandwiched between Russia and China.[1] The native land of the Mongols was a vast territory stretching east to west from the Khingan Mountains to the Altai range and north to south from Lake Baikal to the southern part of the Great Gobi desert along the Great Wall of China. But there was no internal system of administration as the area was inhabited by different warring Mongol tribes who constantly fought among themselves for supremacy and preferred to remain independent.[2] Mongolian traditional culture is based on nomadic heritage and Buddhist culture which suffered greatly during the twentieth century. In the early twentieth century, Mongolia was the second stronghold of Buddhism after Tibet with more than 100,000 monks taking care of the Buddhist tradition in the country. During 1990s, Mongolia's transition from socialism to democracy led to the peaceful revival of traditional culture and values despite modernization of the society. Today, one can find that once again Buddhism has been contributing greatly not only to the preservation of traditional culture but also towards modernization of Mongolia.[3]

This paper has been divided into two parts. The first part deals with Mongolia's traditional culture that is based on Nomadism, Shamanism and Buddhism which received set back during the period of Communist regime in Mongolia. The second part discusses the post-Communist revival of traditional culture in the form of Mongolian identity, language and religion, particularly Buddhism.

Traditional Culture in Mongolia

Nomadism

Nomadism is an important component of identity and livelihood in the post-Soviet Mongolia.[4] Today the Pastoral nomadism is the prevailing form of the land use in Mongolia. One third of Mongolia's population live as nomadic livestock husbandry, while the others work as traders, drivers, government employees or workers in the food and textile industries or they can provide services to the herder's families. The Altai Mountain is the oldest settlement areas, where modern human beings are thought to have appeared between 100,000 and 60,000 years ago. The present lifestyle of pastoral nomadism is thought to have become established in the Mongolian Altai between 2000 and 3000 year ago. The nomad's seasonal migrations are determined by the climate and aimed at work at maximizing the carrying capacity of the pastures in order to feed their livestock in good grazing places and to fatten them up there by increasing their chance to survive the impending Mongolian winter.[5]

Pastoral nomadism in Mongolia is conducted under the difficult conditions of an extreme continental climate and pastures to match. Natural phenomena such as drought (*gan*) in the summer seasons and heavy snowfall accompanied by very low temperatures (*dzud*) in the winter are very common. Actually the large areas of western and central Mongolia were seriously affected by these extreme conditions over a period from 1999 to 2003, causing heavy losses of livestock. But the fluctuations of climate alone cannot be blamed for the death of millions of animals. In spite of having many rural development projects, agriculture-farming as well as livestock keeping, rural infrastructure were severely neglected in the 1990s. This also caused an increasing disparity between the urban central and foremost being the capital of Ulaanbaatar and rural areas. The results have been a heavy migration from rural to urban areas.[6]

Mongolians today give due importance to their nomadic heritage and are against too much of westernization which they think can easily demolish the basic characteristic of their nomadic identity. There have been debates on whether the Mongols need to give up their nomadic identity in order to be competitive in the 21st century. They also maintained that the desire of Mongols to stay as nomads can turn them into "living museum exhibits". Despite positive influence of the country's nomadic heritage on the past two and half decades of reforms, some experts point out that nomadism is not economic in a modern market. Others believe that the only way that Mongols can move forward is to have a proper combination of modernism and traditionalism based on the nomadic culture if they are to avoid being set apart from the residue of the world.[7]

Shamanism

Shamanism is defined as a religious belief system in which the shaman is a specialist whose spiritual knowledge is required to connect to the world of the spirits in order to bring about benefits for other members of the community.[8] Shamanism, the ancient religion of Mongolia was originated in pre-historical times which played a crucial role in the spiritual lifetime of the Mongols up to sixteenth century. Simultaneously, Tibetan form of Buddhism too was playing an important role after it was introduced during the reign of Khubilai Khan (1215-1294), though it did not spread widely. Buddhism made further inroads into Mongolia from the second half of the sixteenth century after it began to be encouraged by the Manchu court, which was anxious to pacify its northern neighbours.[9]

Although Shamanism was suppressed and did not play any important role after the seventeenth century, shamanistic elements were integrated into Mongolian Buddhism. The Shamanist deities became part of the Buddhist pantheon. Thus, Shamanism continued to live on in Buddhist camouflage and the Shamanist prayers collected by scholars in the nineteenth and the twentieth century were full of Buddhist elements.[10] Before Buddhism penetrated in Mongolia Shamanism dominated the political, economic and the spiritual life of the country. The believers of Shamanism believed in one God, Tengri (Eternal Heaven). They revered and worshipped the heaven and believed that everything including happiness and suffering, derived from heaven. At the same time, they also believed that these heavens contained not just one but ninety-nine tengri (almighty spirit). The Mongols who were followers of Shamanism and living in the Daur region believed that there were at least nine levels of heaven.[11] As the Shamanist lacked religious fervour and believed in the right to worship freely, Chinggis Khan formulated a policy of religious toleration for his subjects.[12] Shamanism was there in the post-communist era too. However, the state banned Shamanism in the Communist period. The shamans survived and re-emerged after 1990. In 1998, a crowd of fifty people attended shamanic rituals on the bank of a river nearby town of Moron.[13]

Buddhism

According to the indigenous traditions, Tibet Buddhism (*sang rgyas kyi chos*) first appeared around the fourth century CE during the reign of the twenty-eighth ruler of the Yar-lung principality, *Lha-tho-tho-ri-gnyan-bstan*. At that time Buddhism was already well established in surrounding lands, including China to the east, India and Nepal to the south and the Central Asian city-states to the north.[14] Between Mongolia and India it has been a long history of contacts both culturally and politically. The cultural contact is based on Buddhism which has been the knitting force. Buddhism was introduced in Mongolia late in the Tang period (618-678 AD) although it has been introduced in China during the late Han period (25-200 AD). In Tibet, during the reign of Sangstan Gampo (617-685 AD) Buddhism was introduced through the Chinese and Nepalese princesses who were married to the King. Later Padmasambhava consolidated Buddhism in Tibet. Buddhism in Mongolia came from Tibet during the reign of Ogodei Kan (1229-1241 AD) by Sa-Sakya Pandit, who was the head of Sa-Sakya sect of Buddhism. Along with his nephew Phage-Pa Lama he worked hard to establish Tibetan form of Buddhism in Mongolia by replacing the traditional Shamanism. Consequently, a close relationship was built up between Mongolia and Tibet through Buddhism. In the subsequent period, Buddhist traditions that were earlier introduced in Tibet from India had become a part of the Mongolian society.[15]

After the founding of the Mongolian's People Republic (MPR) in 1924, "a new era began in the country through the so-called socialist revolution".[16] It was the period of Soviet dominance in Mongolia which was responsible for suppressing Buddhism that is a "highly developed system of philosophy."[17] In 1937, there were 110,000 Buddhist monks preaching in over 700 monasteries in Mongolia. But during the late 1930s nearly all Buddhist monasteries and temples were destroyed or secularized and a large number of monks were killed on accusation of being counter revolutionary element.[18] According to Dashpurev and Soni, during two years (1937 to 1939) of most horrible purges carried out under the leadership of Mongolian President Kh. Choibalsan almost 12,000 Buddhist monks were killed in Mongolia.[19] However, "during the Second World War, following changes in the Soviet policy against religion, the Mongolian government too allowed the revival of Buddhism but under strict official guidelines".[20]

Revival of Traditional Culture

Revival of Mongolian Identity

The national identity reflects vastly divergent life experiences, perceptions and methods of expression. According to Uranchimeg (2010), "the essence of our national identity lies in the ability to preserve our heritage, and language which is the most natural symbol of public and private identity."[21] The struggle for democratic reforms in 1989-1990 led the Mongol people to give a call for "the revival of traditional Mongolian culture, re-introduction of old Mongolian script, rehabilitation of Chinggis Khan and encouragement to Buddhism."[22] During this period, adoration of Buddhist past came into head. Both the revival of Buddhism and rehabilitation of Chinggis Khan began to play important roles in the reconstruction of Mongolian culture and identity.[23] In 1992, freedom of religion was assured in the new Constitution, and the separation of religious and secular institution took place.[24] The new Constitution deals with the emblem of national identity consisting of the State Emblem, the Banner, the Flag and the Seal, which are described in a manner that represent both to the traditional religion as well as Buddhism.

It now appears that Buddhism has influenced all aspects of Mongolian culture and the revival of Buddhist heritage is said to be an important factor in the future peace and happiness of Mongolia. In addition, the cult of Chinggis Khan has its connection with Buddhism because Chinggis Khan is accepted by the Mongolian Buddhists as the re-incarnation of the *Bodhisattva Vajrapani*. According to Agata Bareje-Starzynska and Hanna Havnevik (2006), "Chinggis Khan reminds the Mongols of their glorious past." Today one can see the cult of Chinggis Khan being used to strengthen the Mongol national identity, especially by those who have a "Pan-Mongolist" vision. Both the glory of Chinggis Khan as well as Buddhism have now been identified as a pillar of Mongol national identity.[25]

Revival of Traditional Language

The Mongolian traditional language, now known as the national language, was developed after the establishment of the Mongolian People's Republic (MPR) in 1924 on the basis of Khalkha dialects. The traditional script, which originated from the Sogdian letters of Aramaic origin, was used in the MPR until 1941, when a new alphabet based on Cyrillic was adopted.[26] The stories of King Bhoja, Vikramaditya and Krishna were rendered into the Mongolian language which can be heard even in the remote areas of Mongolia. The written language underwent a series of modifications, both in the form of characters and contents, which were related to external influences and to internal social changes. But the written form of Mongolian language has always been a literacy language, fundamentally different from any spoken Mongolian language or dialect.

With Buddhism spreading in Mongolia in the sixteenth and seventeenth centuries the Buddhist monks at first translated from the Tibetan into the Mongol language a phenomenal amount of ecclesiastical literature as well as works on medicine, astrology, philosophy, philology and poetry. One of the collections of stories was even translated from Sanskrit into Mongol and from Mongol into Tibetan. The introduction of an exotic literature resulted in the eliminations from the written Mongolian of many obsolete terms and the inclusions of words from Tibetan and Sanskrit. At the same time, in order to meet the demand for several copies of the new works, created by the spread of Buddhism, the lamas began to produce them in Xylographic form. Cheney (1968) has pointed out that these innovations favoured the adoption of the unified orthography and consistency in grammar which characterizes the written language as it is used today.[27]

The system of writing known as the 'Phags-pa-script' was in official use during the Yuan dynasty. This script, which was based on the Tibetan alphabet, was devised in 1269 AD by a Buddhist monk Phags-pa, on the order of the Mongol Emperor Khubilai Khan. The letter has a quadrangular shape, and therefore this script is often called the 'Square script'. This script, which was never displaced or seriously disturbed the older form of writing, was abandoned when the Yuan dynasty fell in 1368 AD.[28] The script was used in the Mongolian language and became the official language of the Yuan dynasty. The script which contained 44 letters was also used to write in Sanskrit, Tibetan and Turkish languages. In the post-Yuan period, "the Square script appears to have been unable to replace the Uyghur script which was thought to be easier to use and more suited to the linguistic requirements of the Mongolian nomads".[29]

In the 20th century, the Buryat intellectuals like Bazar Baraadin, Elbegdorj Rinchino and Zhamtsarano promoted the idea of Pan-Mongolism, and hence the development of new script also came to light. Baraadin was the script for the Mongolian language used in the Roman letter. This script was used in Buryatia, Outer Mongolia and Inner Mongolia for about thirty years, and is known as the old Mongolian script.[30] In the 1940s, Mongolian script was changed into the Russian Cyrillic script. In 1950, a new generation of Buryat intellectuals started writing in Russian and Mongolian language about Mongolia and the Mongols.[31] According to Batbayar and Soni (2007), "today, the Mongolian language comprises several dialects, including Khalkha, Buryat, Oirad, Chahar, Kharchin, Khorchin, Ordos and others", and "among all the Mongolian scripts, traditional Mongolian is considered to be the most viable and is still used in the Inner Mongolia Autonomous Region of China."[32] The revival of traditional language has been strengthening the modern Mongolian thought about their culture and way of life.

Revival of Buddhism

The revival of Buddhism has received support both from the government as well as from the people across the country. In the post-1991 period, rebuilding of Buddhist sites was started both by city-dwellers in the capital Ulaanbaatar and by nomads in the countryside. As a result, in 1996, there were roughly 2,000 Buddhist monks in Mongolia and more than 155 registered monasteries and temples. However, this figure further increased and by 1998 there were about 3,000 monks and 200 temples in the country, of which 30 temples were built in the capital and provincial headquarters, while others were in the countryside.[33] The Gandanthegchinlin monastery opened new colleges by restructuring the monastic institution on the Tibetan Ge-lugs-pa model. In order to make Buddhist teachings accessible to smaller monasteries in the countryside, the lama was sent to these establishments. In the restoration of old monasteries and building of new temples and stupas International Buddhist institutions as well as Mongolian People helped greatly, mainly through financial support. Much of the temple material has come from patrons in Hong Kong and India, and also from Taiwan, who have also supplied material to several new monasteries around Mongolia.[34] According to Mongolian Statistical Yearbook (2005), there were more than 157 Buddhist temples and monasteries in the country, with 70 churches, seven mosques and six further places of worship belonging to the other regions.[35] However, in the same year it was counted that there were some 2,349 Buddhist monks and nuns, 223 Christian priests and clergy, 349 Moslem imams, and six clergy of other faiths.[36]

Revival of Buddhism is also reflected in the absorption of new elements, mainly since 1990s, i.e., "the establishment of nunneries, the involvement of monks and nun in social welfare, and the lay involvement in the leadership of the monasteries."[37] Prior to 1990s, women were hardly ordained in Mongolia but today ordained female Buddhist practitioners can be seen. In

Ulaanbaatar, there are two nunneries run by Mongolians and one run by Tibetan. By 2008, there were 21 nuns, half of them joined and completed the degree course at Zanabazar Buddhist University. This is the first time when women were granted the Bachelor's degree in Buddhist Studies at the University. Dalma Ling Nunnery was the first residential nunnery in Mongolia that was opened in 2001 on the ground of the Dara Ekh Monastery which is now home of 14 ordained Mongolian nuns.[38] Despite all the developments in the revival of Buddhism, the number of qualified Buddhist teachers in Mongolia is very small. Buddhist monks are sent to Tibetan monasteries in India to get mastery in the Tibetan language which is necessary to qualify for Buddhist teachings. The Lay Mongolian Buddhists in the Association of Buddhist Lay Believers are involved in learning more about Buddhism in order to give it a more national character.[39] There are now constant teaching activities, generally carried out by the Mongolian and Tibetan Buddhist teachers from the Tibetan exile community in India.

Conclusion

The close connection between Buddhism and the Mongolian culture is today seen in the revival of traditional culture in Mongolia. The Mongolian traditional culture is based on nomadic heritage and religious culture like Shamanism and Buddhism. However, Buddhism has come a long way to receive support of the Mongolian masses in the post-Soviet period while compared to Shamanism. This is not to say that the two religions are rivals but they coexist in largely a Buddhist society of today's Mongolia along with other religions like Islam and Christianity. It is encouraging to note that there are now over 50 percent of the Mongolians who are believers of Buddhism which was all about elimination and decline particularly in the late 1930s, when the worst anti-religious persecution was carried out in the country. Several Buddhist monasteries and temples were also shattered which resulted in the decline of Buddhism and bringing the country under severe social and cultural crisis. It was only from the beginning of 1990s that Mongolia's transition to democracy provided opportunity for the Mongolian people to revive Buddhism as part of their traditional culture. The revival of Buddhism alongside the emergence of personality cult of Chinggis Khan has given a new dimension to the socio-cultural and religious life of Mongols who seek their identity in the preservation of traditional culture and values despite modernization that is underway in the country.

Notes and References

1. Tsedendambyn Batbayar and Sharad K. Soni (2007), *Modern Mongolia: A Concise History*, New Delhi: Pentagon Press, p.1.
2. Sharad K. Soni (2006), *Mongolia-China Relations: Modern and Contemporary Times*, New Delhi: Pentagon Press, p. 4.
3. Sharad K. Soni (2009), "Buddhist Factor in Promoting Traditional Culture in Mongolia", *Buddhism and Nordland 2009* , 10 October, p.1.
4. Caroline Upton (2010), "Introduction: Focus on Mongolia", *Central Asian Survey*, vol.29, no.3, September, p.245.
5. Dorjburgedda Lkhagvadorj et.al (2012), "Pastoral Nomadism in the forest-steppe of the Mongolian Altai under a changing economy and a warning climate" *Journal of Arid Environment*, p.2.
6. Batbayar and Soni, *Modern Mongolia*, pp.141-142.
7. Ibid.
8. Marika Namba Walter and Eva Jane Neumann Fridmen (2004), *An Encyclopedia of World Beliefs, Practice and Culture*, vol.1, United State of America, p. XV.
9. Batbayar and Soni, Modern *Mongolia*, p.3.
10. Agata Bareja-Starzynska and Hanna Havnevik (2006), "A Preliminary Study of Buddhism in Present-Day Mongolia", in Ole Brunn and Li Narangoa, eds., *Mongols from Country to City: Floating Boundaries, Pastoralism and City Life in the Mongols Lands*, Copenhagen: NIAS Press p.216.
11. Urgunge Onon (2001), *The Secret History of the Mongols: The life and Times of Chinggis Khan*, London: Curzon Press, p.29
12. See Ibid, p.9.
13. Morris Rossabi (2005), *Modern Mongolia; From Khans to Commissars to Capitalists*, University of California Press, p.192.
14. James B. Apple (2014), "Buddhism in Tibetan History", in Mario Poceski, eds.,*The Wiley Blackwell Companion to East and Inner Asian Buddhism*, West Sussex: John Wiley & Sons Ltd, p.104.
15. C.S.Upasak (1988), "Early Mongolian Miniature Stupa Deposits Vis-à-vis Indian Tradition", in R.C. Sharma, eds., *Perspective on Mongolia*, New Delhi: Seema Publication, p.1.
16. Sharad K. Soni (2013), "Exploring Mongol-Tibetan Relations: The Contribution of Buddhism", *Mongolian & Tibetan Quarterly*, vol.22, no. 2, 2013, p.60.p.58
17. Lokesh Chandra (2001), "Buddhism in Mongolia", *Himalayan and Central Asian Studies*, vol.5, no.1, p.4.
18. Soni, "Exploring Mongol-Tibetan Relations", p.58.
19. See D. Dashpurvev and S.K. Soni (1992), *Region of Terror in Mongolia, 1920-1990*, New Delhi: South Asian Publishers, p.42.
20. Soni, "Exploring Mongol-Tibetan Relations", p.59.
21. B. Uranchimeg (2010), "Mongolian Language and Culture in National Identity ", in K. Warikoo and Sharad K. Soni, eds., *Mongolia in the 21st Century: Society, Culture and International Relations*, New Delhi: Pentagon Press, p.51.
22. Sharad K. Soni (2007 & 2008), "Promoting Traditional Culture in Contemporary Mongolia", *The IAMS Bulletin*, no. 2(40) & 41(1), p.107.
23. Batbayer and Soni, *Modern Mongolia*, p.141.
24. Soni, "Promoting Traditional Culture in Contemporary Mongolia", p.109.

25. Ibid.
26. Batbayer and Soni, *Modern Mongolia*, p.2.
27. George A. Cheney (1968), "Mongols Culture on the Eve of the Revolution", in John R. Kruegar, eds., *The Pre-Revolutionary Culture of Outer Mongolia,* Occasional Paper, no.5, Bloomington: The Mongolia Society, p.73.
28. Ibid, p.73.
29. Soni, *Mongolia-China Relations*, p. 7.
30. K. Warikoo (2010), "Tradition and Culture in Buryatia", in K. Warikoo and Sharad K. Soni, eds., *Mongolia in the 21st Century,* New Delhi: Pentagon Press, p.326.
31. Ibid, pp. 327-328.
32. Traditional Mongolian script is most viable because its graphical peculiarities make it suitable for all Mongolian dialects. See Batbayer and Soni, *Modern Mongolia*, p.2.
33. Bareja-Starzynska and Havnevik, "A Preliminary Study of Buddhism", p.219.
34. See Batbayer and Soni, *Modern Mongolia*, pp.139-140.
35. See *Mongolian Statistical Year Book* (2005), Ulaanbaatar: National Statistical Office.
36. Urantsatsral Chimedsengee et.al (2009), *Mongolian Buddhist Protecting Nature: A Handbook on Faith, Environment and Development,* Ulaanbaatar, p.9.
37. Soni, "Exploring Mongol-Tibetan Relations", p.60.
38. Urantsatsral Chimedsengee et.al, *Mongolian Buddhist Protecting Nature,* p.13.
39. Bareja-Starzynska and Havnevik, "A Preliminary Study of Buddhism", p.225.

CHAPTER 4

Traditional Mongolian Pastoral Livestock Production System: Relevance for Agricultural Sustainability and Food Security

Ritu Jha

The nomads of the world travelled around every inaccessible and accessible corner of the land and established an indepth link with the environment which remains principally based on the mutual interdependence of both the environment and nomads. With the advancement of society, nomads were treated as an eyesore for the civilized and modernized world. They were long seen as barbaric and semi-barbaric people who kept on moving in groups and remained away from the mainstream people who settled in different places and drew boundaries of their territory. But for nomads there were no boundaries as they made their wave of flow in accordance with the natural world of any region. This was typical with the case of Mongolian nomads as well.

Mongolian nomads remain deeply connected with the delicate grassland of Steppes as their livelihood revolves around it. Their attitude to nature has remained an important case study not only for the environmentalists today but also for the policy makers and the planners to rejuvenate the concept of environmental sustainability, long remain embedded in the nomadic livelihood in delicate Mongolian environment. The forced settlement of the nomads as well as restrictions in their mobility due to the farm collectivization schemes under the influence of the former Soviet Union not just led to the erosion of culture but also paved the way for the environmental disruption. The Mongolian nomads further got transformed into an intensive livestock production system following the introduction of market economy after the disintegration of the Soviet Union in 1991. This system of production was highly commercialized and hence high inputs technologies were given priority over the traditional pastoral livestock production system. Ironically, the degradation of grazinglands due to the intensive grazing methods now poses a threat to the food security of the entire Inner Asian region in general and Mongolia in particular.

It is in this context that the paper seeks to assess the traditional system of pastoral livestock production and management strategies involved in it so as to find out its relevance for the agricultural sustainability and food security of Mongolia.

Nomads in Mongolia and their Transformation

Although the history of Mongolia remains full of turbulences, nomadism has always remained a way of life for the Mongolian people. The ancient history of Mongolia was purely dominated by the nomads and their waves of movements on vast land influenced the sedentary civilizations of not just China, Central Asia and Persia but as far as India. Evidences show that Central Asia was primarily divided into two zones: the nomadic and the sedentary. The northern steppes from South Russia to Manchuria were considered as the nomadic zone, while the sedentary zone included the region to the south and the oases of eastern Turkestan. The nomadic zone was further classified into two distinct regions. The region from South Russia up to the valley of Ienessi was occupied by the nomadic hordes of 'Aryan stock' known as Scythians, and the region in the east, which comprised of Outer and Inner Mongolia, Manchuria and further east, was occupied by Turco-Mongol Hordes. The Scythians nomads, which were known by different names in different regions were considered to be closely linked with Vedic Aryans as many researchers have identified close similarities in terms of religious Vedic Deities.[1]

The deep rooted history of Mongolia flourished under the Scythains, Huns, Sien-pi (Serbi), Hephthalite Huns (White Huns), Juan-Juans. Kao-kiu (ancestor of Uigurs) nomadic tribes, etc., all were deeply associated with the ancient past of the Mongols which shaped the social, cultural, religious, political as well as economic domains, in essence the overall way of life of the nomads.[2]

The Three Stages of Transformation in the Livestock Production System

The Mongolian environment is full of extremes, the ecological and climatic factors obstruct the growth of vegetation cover which increases the severity of soil erosion many fold as the soil remain unprotected.[3] Sheehy (1993) investigates the different grazing management strategies as applied to the delicate Mongolian environment which had undergone drastic changes in the political and economic conditions with time.[4] He identifies three basic grazing management strategies which are used in livestock production on Mongolian land devoted to grazing. These management strategies are as follows:

Extensive Grazing Management Strategy

The 'extensive grazing management strategy' formed the basis of the traditional Mongolian pastoral livestock production system. The system is considered well adapted to the natural environmental conditions experienced in the delicate grassland ecosystem. The herd in such grazing system constitute a mixture of both small stocks like sheep and goat and large stock such as camel or horse, cattle and yak with diverse combinations purely according to the adaptability of the animals to vegetation, terrain and environmental conditions. This grazing management is extremely embedded in the concept of environmental sustainability. Grazingland is classified into seasonal pastures which are grazed according to the managerial and production objectives of the livestock producer. The small scale livestock producers graze upland areas having rough terrain during the summer in order to restore body condition and during autumn they are grazed on specific upland plant communities which help them to build body reserves of fat. Whereas large stock from which milk produce are obtained are kept in lowland areas which are close to water sources and rapidly growing mesophytic vegetation well suited to large animal bulk roughage feeders.[5]

The traditional herding practices are closely knitted around the environmental seasonal changes. In this context, a study conducted by Enkhutuvshin and Tumurjav (2011) is remarkable. They identify that the nomadic herders center them on pasture availability, its characteristics and seasonal changes and act accordingly.[6] Herders remain focussed on their livestock strength, weight and flesh. Special attention has been given by herders for increasing the animal's actual flesh and muscles as they believe that fatty animals easily lose their fat during the winter season.

Few key elements of the extensive grazing management strategy which have been identified include livestock mobility, flexible use of land and low-off take from environmentally adapted livestock. The restoration of strong balance between the livestock population and land carrying capacity is the most important characteristic feature of this grazing management strategy.[7] The land managed with extensive management strategy is considered to have been moderate to high ecological stability.

The nomadic art and culture carries deep imprint of the natural environmental settings that can be seen even in the musical instruments and their folk songs. The sand music, a 'mammoth concert' of varying sound which comes out when wind blows away the sand and makes every grain of sand sing. '*Khomy*' melody is the best example of singing of the sand dunes of the Gobi desert.[8] It has been also observed that nomadic herder developed various sounds as signals for understanding their own livestock and the environment. Even animals too understand their signals in terms of when to pasture, graze and drive.[9] If a baby camel is abandoned by his/her mother, the herders sing special folk song and play '*Morin khuur*' a traditional musical instrument, which according to herders induces cow camel to respond positively and express care and love for the abandoned or motherless baby camels.[10] Their everyday way of life, music, musical instruments, folk songs, seasonal mobility are associated with their adaptability to fragile environment.

Semi-Extensive Grazing Management Strategy

The collective livestock production system primarily applies to the semi-extensive grazing management strategy. It relies on the strategies of the extensity of grazing management but also includes the energy inputs into the production system. This livestock production system is primarily for the personal consumption and sale of excess animal products. The mobility of livestock with higher genetic potential to production is reduced because specialization in one kind of livestock is focused on reducing the labour demands and increasing returns from livestock which becomes the core of the system. In terms of ecological stability it varies according to the pastureland: for upland pasture it is considered high, for lowland pasture stability is moderate and for midland pasture the stability is low due to the year-long livestock grazing and increase in the density of livestock population.[11]

Under the influence of the Soviet system of command economy, collectivization of farmland and collective livestock production system was established on a massive scale which transformed the traditional Mongolian pastoral livestock production system. The nomads were forced to settle down or given defined passages by the state for their movement.[12] The movements of nomads were highly restricted and were strictly guided by the state, which remained aloof from the principles of ecological sustainability of the region. It can be assessed from the studies that the forced settlement of nomads was considered as the major blow for the sustainability of the fragile Mongolian environment.[13] Whereas the *negdals* or collective farm system attempted to increase livestock off-take in the traditional pastoral system by using livestock grazing strategies that benefited from high cost modern inputs like supplementary feed for the livestock, specialized livestock breeds replaced the native plants and livestock species.

Scott (1998) in his revolutionary work examines the state's interest to permanently settle the mobile peoples, especially to empower itself in controlling the entire territory and bring them back into a system where they have to pay tax to the state. He remarkably explained that, "...Nomads and pastoralists (such as Berbers and Bedouins), hunter-gatherers, Gypsies, vagrants, homeless people, itinerants, run-away slaves, and serfs have always been a thorn in the side of states. Efforts to permanently settle these mobile peoples (sedentarization) seemed to be a perennial state project—perennial, in part, because it so seldom".[14] He also observes that the complexities of nature was simplified and reduced into figures like coordinates in a map that can be easily identified and controlled by the state. He explains that "Unable to effectively represent the profusion and complexity of real farms and real fields, high-modernist agriculture has often succeeded in radically simplifying those farm and field so they can be more directly apprehended, controlled and managed."[15] On the other hand, Humphrey and Sneath (1999) with their legendary work on nomads argue that the individual initiative of nomadic herders was discouraged under the collective livestock production system. Based on their assessment they narrate that, "... (herders) were instructed where and when to move, so they did not choose places to pasture the livestock themselves. They worked only at the command and direction of their leaders..."[16]

It has been further identified that collective farm system was not considered successful with every crop or every agricultural commodity as the rate of success depends upon many other factors. Scott (1998) compares the wheat crop with raspberry fruit and highlights factors due to which the rate of success varies in the collective farm crops.[17] Wheat crop once planted requires little attention and care until the crop is ready for harvest as most of the operations are highly mechanized and the crop is also easy to store. But in the case of raspberry fruit, the requirements are different, it is grown on particular soil type and requires timely attention. Moreover, it is considered to be difficult to pick up by machines. The perishability is also high and requires extra care in packaging. In his analysis Scott (1998) narrates that "at virtually every stage the raspberry crop needs delicate handling and speed, or all is lost".[18] The success of collective farm and livestock production system varies even with different crops, and hence it is difficult to apply similar production strategy to every food commodity. This system has failed to recognize the deep connectivity of traditional system of livestock production with its environment.

Intensive Grazing Management Strategies

The main focus of this grazing management strategy is to achieve maximization of inputs into livestock production system in order to maximize the off-take from livestock. The specialization of livestock with higher genetic potential for increasing production was the central aim of this production system. However, environmentally adopted livestock and native species of vegetation was not considered necessary. The maximization of production is the only priority for feeding the market economy which ignored the long term ecological stability of the delicate grassland ecosystem. The feed of livestock comes from artificial pastures. Intensive energy inputs in the form of fertilizers, pesticides, irrigational water are all required for maintaining the artificial pastures. The ecological stability in such management systems is low as all the pasture vegetation is grazed by livestock during all the season which poses the problem of overgrazing and makes the grazingland environmentally vulnerable.[19]

After the collapse of the former Soviet Union Mongolian economy got transformed into a market economy. As a result, the livestock production system was also transformed into an intensive grazing management production system. Intensifying the concentration of animals to certain locations benefited the market based livestock production but deteriorated the pastures as they were intensively grazed. It cost heavily to the delicate ecosystem and eroded the nomadic culture as well. It has been identified in the local studies in

Buryatia and Chita in Russia and in Inner Mongolia in China that as much as 75 per cent of the grasslands has suffered some degree of degradation.[20]

Monoculture not just replaced the traditional pastoral livestock production system but also remained concentrated only in sheep and goat rearing for its better suitability for the market economy.[21] It not only transformed the livestock production system but also the traditional herd structure of five kinds of animals called *taranhoshuumal* in Mongolia, which served diverse purpose in nomadic lifestyle.[22] The Modernist livestock production system remains centered to sheep and goat for extracting meat and wool. The development of monoculture resulted into overgrazing of pasture which not only degraded the common property resources (CPRs) but also threatened the biodiversity. It became difficult for the wildlife to find sufficient pasture and water to sustain on the overgrazed land as the sheep and goats are livestock having remarkably high potential for dietary overlap and competition with many wildlife species.[23]

After the collapse of Socialist (collective) system, exponential increase in the livestock population was observed in the Southern Gobi region (SGR) where it increased from about 762,000 to more than 5 million head. Similarly drastic changes have been observed in the livestock composition, especially in goats and camel population. It is further estimated that from 1970 to 2004, goats, which now dominate the national and the SGR herds, increased from 30 to 57 per cent, whereas the camels decreased from 18 to 6 percent in the same region.[24] In his another study conducted in 2009, Sheehy updated his previous study on pastureland sampling which was originally conducted during 1996-1997. After a span of 12 years, he finds that there has been a loss of 34 percent of plant species in the Gobi region and about a loss of 30 percent in forest steppe region.[25] The plant species that had been lost were highly palatable to all livestock, especially to goats. Sheehy with his indepth observation identifies two major reasons behind this catastrophic erosion of biodiversity which he explains in the following words: "Two conditions have created the loss in species: the proportion of goats in the herd in the last 10 to 12 year, and the areas are becoming increasingly arid...".[26] It can well be established from these studies that a drastic shift has occurred in the herd structure which remains a core area of environmental concern today.

The modernist agriculture and livestock production system has locked itself into a 'single-code system', too simple to assess in terms of profit and loss, the core of commercialization process. With deep observation and studies it has been identified that "a modernist agriculture is single coded—it does one thing (produces food) and does it well. It draws on no local traditions; it is placeless, inflexible and monocultural. Divers capes, by contrast, have more elements, more connections between these elements, and thus greater potential for synergies".[27] After 1990s, with the collapse of rural collectives and state farm system and socialist support infrastructure Mongolian economy went to adverse period and transformed into a market economy, but market failure especially in agricultural market and over-dependence on imported staple food have fluctuated the growth and development of the agriculture sector and poses threat to food security of the nation, especially at the household level.[28] The migration of poor herders to the urban areas further adds to the woe.

Globalization, Market Economy and Corporation: The Global Food Politics

In order to understand the global food politics it is essential to learn about how the globalization and market economy have assisted the corporate giants to take the control of world resources in their hands. The agriculture and livestock production system have seen major changes in its spatial relationship with the environment, ownership and control on their food system. Local communities have little or completely no control over the agriculture and food system. The corporations started increasing their hold on the world agriculture and food system and encouraged livestock production close to a few large processing facilities which they operate. Corporates have taken special care in deciding the location of such large processing facilities where there is negligible threat of union activities so that they can successfully maintain low wages for the labour and soft environmental law.[29] Livestock production thus became highly concentrated in regions where large processing and packaging facilities are available under single corporate house. First, the separation of people from the farm and now the separation of animals from cropland that produces their feed have not just disturbed the soil nutrient cycle as well as soil fertility but also added much to breakdown the physical connectedness of animal with its local environment and biodiversity. This transformation has forced the cropland to become entirely dependent on petroleum based agro-chemicals for increasing soil fertility.

The concentration of ownership and control in agriculture little by little shifted from growers to the Transnational Corporations (TNCs) operating in many countries under the umbrella of globalization. Heffernan (2000) observes that horizontal and vertical integration have been the two important ways with which corporate have increased their control on agriculture.[30]

Horizontal Integration and the Expansion of Corporate Control

Most food firms started as small and local firms but as they became profitable they expanded their base in other geographical areas. The expansion occurred through building new facilities, acquisitions and mergers. According to Heffernan (2000), "The expansion of a firm within the same stage of the food system as their original is called horizontal integration."[31]

In this process the small players like small firms, small holders and small farmers got eliminated from the market with the planned horizontal integration of corporations in agriculture which involved two important features: planned overproduction and selling the product below the cost of production. Cargill, a corporate firm, is the best example of horizontal integration, which exposes the relationship of globalization in assisting the corporate world in gaining the economic power of the world food system. Cargill has its operation in as many as 70 countries and can easily absorb the economic losses in one or two countries over a few years as they can manage their losses with the profits in firms in other countries. In this way, the TNCs gain the foothold in new country and devastate the small local firms with single product base and monopolize the market.

Vertical Integration and the Expansion of Corporate Control

For eliminating competition, the second major strategy of large corporate firms is the vertical integration. The firm increases its ownership and has control over a number of stages in a commodity system just like diversifying into different commodity system. This structure gives the firm more economic power. Since in the case of livestock sector animal feed is important, the firms like Cargill which is in the livestock production business and one of the world's largest processors of hog and beef is also one of the three largest global traders in grains that is the main ingredient in animal feed.[32] ConAgra firm, one of the largest food firm in the United States and in the world, owns and controls a major portion of the global food system ranging from the basic raw material for agricultural production to the gigantic retail stores. This is how the vertical integration encourages few TNCs to control the global food system from 'seed to shelf'.[33]

Hence it is imperative for a country's food security to revive its traditional food system based on subsistence in which family control its food from seed to plate, so that entire nation remains food secure. The government's role in controlling a food system has been declining day by day as the TNC's have integrated the global food system which is dependent on their twist and turn.

Relevance of Traditional System for Agricultural Sustainability and Food Security

The regional ecosystem of Mongolian desert and desert-steppe is identified as 'non-equilibrium environment' having features in which environmental factors like precipitation, temperature, winds, etc., influence the ecological condition of the plant community equally or more grazing by livestock. The vegetation developed in such environment is irregular and spatially and temporally diverse communities of plants are developed because of differences in soil and environmental conditions.[34] Environmentally it represents a more delicate ecological system which is more vulnerable in comparison to the 'Equilibrium Environment'. The grass-steppe and forest-steppe regional ecosystem have colder temperature and higher annual precipitation less temporal and spatial diversity of vegetation and soils occur in these ecosystems. The annual production from plant communities is less diverse and has been classified as more 'equilibrium environment'.[35] In both the 'equilibrium' and 'non-equilibrium' Mongolian environment, the livestock grazing management strategies is primarily based on extensive grazing management as was the case in the traditional Mongolian pastoral livestock production system. Due to this reason both the grazingland ecosystems remain in an ecological stable state as the livestock production systems are well adjusted to the local environmental conditions.[36]

Numerous studies have identified that Mongolian grazinglands are gifted with rich biodiversity and considered highly palatable and nutritious for livestock. Over 5000 species of plants have been observed, most of them are grasses which constitute the flora of Mongolian grazingland. While examining the composition of the plant species of grazing ecosystem, over 600 species are of forage, out of which 200 are identified as nutritious and highly palatable to livestock.[37] Traditional Mongolian pastoral livestock production system has for long maintained the sustainability of grazinglands of Mongolian Plateau because the system was based on flexible and mobile use of grazinglands by environmentally adapted livestock which were fed on the diverse native plant species available temporally and spatially on the vast grazinglands.[38] The flexible herding systems also ensure optimal use of the best pastures and water sources.[39]

The vegetation communities are having few delicate characteristic with the seasonal vegetation growth with low productivity and spatially dispersed annual forage standing crop which makes this region vulnerable if highly mobile livestock and flexible grazing management strategies are not followed. The modernization of animal feed and fodder industries has given priority to production system rather than understanding the adaptability of native plants with the delicate Mongolian environment. The common grazinglands are prone to overgrazing which is further going to damage the environment and raises food security concerns, especially for the poor herders which rely heavily on common property resources (CPRs) for feeding their livestock.

Time and again it has been assessed that the traditional Mongolian pastoral livestock production system was well adapted to the delicate grazingland ecosystem. It maintained an ecologically 'steady state' equilibrium that was not altered by grazing of livestock, thus indicating that the nomads have deeper sense of the ecology of delicate grassland ecosystem and so they remained in harmony with nature through ages. It points towards a strong ecological perception, which shaped the nomadic culture and seasonally mobile grazing system was purely the outcome of the flexible adaptability of the nomads with the fragile environment. The traditional Mongolian pastoral livestock production system was embedded in the natural law of sustainability which was purely scientific in nature. In essence, the key for the sustainability and the food security of Mongolia lies in its traditional nomadic culture.

However, the growing economic power and control of transnational corporations (TNCs) on the global food system points to the fact that their main aim remain as not meeting the global demand, but getting foothold on the food system of a country. In the zeal for escalating the economic power, the TNCs drop product prices even below the cost of production and absorb the losses in a country with the profits in other countries until it completely eliminate the small local single-product based firms of that country. This is how the TNCs shift from perfect competition to the state of monopoly in the market and get the control in their hands where even the government of a country has little control over food system. It is a perilous trend under the name of development for the food security of a country.

Conclusion

Few important conclusions can be drawn from the aforementioned discussions. Firstly, the erosion of nomadic culture poses threat for the identity of nomads. Secondly, the strong ecological insight of nomadic culture long preserved the ecological balance in the delicate Mongolian environment and also sustained the food security of the region. Nomads adjusted their livelihood according to their close experiences with sensitivity of the environment which they deeply understood, and for their sustenance they adapted to a mobile and flexible lifestyle which involved frequent seasonal movements. The nomads have well applied the concept of carrying-capacity and mobility in their lifestyle is the outcome of interaction of mankind with its space. Erosion of nomadic culture can jeopardize both the fragile Mongolian environment as well as the food security of the country. Today in Mongolia, the food security especially at the household level is a major concern as the corporate world is growing its control over the food system, and the decision making power of nomadic herders have been shifted to the market giants. Due to the elimination of the global trade barriers, it has become really hard for Mongolia to sustain its own food system. Hence, there is a need to recognize the traditional Mongolian pastoral livestock production system and its relevance in agricultural sustainability and food security of the country.

Notes and References

1. P. C. Bagchi (1955), *India and Central Asia*, Calcutta: National Council for Education, pp. 1-2.
2. Ibid, pp. 3, 5, 9-11; B.N. Mukherjee (1970), "Ta-Hsia and the Problem Concerning the Advent of Nomadic Peoples in Greek Bactria", *East and West*, vol. 19, pp.395-400.
3. W.A. Palmer (1991), *National Report: Mongolia (Draft)*, UN Development Programme, Regional Bureau for Asia and the Pacific, p.55.
4. D.P. Sheehy (1993), "Grazing Management Strategies as a Factor Influencing Ecological Stability of Mongolian Grasslands",*Nomadic Peoples*,no. 33, p.20.
5. Ibid, p.21.
6. For more details, see B. Enkhtuvshin and M. Tumurjav (2011), *Mongolian Nomads and Nomadic Animal Husbandry*, Ulaanbaatar: International Institute for the Study of Nomadic Civilizations, pp. 1-50.
7. Ibid.
8. V. Iyer (1992), "Cultural Perspectives in Modern Mongolia", In K. Warikoo and D. Norbu (eds.),*Ethnicity and Politics in Central Asia*, New Delhi: South Asian Publishers, p. 258.
9. Enkhtuvshin and Tumurjav (2011),*Mongolian Nomads*, pp. 1-50.
10. Ibid.
11. Sheehy, "Grazing Management Strategies", pp. 22-23.
12. This was the result of the abortive *kolkhoz* (collective farm) experiment. For more details see Sharad K Soni (2002), *Mongolia-Russia Relations: Kiakhta to Vladivostok*, New Delhi: Shipra Publications, p. 150.
13. C. Humphrey andothers (1993), "Attitudes to Nature in Monglia and Tuva: A Preliminary Report", *Nomadic Peoples*, no.33, pp.58-59.
14. J.C. Scott (1998), *Seeing like a State: How Certain Schemes to Improve the Human Condition Have Failed*, New Haven: Yale University Press, p.1.
15. Ibid, p.262.
16. C. Humphrey and D. Sneath (1999),*The End of Nomadism? Society, State and the Environment in Inner Asia*, Durham, NC: Duke University Press, pp.39-40.

17. Scott,*Seeing like a State*,p. 221.
18. Ibid.
19. Sheehy, "Grazing Management Strategies", pp. 23-24, 27.
20. B.O. Gomboev (1996), "The Structure and Process of Land use in Inner Asia", in C. Humphery and D. Sneath (eds.),*Culture and Environment in Inner Asia: The Pastoral Economy and the Environment*, vol. 1, Cambridge: The White Horse Press, p.21; Humphrey and Sneath (1999), *The End of Nomadism*, p. 52.
21. D. Sneath (1998), "State Policy and Pasture Degradation in Inner Asia", *Science*, no. 281, pp. 1147-1148.
22. Baohua (2010), "Transformation of Culture in Inner Mongolia", In K. Warikoo and S.K. Soni(eds.), *Mongolia in the 21st Century: Society, Culture and International Relations*, New Delhi: Pentagon Press, p.305.
23. A.W. Allen and others (1984),*Habitat Suitability Index Model: Pronghorn*, Washington, DC: US Fish and Wildlife Service, p.6; D.P. Sheehy and others (2010),*Mongolia: Livestock and Wildlife in the Southern Gobi Region with Special Attention to Wild Ass*, Washington, D.C.: World Bank, 13-14 August, pp. 48-49.
24. Sheehy, *Mongolia: Livestock and Wildlife*, p.12.
25. S.J. Wachter (2009), "Pastoralism Unraveling in Mongolia", *New York Times*, 8 December.
26. Ibid.
27. J. Pretty (2002), *Agriculture: Reconnecting People, Land and Nature*, London: Earthscan, p. 47.
28. World Bank (2009), *Mongolia: Livestock Sector Study*, vol. I, Report No. 50277-MN, World Bank: Sustainable Department, East Asia and Pacific Region. 15 September, pp. 21-25.
29. J.B. Foster and F. Magdoff (2000), "Liebig, Marx, and the Depeletion of Soil Fertility: Relevance for Today's Agriculture", in F. Magdoff, J.B. Foster and F.H. Buttle (eds.), *Hungry for Profit: Agribusiness Threat to Farmers, Food and the Environment*, New York: Monthly Review Press, p.52.
30. W. Heffernan (2000), "Concentration of Ownership and Control in Agriculture", In Magdoff, Foster and Buttle (eds.), *Hungry for Profit*, New York: Monthly Review Press, p.64.
31. Ibid.
32. Ibid, p.68.
33. Heffernan, "Concentration of Ownership and Control in Agriculture", p.69.
34. Sheehy, "Grazing Management Strategies", pp. 23-24, 18.
35. Ibid, p.18.
36. Sheehy, "Grazing Management Strategies", pp. 23-24, 18.
37. Ibid.
38. Ibid, p.17.
39. R. Mearns (1991), "Pastoralists, Patch Ecology and Perestroika: Understanding Potentials for Change", *IDS Bulletin*, vol. 22 (4), p.31.

CHAPTER 5

Rural Economic Transformation in Post-Soviet Mongolia

Alok Kumar

In its early history dating back to 2000 years or even more Mongolia has witnessed a series of rise and fall of its nomadic empires (Hun, Simbe, Nirun, and Kidan). The sporadic nomadic clans were often engaged in the ongoing skirmishes and raids over grazing lands and water sources. In the early 13th century AD, Chinggis Khan unified all the nomadic clans under one flag and reinforced authority over such a vast area that was no less than the area of expansion by Alexander the Great. The empire, however, disintegrated by mid-14th century due to several reasons. Thereafter Mongolia came under Manchu-Qing rule of China in the late 17th century and remained so till the early 20th century when it proclaimed its independence in 1921. After independence it came under heavy influence of the former Soviet Union. It remained closely associated with Moscow until 1990, though it had never been officially part of the Soviet Union. Eventually, in terms of its status Mongolia was referred to as a "Soviet satellite".[1] The governments were actually puppet governments that were controlled by the communist regime of Kremlin. After decline of Russian supremacy, the country underwent its first democratic elections in 1990 which gave way to the establishment of a multiparty parliamentary system. In the post-Soviet period, a paradigm shift was observed from central planning and state ownership to a private and market based economy, despite the fact that private ownership had never been attributed to the traditional Mongolian Economy.[2] In the last two decades, Mongolian economic transition has proceeded successfully which is evident by rapid economic growth in real terms at an average annual rate of 6.3 percent. It was even faster during the period 2004-06 averaging 8.4 percent, which reached its peak in 2011 with a growth rate of 17.3 percent.[3] The major source of real economic growth has been primary sector only with heavy dependence on mining and livestock ranching.[4]

Land and People

As officially claimed, Mongolia preserves some of the unspoiled patches of earth's landmass, and hence it is referred to as paradise for ecotourism. It has close linkages with Central Asian Republics (CARs) in terms of language, culture and a shared history, therefore, it is arguably, a Central Asian state.[5] Geographically, Mongolia is spread over a vast territory of 1,564,100 sq. kms., almost three times larger than the size of France, resided by 2.78 million (2010) population which makes it the least populated country of the world. Almost 90 percent of land area of the country is pasture land or desert of which only 1 percent is arable and merely 9 percent is forested. Most of the Mongolian territory is dominated by undulating terrain of semiarid grassy steppe lands. The mountains are in west and southwest which reach over 4,000 meters height. It also contains vast semi desert and desert plains and the famous Gobi desert where population density is as low as 0.3 persons per square kilometres. The ethnic composition of the country is constituted mainly by 86 percent of Khalkha Mongols, 3.9 percent by Turkicspeaking Kazakhs and the rest 10.1 percent are others including Oirats, Buryats, Chinese and Russians. The 94 percent population follows Tibetan Buddhism, while the rest 6 percent follows Islam and Shamanism. Literacy is above 90 percent. People grow wheat, barley, vegetables, forage crops in their farmlands as well as animal products are produced through rearing of sheep, goats, cattle, camels and horses.

At the industrial level, oil, food and beverages, processed animal products, cashmere and natural fibres are produced. Mongolia is also bestowed with a variety of mineral resources. The transition of economy from state ownership and central planning to a private, market-based economy[6], Mongolia's road has not been smooth enough. It has been further complicated by heavy dependence on a few primary exports, particularly minerals (copper and gold) and agricultural produce (cashmere). Copper is the main mining produce and it is the leading export commodity followed by gold. It has some reserves of petroleum which needs further exploration. Other natural resources available are coal, molybdenum, tungsten, phosphates, nickel, zinc, fluorspar, silver and iron but they are in limited pockets. The climate of the country is classic "continental" which is characterised by low rainfall and extreme variations in seasonal temperature between winter and summer (average summer temperature +17°C, average winter temperature –26°C).[7]

The climatic characteristic of Mongolia severely limits its potential of crop production but it has no significant effects on livestock herding. Nonetheless, apart from restricted crop production, its vast territory and undulating terrain presents a major challenge in developing adequate infrastructure, and it becomes more difficult when the rural population is widely disbursed. Geographical isolation affects rural development both politically and economically. As it will be discussed later, in the given condition, providing rural infrastructure services such as transportation, health facilities and education put greater challenge than rural financial services.[8] Since 1990 when economic transition was started, the percentage share of the private sector in GDP has gradually risen from 57 percent in 1996 to 75 percent in 2001 and now most economic sectors are privatized more than 90 percent. At times contribution of manufacturing sector to gross domestic product (GDP) rose to more than 35 percent surpassing agriculture's proportion to the GDP but again it fell sharply to 15 percent in recent years and the agriculture and mining have regained its importance.[9] Following transition to market economy, poverty has decreased but as high as about 40 percent (2009) of the population is still living below the poverty line. The gap between the rich and the poor is very high as the richest 10 percent are occupants of 24.5 percent of the national GDP in 2009.[10]

Transformation of Rural Economy

Agriculture is considered to be the backbone of rural economy of Mongolia.[11] In fact, Mongolian herders strongly resisted centralised planning and agricultural collectivisation in the early 1930s because it eventually restricted the movements of nomadic pastoral and herding families to a limited single local area. The process of collectivisation went on and by 1960s almost 75 percent of livestock were owned by herding collectives and less than 25 percent were owned by individual members of the same collectives.[12] At times, Mongolia was making efforts to become self-sufficient in crops production. The state farms such as wheat were allocated relatively more capital for mechanization as well as focussing on better productive lands near population centres. However, when private property and market incentives arrived, the production of wheat, particularly in 2007 fell to less than one third of its 1990 production level due to shortcomings on the input side and fragmentation of land, while production of vegetables have risen.[13]

Another major change in rural economic activities was the spectacular increase in the number of livestock and herding families. These families returned to nomadic pastoral traditions. The number of herding families increased from 75,000 in 1990 to 190,000 in 2000. In the same period, number of livestock increased from 25.8 million in 1990 to over 33.5 million in 1999. It was partially attributed to the occurrence of a natural phenomenon namely "dzuds" (excessive winter cold and snow, combined with summer droughts) in a series in the beginning of 1999; partially it was due to exceeding carrying capacities of pasturelands, especially near population centres. With Mongolia facing socio-economic transition poverty has increased many folds due to increasing inequality in income distribution, leaving the key question unanswered as whether poverty and income gap between urban and rural area can be reduced. Here one has to understand that situation of urbanisation is not actually as it is depicted by Government of Mongolia. It is not 58.5 percent urbanised as reported officially in population figures. The problem remains with assessment in which all the 21 *aimags* (provinces) are counted as urban centres. Indeed 9 *aimags* have populations below 20,000 another 10 have populations between 20,000 and 40,000 and only 2 have populations around 70,000. Considering this, by most criteria used in the world, Mongolia is more than half rural.

Ironically, the incidence of poverty is rather higher in *aimags* if the definition of urban centres were to be adjusted. The rate of unemployment is significantly higher in rural areas among the poor. According to the Mongolian poverty estimates, herding families need a minimum of 200 herds to be above the poverty level. By this standard about 90 percent of herding families were below poverty line in 1991. Only silver-line was the fact that some 28 percent of herding families were not dependent on income solely from livestock. This states the need of income diversification for rural poor.[14] However, pastoralism with all diversified species is a natural and effective economic activity for the given ecological conditions. Furthermore, the vast natural pastureland, its climate conditions and its limited population naturally favour extensive livestock ranching.[15]

Main Actors of Rural Finance in Mongolia

Commercial Banks (CBs) are the largest constituent of rural financial markets of Mongolia. As a part of economic transition, Mongolia quickly moved from a mono-banking system to a "Western-style" system in order to create a sustainable banking system. Initially the commercial banks remained largely under government control and the loans were directed according to government priorities. Moreover, these commercial banks faced problems due to lack of understanding of risk and risk management skills. As a result, the country had to suffer from a series of banking crises during the 1990s, aggravated by the Asian and Russian financial crises. When this period of crisis was over, Mongolia's economic situation started improving remarkably. Currently, the country has 16 private commercial banks along with the state-owned Savings Bank. Among private banks, Anod Bank and Golomt Bank are larger and more successful. Each of the Savings Bank and recently privatized Trade and Development Bank (TDB) have some 10 branches outside the capital Ulaanbaatar, but neither of them is significantly involved in rural lending. However, the Savings Bank has many rural depositors and it has recently been involved in ADB's 'Agricultural Sector Development Program' for rural loan disbursement. Anod Bank also has rural borrowers, so it may play some future role in rural finance sector.[16]

There are two other private banks namely Zoos Bank and Mongol Post Bank that are expanding remarkably into rural finance. The Zoos Bank considers Ulaanbaatar market as saturated, therefore, plans are afoot to expand into all *aimags*. It has now seven branches outside Ulaanbaatar, which have considerable number of micro-borrowers in rural areas. It has been involved in microfinance projects in rural Mongolia with the support of international donor agencies like Asian Development Bank (ADB), World Bank (WB) and United States Agency for International Development (USAID). Mongol Post Bank (MPB), which was separated from Post Office in 1998, has branches in all *aimags* and it has the second largest network with 62 branches all over the country due to its postal origins. MPB is substantially involved in microfinance in rural areas in participation with ADB, WB, and Kreditanstaltfür Wiederaufbau (KfW). These international donor agencies facilitate relatively sophisticated risk management techniques and a broad outreach. There are two relatively smaller but significant banks in terms of micro and rural finance. They are Xac Bank and Xaan Bank. Xac Bank was created in 2001 by the merger of two Nonbank Financial Institutions (NBFIs). Basically the Xac Bank was a NGO-MFI which is globally recognised as an example of transformation of NGO-MFI to a bank.[17] Both the Xac Bank and Xaan Bank were deeply involved in microfinance in rural areas, of which one was founded by Mercy Corps with financial assistance from USAID and the other constituted by a group of six NGOs which were carrying out the UNDP's Microstart Program in the rural areas.,

With its 20 branches the Xac Bank is present virtually in every *aimag* and it uses international best practices in lending techniques with a flexible approach in terms of collateral from solidarity groups. It primarily lends to herder's solidarity groups, micro or small clients, under the USAID's 'Gobi Regional Economic Growth Initiative'. The Xac Bank has a promising sustainable future in both funding and profitability as the Bank was serving 18,610 borrowers with average loan amount of US $640 and 25,666 depositors with average deposit of US $333 by the end of 2003. The erstwhile Agricultural Bank is now known as Xaan Bank. The state owned Agriculture Bank became insolvent due to bad debts and inefficient officers, was subsequent privatised. A new independent management team was set up to rehabilitate Xaan Bank with support from USAID primarily and various other donor agencies such as Deutsche Gesellschaftfür Technische Zusammenarbeit (GTZ), KfW, WB, and ADB. The new management designed simple and attractive loan products with low administrative costs so that even the smallest branches could be able to make profits instead of closing the small and non-profitable branches. A series of other managerial reforms were also incorporated as management information systems (MIS), information technology (IT) and recruitment of local staffs with high incentives on their performances. However, it was criticized for sideling its original mandate of financing agricultural and rural development. Remarkably, by the end of 2003, the bank had around 130,000 outstanding loans with an average amount of US $350, of which 30,000 were to small and microenterprises and 10,000 were to herding families.

The Microfinance market of Mongolia is very small, that is why any specific law for deposit taking MF has not been created. In fact there is hardly any specific microfinance enabling law. In 2001, X.A.C. Co. Ltd. wanted to mobilize deposits from the public and for this purpose it had sought licence as a full scale commercial bank. The minimum capital for bank licensing was out of the reaches of Xac Bank so the company opted for merger with Mercy Corps owned Goviin Ekhel LLC (GE), which was the leading loan provider for small and medium enterprises. With this merger in October 2001, the two companies' combined capital was sufficient for minimum requirement and Xac Bank, the successor, was licensed. By 2005, it had mobilised about

US$ 20 million equal to 83 percent of its loan portfolio.[18] The Xac Bank has asserted remarkable growth which is observable on several performance indicators. Its assets grew by 26 times, loans increased by 43 times and savings by 25 times during the period between 2002 and 2010. Now it has an asset of over US$ 450 million. At times, the Xac Bank was UNDP beneficiary which has been now promoted to an implementing partner.[19]

The Nonbank Financial Institutions (NBFIs) are present in considerable number but they are relatively unimportant as far as Mongolian financial sector and especially rural finance is concerned leaving aside the large NBFI Chinggis Khaan, which has become a bank. The Savings and Credit Cooperatives (SCCs) are somewhat twice the size of NBFIs in total assets but they are also a minor part of the Mongolian financial sector as compared to banks. The SCCs have also expanded rapidly in number like NBFIs but when we compare between SCCs and NBFIs, the former has more relevance for rural finance and potential to grow. Like in other countries, informal source of finance are very common, for example moneylenders, pawnshops, friends, relatives etc. Particularly rural finance involves relationship between agriculturist and traders mainly for meat and cashmere. The meat processors usually make contracts with herders in the spring which includes the type and quantity of meat and price to be paid at delivery in the fall, with three months advanced finance. Same process applies to agricultural products and cashmere. Since it is based on long term traditional relationship so the collateral normally is not required and it is done verbally. However, the larger traders usually borrow from commercial banks, while the smaller traders obtain loans either from banks or from larger purchasers. In case of collateralised loans the average interest rate varies between 8 and 15 percent per month which quiet higher.[20]

Government Policies and Regulatory Environment

Mongolian government policies have always been conducive towards rural finance. There exist no serious impediments at policy which could hampera bank at entering or branching or for their foreign ownership. Importantly, there is no cap over interest rates and no targeted subsidised government credit program which would discourage the participation of private financial institutions in rural finance and their sustainability. The central bank has made significant efforts for a genuine supervision system but they have never been obstacle in general operations. The central bank is required to supervise NBFIs, which cannot legally take deposits but there are reports of disguised deposit takings. If central bank makes efforts to bring transparency in NBFIs' operations it could provide a multidimensional improvement.[21] The central bank has become highly concerned about the SCCs for their irresponsible behaviour but at the same time doesn't want to take primary regulatory responsibility. With the technical assistance of ADB's Rural Finance Project, SCC laws and bylaws were drafted as a set of regulations and recommendations. There are some aspects that could be improved to make the SSCs at par with the formal banking system. Like most of the countries that underwent transition from state ownership and central planning to a market-based private economy, in Mongolia too the issues of contracts and collateral have risen in importance, although it has made significant progress in this direction. After economic transition most rural land remains under state ownership because the rural Mongolians return to their traditional nomadic herding, thus so far as land is concerned it is not available as physical collateral. The animals and other moveable property do not provide alternatives, therefore, it implies a need to assure the registry of moveable properties so that the defaulting borrowers could be brought to the rule of law. In this regard, Mongolia could follow the steps taken in this direction by major Central Asian countries to improve its legal infrastructure for leasing and other alternatives for moveable collateral.[22]

Major Challenges and Possible Interventions to Overcome Problems

Mongolia is sandwiched between Russia and China hence, it is a landlocked country. Economically, it is heavily dependent on both the riparian states. Mongolia has always been in good relations with Russia. The socially sensitive Russia supplied subsidized fuel to run Mongolian economy apart from other assistance. The situation with China is quite different. China always imports raw materials from Mongolia and in return pushed their cheap manufactured products. The Mongolian countryside is flooded with low priced footloose products that put serious threats to the indigenous Small and Medium Enterprises (SMEs). The Mongolian SMEs are unable to compete with Chinese products which are major hindrance in development of microenterprises in rural areas. It is partially attributed to the traditional nomadic pastoral culture as the people do not tend to accept innovations related to microenterprises or any other income generation activities. Keeping this in mind the National Agricultural Extension Centre (NAEC) was established in 1996 as the first official agriculture extension organisation of Mongolia with technical support from the Asian Development Bank (ADB).[23]

The rural areas are mainly confronting problems related to financial services. The Xaan Bank and Xac Bank are leading in this direction, especially in terms of potential profitability. Considering the fact, other banks are also beginning to move into rural areas. Since the formal financial services have not been adequately explored so far, the informal finance is still very significant in rural areas. To enhance the role of formal financial institutions, SCCs needs to be sharpened in trainings and technical assistances including transparency. Implementation of a proper regulatory framework for SCCs and NBFIs could definitely help expand financial infrastructure in rural areas. Diversification of rural areas is also much required. For diversification of rural areas, tourism suddenly spirals out in mind especially ecotourism given its geography and traditions of herder hospitality. For this purpose better transportation facilities need to be developed in the countryside along with education and training to understand what free spending foreign tourists demand, such as proper sanitary and hygienic condition for food and stay.[24]

Conclusion

Mongolian economy is based on agriculture, if mining is also included then it could be said that it is largely based on primary sector only. Due to the gradual economic transition more than 90 percent of the economy is now privatised. Therefore, the economic transition has definitely and positively impacted on the rural economy of Mongolia. But heavy reliance on primary sector is never considered as a good sign for the healthy development of an economy. Once the raw materials are over, given the location, the country has to depend economically on the riparian states. When it falls into economic crisis or debt trap, it is no surprise that the expansionist dragons might start crawling over Mongolian territories. Against this backdrop, Mongolia needs to develop economic situation of rural areas by involving the rural populace into income generation activities, commercial cropping and industrial scale livestock ranching. For this purpose it has to inject more funds by improving financial infrastructure. It has to make international collaboration for training and implementation of technologically advanced small and medium industries to check and utilise its own resources. Considering the aforementioned discussion it may be concluded that the rural landscape of Mongolia is full of opportunities, whether for industrial development or tourism, that can provide a promising future to the country.

Notes and References

1. Sharad K. Soni (2002), *Mongolia-Russia Relations: Kiakhta to Vladivostok*, New Delhi: Shipra, p. 7.

2. R.C. Vogel and Dennis Sheets (2006), "Rural Finance in Mongolia", *Beyond Microfinance: Building Inclusive Rural Finance Markets in Central Asia,* Asian Development Bank, p.159.
3. Sharad K. Soni (2013), "Evaluating Mongolia's Experience of Democratization: The Post-Soviet Scenario", *The Mongol Journal of International Affairs* (Ulaanbaatar), vol.18, 2013, p.31.
4. E. Ianchovichina and S. Gooptu (2010), "Growth Diagnostics for a Resource-Rich Transition Economy: The Case of Mongolia", *The World Bank*, p. 2, http://siteresources.worldbank.org/INTDEBTDEPT/Resources/468980-1206974166266/4833916-1206974192224/IanchovichinaGooptuwps4396.pdf (accessed on June 6, 2014).
5. M.B. Lamberte, et. al., eds. (2006), *Beyond Microfinance: Building Inclusive Rural Financial Markets in Central Asia,* Philippines: Asian Development Bank, p.ix.
6. UNDP (2010), *Microfinance in Mongolia,* http://www.undp.org/content/undp/en/home/ourwork/povertyreduction/projects_and_initiatives/microfinance-in-mongolia/ (accessed on June 6, 2014).
7. Nations Online: Mongolia, http://www.nationsonline.org/oneworld/mongolia.htm(accessed on June 6, 2014).
8. O. Shagdarsuren (2007), "Tackling Isolation in Rural Mongolia: Use of Information Communication Technologies in Agricultural Extension Services", *Geographical Paper,* No.181, p.1, http://www.reading.ac.uk/web/FILES/geographyandenvironmentalscience/GP181_Oyuna4_final_from_Oyuna_B.pdf (accessed on June 6, 2014).
9. Vogel and Sheets, "Rural Finance in Mongolia", p.160.
10. Mongolian State Statistical Office, *Statistical Yearbook 2009,* Ulaanbaatar: Central Intelligence Agency, CIA Factbook, 2010. p.300.
11. Shagdarsuren, "Tackling Isolation in Rural Mongolia".
12. Vogel and Sheets, "Rural Finance in Mongolia", p.162.
13. ADB (2007), *Annual Report-2007,* vol.1, Manila, pp.42-49.
14. Vogel and Sheets, "Rural Finance in Mongolia", p.163.
15. R.C. Sharma (1997), "*Mongolia: Tryst with Change and Development*", Patiala: Vision and Venture Publishers, p.248.
16. Vogel and Sheets, "Rural Finance in Mongolia", p.164.
17. World Bank (2004), *Microfinance and the Poor in Central Asia: Challenges and Opportunities,* p.xv, http://documents.worldbank.org/curated/en/2004/05/5715225/microfinance-poor-central-asia-challenges-opportunities (accessed on June 6, 2014).
18. J. Ledgerwood, and V. White (2006), *Transforming Microfinance Institution,* Washington DC: The International Bank for Reconstruction and Development/The World Bank, p.29.
19. UNDP (2010), *Microfinance in Mongolia,* http://www.undp.org/content/undp/en/home/ourwork/povertyreduction/projects_and_initiatives/microfinance-in-mongolia/ (accessed on June 6, 2014).
20. Vogel and Sheets, "Rural Finance in Mongolia", pp.171-174.
21. A. Saffery, et.al. (2010), *Mongolia Economic Growth Assessment,* Washington, DC: USAID/EGAT/EG, p.59.
22. Vogel and Sheets, "Rural Finance in Mongolia", pp.172-174.
23. Shagdarsuren (2007), "Tackling Isolation in Rural Mongolia".
24. ADB (2004), *Private Sector Assessment for Mongolia,* Box 7: Tourists' Perceptions of Mongolia, p. 46. http://www.forum.mn/res_mat/privatepercent20sectorpercent20assessment.pdf (accessed on June 10, 2014).

CHAPTER 6

Socio-Economic and Political Status of Women in Mongolia

Jyoti Pandey

The last decade of the twentieth century, soon after the collapse of the former Soviet Union in 1991, saw Mongolia going for transition from communism and centrally-planned economy[1] to democracy and market economy.[2] In addition, it also paved the way to transform Mongolia from a semi-nomadic pastoral society to one based on settled industries in an urbanized environment. Such transformation led to many changes in Mongolia's polity, economy and society which also left tremendous influence on the status of women in the overall transitional society of Mongolia. Significantly, Mongolia of today is considered to be a relatively gender-equal society, in which men and women have similar access to social services, apart from having basic human rights. Mongolian women, in comparison to men, enjoy similar levels of health, higher life expectancy, higher levels of education and lower but relatively high levels of participation in the labour force.

According to 2010 Census, women account for almost 50 per cent of Mongolia's total population of 2.7 million with 43.5 per cent of female population being under 15 years of age.[3] In addition, women comprise 45.5 per cent of the economically active population with 83 per cent working in the formal sector. Although Mongolia has gender-equal society and the female literacy rate is 97.5 per cent,[4] their political, social and economic rights are much lower in practice than the men. Mongolia has introduced several laws, policies and programmes to promote gender equality and to address domestic violence. Despite these commitments there are hindrances to substantive gender equality.[5] Although gender parity or near parity in primary, secondary and tertiary education has been achieved, this has not been translated into equality in economic opportunity or political participation.[6] It is in this context that this paper deals with the socio-economic and political status of women in Mongolia, particularly in the post-1991 period.

Mongolian Women in Historical Perspective

A unified Mongolia was forged in 1206 AD with the creation of the Mongol empire by Chinggis Khan. But when the Manchus established their Qing dynasty in China, the Mongols were brought into submission in 1691.[7] Soon after feudal relations were institutionalized that influenced the status of women as well. Historically, Mongolian women have been known for their physical strength, bravery and devotion to family. Their role in Mongolian society and culture has been prominent in the large part of Mongol land due to the need for sharing the nomadic life style's laborious herding and household workloads in an extreme climate.[8] They were fighters as well. Under Chinggis Khan's rule, every man and woman was trained to keep the nation ready for battle. Mongolian women knew how to use a bow and arrow, and were expert horsewomen, and even took part in wrestling contests.[9] Probably the most famous of these women was Kublai Khan's mother and Chinggis Khan's daughter-in-law, Sorghaghtani Beki. She has been mentioned in several sources as one of the great figures of the thirteenth century. European missionaries who visited the Mongol court in the middle of the thirteenth century observed that she was the most renowned among the Mongols.[10] A Middle Eastern physician wrote that "if I were to see among the race of women another who is so remarkable a woman as this, I would say that the race of women is superior to the race of men".[11] However, except for queens and wives of noblemen, who were involved only as consorts and mothers of rulers, most women were not involved in macro-level decision-making and were excluded from the public life.[12]

From the perspective of Mongolian women today, representations of women in Mongolian history and culture, thus, reveal many contrasts, forged by both the nomadic culture and a feudal social organization. In contrast to neighbouring cultures, they do not convey a picture of women's subordination but are dominated by the icons of noble women.[13] In the traditional society of nomadic livestock breeding, the women did not have political, economic, social or the spiritual rights.[14] There was not even a single legal act which protected women's civil rights. Moreover, there existed a whole set of rules and dogmas, particularly religious ones, which restricted all social freedom of women. They had no right to choose even their life partners, nor could they divorce. They were completely dependent on their husbands. Notwithstanding the denial of political and social rights, women played a crucial role in the economic life. In addition to housekeeping and childcare, the task of livestock breeding as the key economic feature of the society had also to be performed by the women.[15]

In 1921, with the collapse of the Qing dynasty and the proclamation of the People's Republic, Mongolia became the first country in Asia after the Soviet Union to declare itself a socialist state.[16] Thereafter, constitutional, social, economic and political changes took place under the Soviet influence, transforming Mongolia from a nomadic pastoral economy and a feudal theocracy to an urbanized industrial and centrally-planned one-party state. Livestock production was collectivized into state farms and mechanized. The state-provided economic and social infrastructure and services in rural areas led to the creation of urban settlements in rural provinces.[17] Such developments brought major changes for Mongolian women. They became literate and were provided with opportunities to participate in the political, social and economic life of the country.

The first Constitution of Mongolia adopted in 1924 stated that "all citizens of Mongolia are entitled to equal rights irrelevant of their ethnic origin, religious belief or sex." Arranged marriage was prohibited by law in 1925, providing the legal framework for women to choose a husband. Women's civil rights were enshrined in the 1926 legislation, which ensured equal rights to work, education and political participation.[18] Women began to receive primary, secondary and tertiary education much the same way as did men. Furthermore, they worked in all sectors of the public sphere similar to men. Yet this did not extend to decision-making where men still dominated top management as prescribed by social norms and customs. Due to gender quotas set by the ruling Mongolian People's Republican Party (MPRP), women were represented in the State *Ikh Khural* (Parliament) at the levels as high as 20-23 per cent. But only one or two women worked as Deputy Ministers and no woman was a Minister. Under centrally-planned economy socialist state guaranteed employment and implemented a formal equitable labour policy. However, the so-called women's occupations were defined when health care sector, education, child daycare and other sectors began to be dominated by female workforce.

Between 1960 and 1970 government's emphasis was on social welfare, health condition, pension benefits and establishment of professional training centers where women could get training. These measures obviously helped women in building up their social roles and identities. On the other hand, they were manifestations of an attitude that women are not active participants of social development, but passive recipients of social wealth. Such vision of women's role and place has not been changed in Mongolia even in the post-1991 transition to democracy and market economy.[19] But during the initial years of Mongolia's transition the first major development in the country was the adoption of a new Constitution in 1992. Civil and political rights as well as economic and social rights were guaranteed by the Constitution, and accordingly both men and women citizens enjoyed extensive state-provided health and education, along with social and employment protection.[20] These developments led to significant transformations in the socio-economic and political status of women.

Socio-economic Status of Mongolian Women

During the democratic transition, Mongolian women were found to have started to unify their efforts in the struggle for their civil, economic and social rights. These women experienced significant changes in their socio-economic status as compared to the socialist period. The growing problem of domestic violence against women was one of the serious reasons restricting women's participation in political, economic and social life of the country. Common forms of violence against women included physical violence and emotional abuse within the family as well as sexual harassment or rape that was found both within and outside family. It has been found that 51.2 per cent of domestic violence was caused by family quarrel, 24.8 per cent by jealousy and 40.3 per cent by alcoholism. The main perpetrators of domestic violence were men and in view of the research on crimes which were committed in the family sphere, violators often included, as per Table 1, husbands (64.1 per cent) , former husbands (2.8 per cent), partners residing together (3.4 per cent), boyfriends (17.1 per cent) and fathers (4.9 per cent). It was revealed that for three years (1997-99), 58 to 64 per cent of the perpetrators of domestic violence were husbands.[21]

Table 1: Perpetrators of Domestic Violence (In percentage)

Perpetrators	**Domestic violence (%)**
Husbands	64.1
Former Husbands	2.8
Partners Residing Together	3.4
Boyfriends	17.1
Fathers	4.9

Source: Compiled by the author from *Journal of Women's Health*, vol.18, no.11, 2009.

Though such crimes are punishable under the Mongolian laws, there have been severe cases witnessed during the early years of transition. Women victims have often been found to have felt the pressure of "saving face" for the family. Among three hundred women in six districts of Ulaanbaatar or one in three women has experienced such violence. As such, a National Center Against Violence (NCAV) was created in 1995 with financial support from the Australian Government. This is the only organization so far in Mongolia working to protect women and children from domestic violence, though some NGOs especially led by women are also trying to reduce the violence against women. This was the result of proper education acquired by women as they banded together to form non-governmental organizations to criminalize domestic abuse to improve conditions for women in the labour force, to conduct research on employment, prostitution, child labour, and inequalities in wages for women.[22]

Due to transition to an open-market economy, privatization, retrenchment and structural adjustment have been disproportionately borne by women. During the socialist period, they accounted for almost half of Mongolia's work force and dominated in banking, health and education sectors. They also pre-dominated in several sub-sectors notably communication, trade, technology, utility services, public canteens and insurance. Thus the professional gap between men and women remained narrow. However, as the socialist system collapsed, so did the rights and voices of women in Mongolia. Despite their higher educational levels, there has been a persistent wage gap between men and women. In 2000, women earned an average 8 per cent less than men.[23] Salary levels were higher in sectors like mining and transportation that were pre-dominated by men. Furthermore, despite lower levels of education and training, men held significantly higher proportion of managerial positions even where there were high concentrations of female workers. For example, there were few women school principals, although women made up 75 per cent of the educational workforce.[24]

Figure 1: Employees Holding Managerial Positions by Sex in Mongolia (2004)

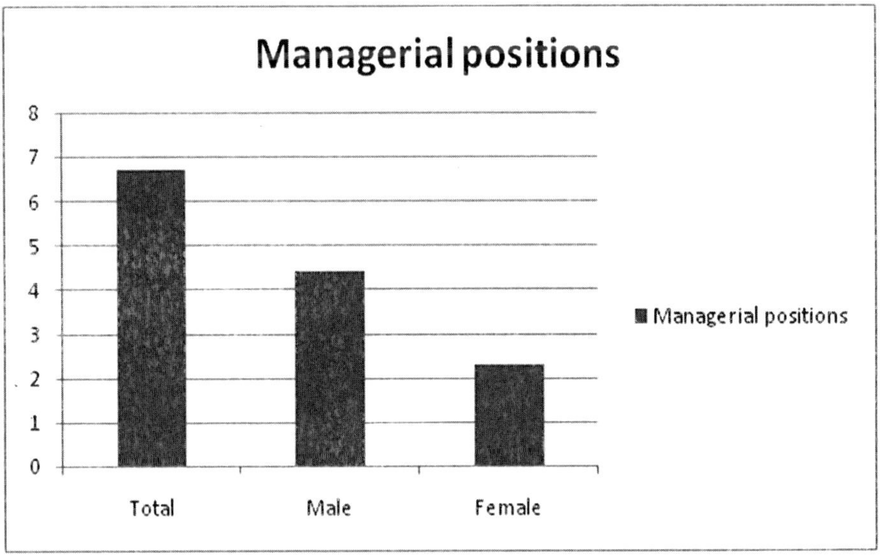

Source: Based on Sample Survey of Employees in Enterprises and Organizations, NSO, 2000, 2001, and 2002.

In the educational, health and banking sectors they also lost their jobs and were pushed away from the political and social life of the country through early retirement. An estimated 20,000 women aged 35-55 were pushed to early retirement on the grounds of having given birth to four or more children. Women, who were rewarded for having many children and were called the "glorious mothers" during the socialist period, were now reduced to poverty. On its part, government failed either to generate new jobs for these women or to provide them with loans or aid. Furthermore, no policy was implemented on training or retraining in order to improve skills or change profession through formal or informal education.

Since Mongolian women had fewer opportunities outside the state sector than men, the National Programme of Action for the Advancement of Women stressed that "mechanisms ensuring equal opportunities and improvement of women's participation in distribution and ownership of property, loans, technologies and information should be created". Despite this the women were initially unable to get any loans. In rural areas, though privatization of livestock allowed herders to meet their needs for food and other goods, the workload of women-herders increased significantly. Women-herders spent more time on processing products of animal husbandry, child-rearing activities and household work. These women in rural areas were restricted in the enjoyment of their legitimate rights in terms of working hours, wages and paid annual leave. Moreover, their contribution in the economic development was not recognized and rewarded properly. In urban areas, because of high rate of inflation women had no option but to work for more hours to earn additional income. Public servants ran private businesses after office hours. Domestic responsibilities and need for household subsistence further added to such double and even triple burden on women.

However, at the same time self-employment made a significant contribution to the household and national economy despite the fact that majority of these self-employed women remained uncovered by social and medical insurance and even did not get paid maternity leaves and other benefits related to reproductive function. In health care, the government implemented a number of national programmes in collaboration with international organizations for improving women's health, particularly reproductive health but no concrete results was seen. Although there had been an improvement in women life expectancy, the mortality rate continued to remain high due to other health factors. According to a news report published in the *UB Post* on 5 January 2001, occasional sex relations and prostitution of women abroad increased risk of getting infected with HIV and other sexually transmitted diseases, which both the government as well as Women NGOs tried to prevent. In a 2002 report of the US State Department, Mongolia was already identified as a source of country for women and men trafficked for the purposes of sexual exploitation and forced labour. Mongolian women were trafficked to China, Macau, South Korea, Turkey, Israel, Hungary, Poland and other East European countries as well as France and Germany for commercial sexual exploitation. Yet, education favoured women in the post-2000 period. More than 70 per cent of students in higher education in mid-2001 were women, offering hope for their rise to managerial positions in the economy, health, education, and government. This has helped address the problems faced by Mongolian women today in the socio-economic sphere.

Mongolian Women in Politics

Since 1991 Mongolian women together with men have been actively involved in the democratic transformation of the whole society. In the process, they also started unifying their efforts in the struggle for their political, civil, economic and social rights which were finally documented in the new Constitution adopted in 1992. The Mongolian Constitution states "Men and women enjoy equal rights in political, economic, social, and cultural fields as well as in marriage". While legal provisions were made for equal opportunity for both men and women, the decision-making power and visibility of women in public affairs got significantly reduced in the transition period. While considering Mongolian women's political participation, three arenas of access to politics have been observed: The first arena is for women Parliament members, the second is for women members of political parties, and the third belonged to the women at the grassroot level. Each arena has its own specifics and differs from each other by the numbers of participating women, their role and responsibilities in society, educational level, awareness of politics, and the ways of participation in politics. Women were found to have less influence in policy-making bodies and forums. Even today their representation in Parliament is getting reduced as evident by the fact that only 9.2 per cent of MPs are women.[25] This shows that there is threefold reduction in women participation as compared to the previous Parliament. No woman holds a ministerial portfolio and there are no women State secretaries, ambassadors or provincial governors.[26]

Women's representation in the Boards of Political Parties has been one of the important indicators of their political participation. Initially, women seemed to be fairly represented in the three largest and most influential parties, i.e., Mongolian National Democratic Party (MNDP), Mongolian Social Democratic Party (MSDP) and Mongolian People's Revolutionary Party (MPRP). But later the MPRP, the oldest party with 70 years history of ruling the country,[27] significantly lost women membership.[28] Hence, there has been a wide gap between women's entry into a political party and their inclusion in its leadership. There were no women at the top leadership positions in any political parties such as party chair, deputy chair or general secretary except one woman who was given the charge to perform as acting general secretary of the MNDP. Very few women have been elected in the national executive councils of the political parties: MPRP—10 per cent, i.e., 1 woman out of 10 members; MNDP—9.5 per cent, i.e., 2 women out of 21 members; MSDP—10 per cent, i.e., 3 women out of 30 members.[29]

The figures in Table 2 show a significant step forward in bringing up the proportion of female legislators in the National Parliament of Mongolia. Women accounted for 3 per cent in 1992 which increased to around 11 per cent following the 1996 and 2000 elections. In 2012 elections, the total number of women candidates in the Parliament rose to 11 which included 10 elected members and one member who replaced a male member of the

Mongolian People's Party after his resignation in November 2012.[30] The gender inequality in political participation can be attributed to the opinion of a small segment of society dominated by men which indicates that "women members of the Parliament cannot work on making gender sensible all newly approving laws, regulations, and overcome influences and restrictions of political parties which they belong to". These people supported by existing women parliamentarians did not join the women's efforts for allocation of financial means in the state budget to implement the National Program on Women's Advancement.

Table 2: Distribution of Seats in National Parliament (1992-2012)

Year	Male	Female	Total
1992	73	3	76
1996	70	6	76
2000	68	8	76
2012	62	10	76

Source: Compiled by the author on the basis of data taken from Inter-Parliamentary Union (IPU) PARLINE database (various years).

But there are also people with another point of view who thought that it was not right to blame the women parliamentarians in the relative failure of the National Program implementation. According to them, there were other causes also including the still existing wrong mechanisms or political and economical structure in the country. Regarding education and level of understanding politics among women at the grassroot level, it has been very low which has added to strong backwardness in public mentality on women's leadership capacity as well.[31] In short, it can be said that women citizens even after more than two decades of transition lack their own belief and opinion on politics and are not aware of how to participate in politics, and what benefits they can achieve from their political participation.

Situation in 2012 Parliamentary Election

A total of 544 candidates from 11 parties and 2 coalitions contested the 76-seat Parliament in Mongolia's 2012 parliamentary elections.[32] Preliminary results show that the opposition Democratic Party (DP) became the largest party in Parliament, taking 32 of the 76 seats followed by the current ruling party, the Mongolian People's Party (approximately 27-28), and the Justice Coalition (11). The Civil Will-Green Party won two seats and independent candidates won 3 seats.[33] However, the new government was formed with a coalition of three parties, i.e., the Democratic Party (DP), the MPRP-MNDP "Justice" Coalition and the Civil Will Green Party.[34] A new mixed electoral system (a combination of the majority and proportional system of voting) was used for the first time in 2012 parliamentary elections. In order to facilitate the rapid publication of results and avoid allegations of fraud, electronic voting was also introduced, though technical problems delayed the release of the final election results. The new election law introduced a quota system to ensure that no less than 20 per cent of the candidates are women. A record number of 174 women (32 per cent) stood for election in 2012, of which 10 were elected, up from 3 in 2008 elections.[35]

Meanwhile, the proportion of female candidates was nearly 32 per cent, well above the quota. The main reason for the increase was not the quota system but the increasing discontent with the male-dominated corrupt leadership and the perception that female leaders were less corrupt and more principled. Despite unfavourable listing on party ballot lists, 4 women won the election through the proportional system, which suggests that voters made conscientious candidate choices.[36]

Civil Society and NGOs for Protecting Women's Rights

The Women's NGOs in Mongolia have played a crucial role in moving the society towards democratization. Since transition the Women's NGOs have been grappling with the issue of women's representation in politics and a woman's share in the decision-making. With active involvement of these NGOs National Policy on Gender Empowerment was adopted in 2002 the implementation of which was overseen by the National Committee for Gender Equality headed by the Prime Minister.

After two decades of struggle to pass a law on gender equality, Law on Promotion of Gender Equality was adopted by the Mongolian Parliament on February 14, 2011. The aim of the new law is to ensure the equal participation of women and men in all political, legal, economic, cultural, and social spheres as the law prohibits any forms of discrimination in these spheres and in family relations.[37] Women's NGOs like Mongolian Women's Fund and other women leaders in a coalition of 17 women's groups played significant roles in adoption of this law.

It was, in fact, the last decade of the twentieth century that was marked by a profound emancipation of Mongolian women, the elevation of their educational and professional status and their ultimate and fortunate inclusion into the social, economic, political and cultural life of the nation. Since then various Mongolian women's organizations have been focussing on the improvement of women's status specifically ensuring the gender equality in education, employment and politics. Most of the women's organizations are now form the part of active NGOs focussing on the social protection and social security for women that were earlier not provided by the state. They have also started evolving new strategies that could bring positive results on enhancing the status of women.

Establishing gender equality in diverse social institutions has been one of the most important objectives of women's organizations worldwide. Paralleling this worldwide phenomenon, the number of women's organizations in Mongolia has increased dramatically with the government establishing national mechanism on issues related to women.

Conclusion

The conclusion that can be drawn from the above-mentioned discussions is that the overall status of women in today's Mongolia owes much to country's transition to democracy and market economy which has had both the positive as well as negative impact on the women's cause. The status of women is an important factor influencing the overall development of a country. In any civilization it shows the stage of its evolution at which the civilization arrived. The term 'status' not only includes personal and proprietary rights but also includes duties, liabilities and disabilities. In the case of Mongolian women, it means her personal and proprietary rights as well as her duties, liabilities and disabilities vis-à-vis the society and her family members. Over the ages, the status of women in the society has always been secondary to that of men. This is actually surprising as historical evidence shows that during the prehistoric times, it was the woman who was the leader in the house.

There is a clear revelation that although the women in Mongolia enjoy equal freedom and political, economic and social rights with men, their situation has deteriorated in the post-1991 period. The low level of employment, violence against women, lack of political representation, and poverty are the most worrying issues confronting the Mongolian women today. In fact, the Mongolian Constitution of 1992 prohibits all forms of discrimination, stating that "no person may be discriminated against on the basis of ethnic origin, language, race, age, sex, social origin or status, property or post, religion, opinion, or education."[38] Even in 1981, Mongolia was one of the first countries to ratify the Convention on the Elimination of All Forms of Discrimination against Women.[39] But reports show that the country has yet to address several important articles as discrimination of women existed in the legislation as well as in reality in the transitional Mongolian society. Thus, Mongolia needs improvement in and reinforcement of its laws and policies more favourable to women so that gender disparities could completely be eliminated.

Nevertheless, it is to be noted that the improvement in the overall situation of Mongolian women has been seen in the second decade of country's transition or beyond, i.e., in the post-2010 period. Women have now familiarized themselves with personal empowerment, advanced global education and social networking. They seem to be more actively involved in social causes, environmental issues and community development. Increasing numbers of women are earning advanced degrees, studying abroad and taking advantage of progressive opportunities in organizations such as Brandeis University's WSRC.[40] In addition, they are now financially capable of creating improved living conditions, seeking greater educational opportunities for their children, and spending more time in their social lives. With the current efforts of women empowerment by the government and related organizations, the future of Mongolian women seems to be bright.

Notes and References

1. A centrally planned economy is an economy where decisions on what to produce, how to produce and for whom are taken by the government. This type of economy was prevalent during the pre-1991 period in the Soviet and East European societies. Mongolia too experienced a centrally planned economy for almost seven decades under the influence of the former Soviet Union. For details see Sharad K Soni (2002), *Mongolia-Russia Relations: Kiakhta to Vladivostok*, Delhi: Shipra Publications, pp.145-147.
2. Market economy is an economy in which there is free competition and prices are determined by the interaction of supply and demand. This is the post-1991 global phenomenon existing in the democratic societies.
3. *Population and Housing Census of Mongolia 2010*, http://ancsdaap.org/cencon2011/Papers/Mongolia/Mongolia_slides_2011.pdf (accessed on 17 December 2014).
4. United Nations ESCAP 2007 Statistical Yearbook, http://www.unescap.org/publications/detail.asp?id=1275 (accessed on 6 January 2015).
5. National CEDAW Watch Network Centre (2008), *Implementation of the Mongolian National Programme of Action for the Advancement of Women*, Ulaanbaatar: NCWNC.
6. World Economic Forum (2010) Global Gender Gap Report, http://www.weforum.org/pdf/gendergap/report2010.pdf (accessed on 22 December 2014).
7. Sharad K Soni (2006), "Mongolia's March Towards Democracy (1989-2005)", *Mongolica* (Ulaanbaatar), vol. 19, no. 40, pp. 284-86.
8. Mongolia Culture Blog, http://mongolculture.blogspot.in/2007_09_01_archive.html (accessed on 14 February 2015).

9. David Morgan (1986), *The Mongols,* New York : Blackwell Press.
10. *Ancient Mongol Women*, http://www.mongolia-attractions.com/ancient-mongol-women.html (accessed on 14 February 2015).
11. *Women of the Mongol Court*, http://danielroy.tripod.com/cgi-bin/alternate/mongolia/opi10.html (accessed on 2 March 2015).
12. *Women in Mongolia*, http://iknowpolitics.org/sites/default/files/women_in_mongolia_ch2 socialstatus.pdf (accessed on 4 January 2015).
13. *Mongolia Gender Analysis*, Background Paper No. 1 in preparation for USAID/Mongolia's 2004-2008 strategy Prepared by Christopher Finch, January 2003, http://pdf.usaid.gov/pdf_docs/PNACR953.pdf (accessed on 23 December 2014).
14. A.F. Benwell (2006), "Facing Gender Challenges in Post-socialist Mongolia". In O. Bruun & Li Narangoa (eds.), *Mongols from Country to City: Floating Boundaries, Pastoralism and City Life in the Mongols Lands,* Copenhagen: NIAS Press, p. 217.
15. UNESCO, *Status of Women: Mongolia*, http://unesdoc.unesco.org/images/0008/000871/087165eb.pdf (accessed on 7 February 2015).
16. *Mongolia*, http://en.wikipedia.org/wiki/Mongolia (accessed on 17 February 2015).
17. *Women in Mongolia: An Overview*, http://www.unifem.org/attachments/products/163_chap1_1.pdf (accessed on 29 December 2014).
18. *Women's Social Status*, http://www.unifem.org/attachments/products/164_chap2.pdf (accessed on 9 January 2015).
19. Martha Avery (1997), *Women of Mongolia*, Washington: Asian Art & Archaeology/University of Washington Press.
20. *Women in Mongolia: An Overview.*
21. SOROS Foundation (2003), "Ways for Prevention of Domestic Violence", Mongolian Women Lawyer's Association, http://www.soros.org/initiatives/women/articles_publications/publications/domestic_handbook/dv_handbook.pdf (accessed on 28 January 2015).
22. *Women in Modern Mongolia*, Asia Society, http://asiasociety.org/countries/traditions/women-modern-mongolia (accessed on 22 December 2014).
23. B. Robinson and A. Solongo (2000), "The Gender Dimension of Economic Transition in Mongolia", In F. Nixson, B. Suvd, P. Luvsandorj, B. Walters (eds), *The Mongolian Economy: A Manual of Applied Economics for a Country in Transition,* Edward Elgar Publishing Ltd., pp. 231-255.
24. Selim Jahan and N. Batnasan (2007), *Poverty Research and Employment Facilitation for Policy Development,* UNDP Project, Ministry of Social Welfare and Labour, Government of Mongolia, Ulaanbaatar.
25. National Statistical Office of Mongolia, http://www.nso.mn/index2.php (accessed on 27 February 2015).
26. Committee on the Elimination of Discrimination Against Women, 504th & 505th Meetings, http://www.un.org/News/Press/docs/2001/WOM1258.doc.htm (accessed on 5 January 2015).
27. *Women in Decision Making and Management,* http://www3.uakron.edu/worldciv/worldciv/images/Asia/Mongol/page14.htm (accessed on 21 November 2014).
28. Ibid.
29. IPU Parline Database, http://www.ipu.org/parline-e/reports/2219_E.htm (accessed on 29 November 2014).
30. Asian Development Bank and World Bank (2005), "Country Gender Assessment", cited

in Combined Fifth and Sixth Periodic Reports of States Parties: Mongolia, CEDAW/C/MNG/7 2007, CEDAW, New York, NY., p. 34.

31. Ibid.
32. Li Narangoa (2012), "Mongolia's 2012 Parliamentary Election", *Eastasiaforum*, 10 July, , http://www.eastasiaforum.org/2012/07/10/mongolias-2012-parliamentary-election/ (accessed on 3 December 2014).
33. IPU Parline Database, http://www.ipu.org/parline-e/reports/2219_E.htm (accessed on 18 January 2015).
34. Sharad K Soni (2013), "Evaluating Mongolia's Experience of Democratization: The Post-Soviet Scenario", *The Mongolian Journal of International Affairs* (Ulaanbaatar), vol.18, p. 37.
35. IPU Parline Database.
36. Ibid.
37. Channel Foundation-MONES, http://www.channelfoundation.org/mones.html (accessed on 2 February 2015).
38. *Mongolia: Constitution*, 13 January 1992, http://www.servat.unibe.ch/icl/mg00000_.html (accessed on 23 November 2014).
39. *Mongolia Country Profile: National Implementation of Agenda 21*, http://www.un.org/esa/earthsummit/mong-cp.htm (accessed on 14 December 2014).
40. Women's Studies Research Center, http://www.brandeis.edu/wsrc/research/docs/spring2012.pdf (accessed on 21 January 2015).

PART II

Connotations of Internal Changes

CHAPTER 7

Political Agencies and the Growth of Procedural Democracy in Mongolia

Raj Deep

The third wave of democracy has engulfed within its ambit many countries that were earlier ruled by military government, one party system and personal dictatorship and this has significantly changed the global political order in the last thirty years. What is democracy and what constitutes the democratization process has been the most debated and discussed issues of contemporary world. The importance of a democratic regime lies in its very system of functioning that provides a citizen with the choice of choosing the policy makers in the public domain. This is facilitated by free and competitive elections that offer them a rational choice between political parties and contending parties which strives to provide a set of institutions that allows the citizens to choose the makers of public policy in free competitive elections.[1] Henceforth, democracy can be considered as one of the ultimate principles that modern civilizations strive to create and preserve. Democracy as a form of governance is expected to provide extensive inclusiveness and representation to a wide array of population that acts as a positive catalyst for the functioning of a fair and just society. Importantly, democracy serves as a platform to check unaccountable power and manipulation by the few at the expense of many, thereby making democracy as a form of governance by the people and for the people. This is often implemented through elected representatives, which therefore requires free, transparent and fair elections, in order to achieve legitimacy.

The whole idea of this article is to outline and elaborate the features and factors which specifically absorbed the external shocks and make the transition peaceful and sustainable in Mongolia. In today's context, the role of political agencies, especially the rise of political parties which themselves were the product of the transition must be credited for filling the void, which was left vulnerable by the transition. Growth of multi party system and regular elections and consequent to it the adoption of a new Constitution in 1992 was conducive to the development of procedural democracy in Mongolia, bringing about a kind of paradigm shift in the structural and functional role of the agencies. Moreover, Mongolian democracy has been successful at least in the political realm as the implementation of electoral democracy combined with political and civil liberties i.e. liberal democracy and creation of an independent political identity bears a testimony to this fact.[2]

Procedural Democracy: A Theoretical Perspective

Proceduralist vision is considered as the best normative defense of democracy in the modern world. Since the inception of democracy, one distinguishing feature which forms its core is the pursuit of 'equal liberty'. The pursuit of 'equal political liberty' is what characterizes democracy as a distinct form of government[3]. This 'equal liberty' can be defined as the participation by the people in the decision making process without being discriminated on any grounds and making equal contribution to the establishment of majority view. Procedural aspect defines equal political liberty as the most important good for which democracy should work. And it posits that the modern democratic procedure based on every individual's equal participation in fair and competitive elections for selecting political representatives and thereby contributing to the production of decisions via majority rule—is the best way of respecting equal liberty in a context of pluralism and dissent.[4] The term equal political liberty has wide connotations and includes not just only participation through voting and making their choices independently but creating environment which promotes equal conditions of opportunity with the larger aim of protecting civil, political and social rights, complying with a meaningful equal participation.[5] David Held has defined procedural democracy as having a set of institutions encompassing of an inclusive citizenship, the rule of law, the separation of powers (executive, legislature and judiciary), including an independent judiciary capable of upholding a constitution, elected power holders, free and fair elections, freedom of expression and alternative sources of information, associational autonomy, and civilian control over the security forces.

Robert Dahl has defined procedural democracy in terms of five important characteristics which are as follows: Effective Participation, Voting Equality at the decisive stage, Enlightened Understanding, Control over the agenda & Inclusion.[6] Trailing John Rawls in 'A Theory of Justice' (1971) he argued that it was immaterial whether there was any debate between substance and procedures, but the important thing to consider was the priority of procedures over substantive goods. Further, Dahl highlighted that the democratic process in itself consisted of an array of democratic goods which are actually inherent in the procedures themselves. The procedural democracy is not oblivious to substantive issues, Dahl claims but rather endorses and ensures certain goods like freedom of speech and freedom to assemble: 'So though my explicit concern is with political equality, he writes, ' my implicit concern is with freedom, human development and human worth.'[7] As the procedural democracy is deeply committed to the goal of equal political liberty it is considered as the most expressive and widespread definition of democracy in the modern contemporary societies.

Elections and the Role of Political Parties

Political parties play a pivotal role for the representative democracy and to the process of democratization and act as a connecting link between the society and the state. Political parties perform a number of important functions that are must for the proper functioning of democracy in a modern state. They organize voters, aggregate and articulate interests, crafts policy alternatives and provide the basis for coordinated electoral and legislative activities. Thus political parties are central not only to the representative government but also to the process of democratic development in transitional democracies.[8] Strategies to establish and consolidate democracy that ignore the central role of parties cannot hope to be successful, no matter how much attention they pay to other vital matters such as building civil society and the institutions of good governance.[9] This section highlights how the void created by the transition in Mongolia was filled by the political parties and what role do they play in the evolution of procedural democracy in Mongolia.

Elections of 1990: Beginning of a New Era

The first general election (Multi Party elections) for the People's Great Hural took place on July 29, 1990. The total voter turnout was around ninety five percent. The parties which were in opposition to MPRP acquired around 40 percent of the seats of Small Hural, though the Great Hural was dominated by the MPRP as it acquired 85 percent of the seats. The first meeting of the Great Hural were held in September 1990 and which elected a President from the MPRP, Vice-president from SDC (Social Democrats), Prime Minister from the MPRP, and 50 members to the Little Hural.[10] Thus the first sign of cooperative federalism was found evident when despite being in overwhelming position in the Great Hural, the MPRP agreed to form a coalition government with the opposition and four cabinet posts were assigned to them. The Vice President was also the Chairman of the Little Hural. With all the political arrangements done, the Great Hural in November 1991 started discussion on a new Constitution. The new constitution was finally adopted on January 13, 1992 replacing the 1960 Constitution, which brought considerable changes in Mongolia's political system.[11]

The most important change made in this Constitution was the replacement of the two-chamber Parliament (bicameral) known as the Great and Little Hurals with that of a single chamber (unicameral), which came to be known as the State Great Hural (SGH) comprising 76 Deputies.[12] The New Constitution adopted in 1992 in Mongolia, became the structural and functional framework of actions and policies of post-socialist, democratic Mongolia in the twenty first century, providing people the freedom of political choices, respecting human rights and equality of all forms of property ownership.[13]

1992 Parliamentary Elections: A Litmus Test for the Mongolian Democracy

The elections of 1990 and adoption of a new constitution in 1992 had set the stage right for the next parliamentary elections to be held in June 1992. The MDU has provided people a sense of viable alternative and the multi party elections of 1990 have provided the necessary background for the evolution of procedural democracy in Mongolia. The 1992 parliamentary elections were a kind of litmus test for the nascent and evolving democratic and institutional set up of the country. Though the elections were not new to Mongolia but the structures and the agencies which were created by the new Constitution of 1992 brought a kind of radical transformation in the nature and working of the electoral mechanism.

Figure 1: 1992 Parliamentary Election Results

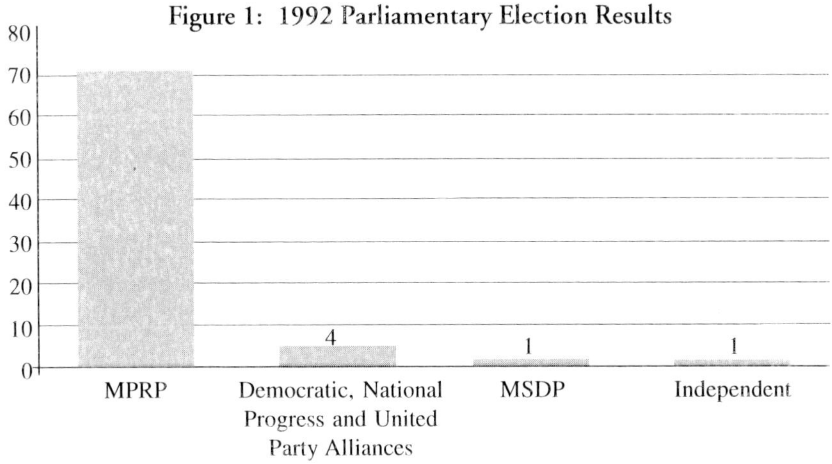

Source: J. Yadamsuren (2002), Democratic Election Data, Election Commission (Ulaanbaatar), pp. 3-59; International Republican Institute (2000), *Mongolia Parliament Election Observation Mission Report*, Washington D.C.: IRI, July.

The results were very surprising both for the MPRP and the opposition as the percentage of votes share declined for the MPRP from 62 percent of the votes cast in 1990 to 57 percent in 1992. Even the votes share for the three major opposition parties which had got 35 percent of the votes in 1990 were able to manage only 27 percent of the votes in 1992. The remaining votes were split among the independents (3 percent) and the numerous opposition parties. As the opposition were divided and splinted, the MPRP was able to win the election with 70 seats out of 76 seats.[14] Though the result of 1992 elections were more or less on the same pattern as earlier but the kind of participation and representation presented a kind of evolution and maturation in the style of procedural democracy in Mongolia. The experiences taken from the 1992 elections made the opposition well versed with the nuances of electoral dynamics and the kind of unity and maturity shown in the 1996 elections and thereafter, which is discussed below bears a testimony to this fact.

The 1996 Parliamentary Elections

In January 1996, article 26 of the Election law was revised which divided Mongolia into 76 single member districts with one candidate chosen from each constituency.[15] Elections took place in June 1996 and the results presented a kind of watershed in the history of parliamentary democracy in Mongolia. The voter turnout was 92 percent which reflected the mood of the Mongolian people and their rising trust on the procedural dimension of democracy. The results brought an end to the seventy five years dominance of MPRP and ushered a new sense of hope for the nascent democracy in the region. The Democratic Alliance (DA) consisting of Mongolian National Democratic Party (MNDP) and Mongolian Social Democratic Party (MSDP) captured 65.8 percent of the 76 seats at stake in the Great State Hural, Mongolia's Parliament. There was a marked rise in the number of seats won by the Democratic Alliance from a mere six in 1992 to fifty in 1996. On the other hand MPRP lost 45 of the 70 seats that they won in the previous election. Almost all the seats were won either by the Democratic Alliance or the MPRP except one which was won by O. Dashbalbar of the Mongolian United Heritage Party (MUHP). Fig. 2 represents the results of 1996 parliamentary elections.

Figure 2: 1996 Parliamentary Election Results

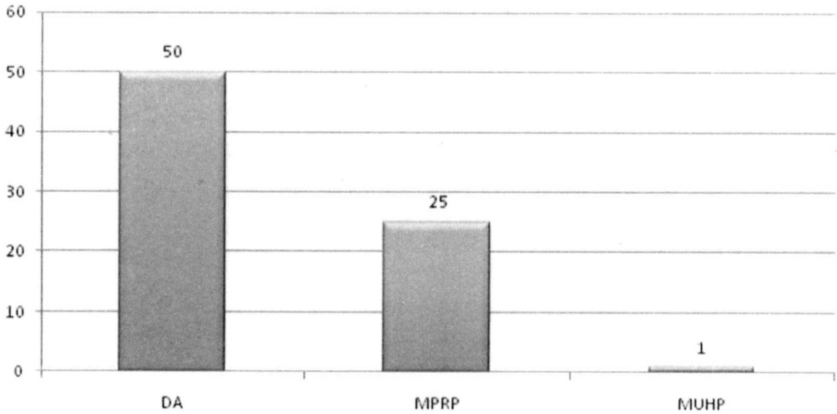

Source: General Election Commission of Mongolia, 1996.

Uncertainty which has been one of the important dimensions of procedural democracy was at its best in the 1996 parliamentary elections. Thus the elections of 1996 brought for the first time a major shift of the political power in Mongolia in 75 years of history. When it comes to deliverance the new government introduced judicial reforms and radical economic reforms, freed the media and strengthened the legal system. However the four years stint of Democratic Alliance in power was severely faced with a stiff resistance from MPRP which by that time had learned the parliamentary procedures to obstruct and attack the coalition's reform agenda. Moreover the Democratic Coalition itself was encircled with the problems of corruption, a political infighting within coalition itself and an attitude among the Coalition members that seemed to put their personal ambitions prior to the Coalition or national interests. All these factors went against the coalition and the election of 2000 brought back MPRP again in power. But fortunately the transition from MPRP to the Democratic Union in 1996 elections proved to be peaceful and smooth signifying the importance of political parties in the democratic consolidation in Mongolia. Procedural democracy provided the people with an opportunity to vote out the Communist party and vote in the Democrats and the voter turnout and the election results bear a testimony to this fact.

The 2000 Parliamentary Elections

The July 2000 parliamentary elections brought MPRP back in power with 72 of the 76 seats (95%) won by them and creating another one party government. The total voter turnout was 82.43%. Though the results were not much surprising looking at the four years stint of Democratic Alliance but the magnitude of victory was amazing. It completely wiped out the Democratic coalition from the political scene and reflected the mood of the country. The New Democratic Coalition and Social Democrats acquired 13% and 9% of the votes respectively but were not able to won a single seat.[16] Thus we found that MPRP completely overshadowed the presence of all the other parties and succeeded in projecting itself as the sole harbinger of people's interests. This shift in the hands of power strengthened the belief that a meaningful opposition always has the chance of capturing power and forbids the mistakes from becoming permanent. Fig. 3 represents the 2000 Parliamentary Election results.

Figure 3: 2000 Parliamentary Election Results

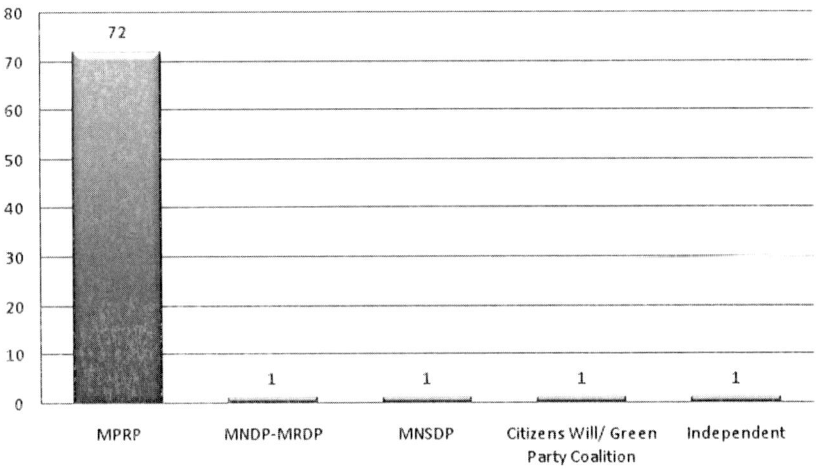

Source: General Election Commission of Mongolia, 2000.

Though the reasons were manifold for the defeat of the democrats but the core factor was that the Coalition was not able to deliver the promises made during its tenure. Responsiveness which is one of the crucial elements of procedural democracy figure in and the MPRP projected itself as a viable political alternative for the people. Other factors responsible for the defeat of democrats were the formation of four governments in four year period i.e. revolving door to door government. It resulted in a degree of instability and its failure to provide a stable leadership. Secondly, there were serious pitfalls in the economic policies of the Democratic Alliance. Thirdly, the coalition could not keep its strings attached and resulted in the split of the same with each party running its own list of candidates. Fourthly, the experience of MPRP in policy matters outweighs the newly elected MPs of the Democratic Coalition which was evident in most of the cases during the later regime.

The 2004 Parliamentary Elections

The election of 2004 brought a kind of coalition unique and first of its kind in Mongolia as both the MPRP and the MDC were short of majority and hence decided to forge an alliance between them. Seven political parties and fifteen independent candidates ran in the 2004 parliamentary elections.[17] The elections took place on June 27, 2004 with the MPRP winning 36 seats and the MDC winning 34 seats with neither of them having the minimum required seats of 39 to form a government. Mongolian Republican Party won 1 seat and 3 seats were won by the independents with 2 seats being declared as invalid. As no party had the absolute majority and the situation was that of a hung parliament the solution provided was to form a coalition government instead of relying on the support of the three independent candidates. Hence the grand coalition was formed between the MPRP and the MDC under the Prime Minister ship of Tsakhiagiyn Elbegdorj of the Democratic Party to save the country from going into another election which was not very conducive looking at the economic situation. But the fragile coalition government did not remained intact for long and lastly on January 11, 2006 collapsed altogether when all the MPRP cabinet members resigned in protest to what they described as "the coalitions ineffective governance and loss of public support".[18]

The voter turnout was 82.2 percent more or less on the same pattern of 2000. The parties of MDC won around 44 percent of the vote with an increase of seven percentage points from the previous election, whereas the MPRP party won 49 percent votes with an eight percent decrease from the previous election. Though the MPRP had a slight edge over the MDC in terms of vote percentage and seats won but the real winner was the later as it managed to capture the imagination of the masses despite having a strong presence of the former. Fig. 4 represents 2004 parliamentary election results.

Figure 4: 2004 Parliamentary Election Results

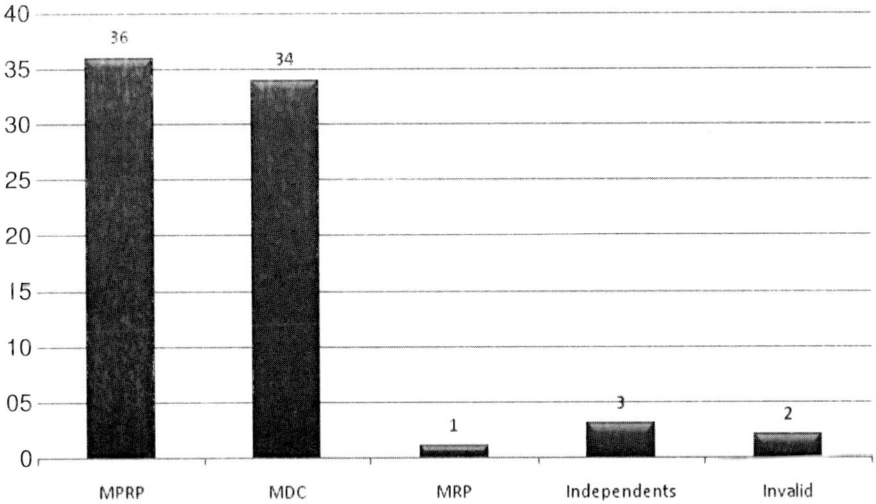

Source: General Election Commission of Mongolia, 2004.

The 2008 Parliamentary Elections

The year of 2008 was a low point in the democratic history of Mongolia. Elections took place on June 29, 2008 with 356 candidates running for the 76 seats in the State Great Hural. However the turnout dipped down to 74.3% in 2008 from 82% in 2004. The results shifted the power in the hands of MPRP which won 46 seats, 27 seats went to the main opposition party, the Democrats (DP), and one each was shared by Civil Will Party, Civil Coalition and Independent. Violence erupted just after the election results in which around five persons were killed and around mid night a four day state of emergency was declared. This event was a kind of black spot in the democratic evolution of Mongolia which promoted the authoritarian tendencies and tried to malign the democratic credentials of the region. Despite all these S. Bayar was elected as the new Prime Minister of the coalition government between MPRP and DP.[19]

Figure 5: 2008 Parliamentary Election Results

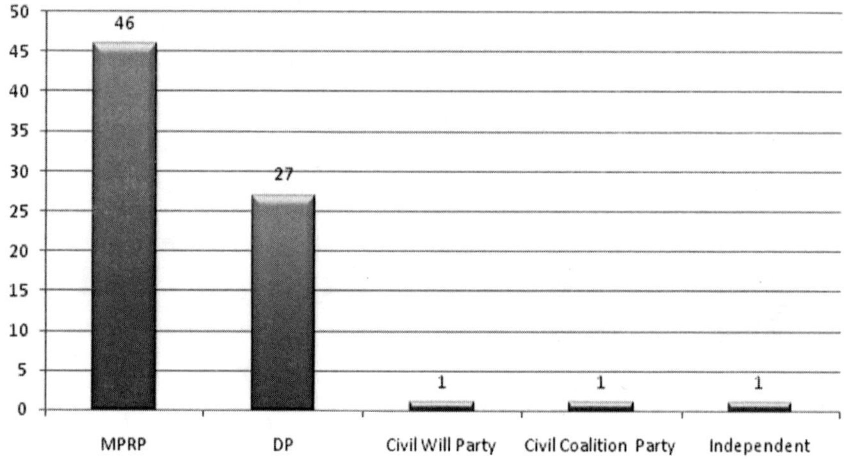

Source: General Election Commission of Mongolia, 2008.

The 2012 Parliamentary Elections

The latest parliamentary election took place on June 28, 2012 in which the Democratic Party won 34 seats and the incumbent Mongolian's People Party (the new name of MPRP changed in 2010) captured 26 seats with neither of them having the required majority to form the government. The Justice Coalition got 11 seats; the Civil Will-Green Party got 2 seats whereas the rest 3 was captured by the independents. A total of 544 candidates from 11 parties and 2 coalitions contested the 76 seats parliament in Mongolia's 2012 parliamentary elections. The fractured mandate led to the formation of a government based on the coalition of three parties i.e. the Democratic Party (DP), the MPRP-MNDP "Justice" Coalition and the Civil Will Green Party. The election of 2012 was epoch making in many ways for Mongolia which implemented new election laws. For the first time in history electronic voting machines were used in order to avoid the charges of fraud and manipulation that took place during the 2008 elections. A new election system based on the combination of the majority and proportional system of voting was introduced which benefitted the smaller parties and helped them to prove their stake in the electoral process. Thus we saw that the parliamentary elections of 2012 brought about a significant number of changes like introduction of new parliamentary election law, especially the introduction of proportional voting that facilitated the rise of smaller political parties and ad-hoc coalitions which promoted the democratic consolidation of Mongolia and once again proved it to be the only post socialist democracy in the region. Fig.6 represents the results of 2012 parliamentary elections.

Figure 6: 2012 Parliamentary Election Results

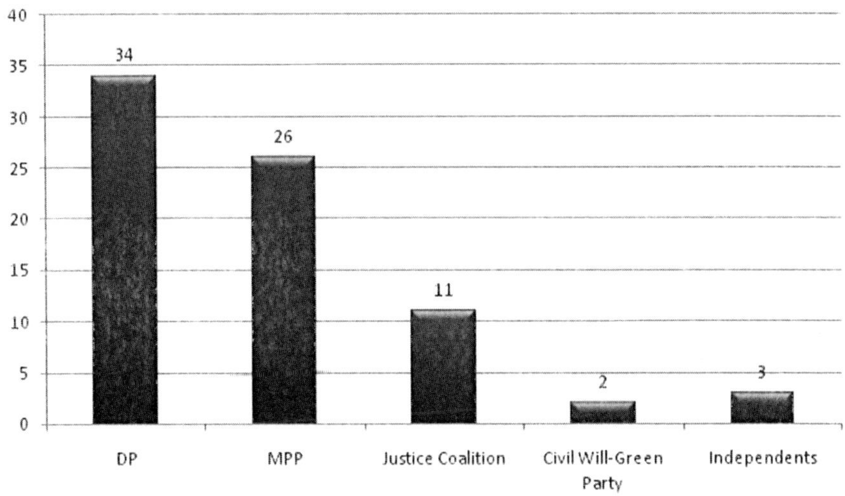

Source: General Election Commission of Mongolia, 2012, UB Post, Mongolia Today, News.mnRevote (News.mn)

Looking at various electoral outcomes with the evolution of procedural democracy in Mongolia one can find that the elections from 1990 to 2012 have resulted in significant changes thereby making the political agencies and political actors well versed with the nuances of democratic ideals. This facilitates a kind of restructuring of the political space making it conducive for the democratic transition in Mongolia. Moreover the popular support and the high voter participation in the parliamentary elections seemed to be an encouraging factor for the evolving procedural democracy in the region.[20]

Assessing Procedural Dimension of Democracy in Mongolia

Mongolia has a representative model of democracy with indirect elections taking place every fourth year for parliamentary seats. The adoption of a new constitution in 1992 brought about structural and functional changes in the institutional set up of Mongolia. Institutions such as judiciary, parliament and political parties got a new boost and catered to the new demands and aspirations of the Mongolian people. The institutional changes like the adoption of a new Constitution in 1992 led to the growth of political parties other than the MPRP and consequent to it the multi party elections provided people with alternatives, thereby promoting the "Politics of Difference". This 'Politics of Difference' promotes diversity conducive for the development of democratization process. This section analyses how far the political agencies have helped in evolving the procedural democratic discourse in Mongolia.

As the existence of procedural democracy requires a minimum of two contenders vying for the political space, the very establishment of a multiparty system in Mongolia in 1992 proved to be a decisive step towards this direction. Though the results of 1992 parliamentary elections were in favour of MPRP but still the presence of other opposition parties and their way of effective participation and contestation supports the existence of procedural democracy in Mongolia. The 1996 election results and thereafter the regular shift of power shows how the emergence of multi party system helped in the evolution of procedural democracy in Mongolia. It highlighted the importance of opposition for the successful working of democracy. Both quantitatively and qualitatively there was a marked shift in the nature and functioning of the opposition.

Prior to the amendment of Constitution in 1992 the elections were merely of minimalist type where the role of opposition was only limited to the contestation and where method was given the sole priority without any adherence to the values. As equality was not an important dimension for the minimalists, the opposition stands redundant with all the rules suiting to the interests of MPRP. However the situation changed after 1992 with meaningful opposition and meaningful pluralism of proposals emerging on the political scene. MDU projected itself as a strong and viable alternative against MPRP. The elections of 1996 put MPRP in the role of opposition and their four years stint made them aware of the importance of meaningful opposition in a parliamentary democracy. MPRP which did not care for the democratic procedures in the past learned quickly the nuances of parliamentary procedures and used it to attack MDU reflecting a sense of maturity in the understanding of procedural democracy.

The essence of democracy is the factor of uncertainty which makes it more mystical. The emergence of MDU and other parties made the political space competitive and outcomes unpredictable which were evident in the elections of 1992 and thereafter. In 1992 despite having an end number of contenders MPRP dominated the political scene which was other way round in the 1996 parliamentary elections as the MDU coalition won with a landslide majority. Same kind of uncertainty prevails in the later elections and this environment of uncertainty acted as a booster for the parties to work effectively in order to gain the electoral majority. This uncertainty promotes the feeling of responsiveness among the political parties and urged them to work for the benefit of people either being in power or in opposition. The manifestos were designed to suit the local and national demands of the Mongolian people who voted in favour of a particular party if their demands were met or vice versa. In a democracy power is constantly changing its hands and there is a kind of uncertainty which acts as an incentive for the participants to win the game or to contain the winner. This regular shift brings a kind of course correction and prevents the mistake from becoming permanent, which was quite evident from the successive election results of 2000 to 2012.

Moreover, the presence of a strong opposition provides the public with informed choices and enlightened understanding as the election campaigns brought into forefront various issues catering to the demands of the people. The election results of 2012 parliamentary elections brought a kind of unique coalition of Democratic Party (DP), MPRP-MNDP 'Justice' Coalition and Civil Will Green Party as the mandate was fractured and no single party had the numerical majority to form the government. This kind of rainbow coalition reflects how the procedural democracy since 1992 has gradually evolved with the time and stands firm in its commitment to the ideals of 'equal political liberty'.

Conclusion

The procedural democracy in Mongolia has evolved maturely with time and has successfully consolidated the democratic ideals, as the multiparty system and regular elections with consequent shift of power bears a testimony to this fact. Unlike other Asian countries, Mongolia is challenging and breaking the stereotype of alternating between authoritarianism and democracy. In the past few years, the development of political parties in Mongolia reveals that these have undoubtedly played a decisive role in the evolution of procedural democracy in the region. Parties acted as the principal agents around which contestation and mobilization are organized, working to structure political alternatives and formulating policies and translating them into effective choices for the people. Political parties display numerous contradictory features which reveal the blending of different forms of modern organization and participatory politics with indigenous practices and institutions. Hence, the third wave of democratization process in Mongolia could be seen as an outcome of the shifting role of political parties and various electoral outcomes leading to the coalitions and alliances bear a testimony to this fact. Indeed the political parties have acted as an agent of change, thereby facilitating the growth of procedural democracy in Mongolia. This, in turn, helped much in running a stable government so far as accountability and responsiveness are concerned. More than two decades have passed since transition but still Mongolia stands firm in its commitment to the ideals of democracy displaying how the process has constantly evolved withstanding the test of time. The democratic values have imbibed within the structures and agencies to such an extent that thinking of life without democracy seems to be uncertain in Mongolia.

Notes and References

1. G. Bingham Jr. Powell and Eleanor N. Powell (2005), "Democratization: A Briefing Paper for AP Comparative Government and Politics", at http://apcentral.collegeboard.com/apc/public/repository/ap05_comp_govpol_demo_42252.pdf(accessed on 12 September 2014).
2. Sharad K. Soni (2013),"Evaluating Mongolia's Experience of Democratization: The Post Soviet Scenario", *Mongolian Journal of International Affairs*, no.18, p. 43.
3. As Bobbio put it: "Liberty and equality are the values that lay at the foundation of democracy" as "a society that is regulated in a way that the individuals who compose it are freer and more equal than in whatsoever other form of coexistence"; Norberto Bobbio (1995), *Eguaglianza e liberta,* Turin: Einaudi, p. xii (authors' translation).
4. Hans Kelsen (2005), *The Essence and Value of Democracy*; Norberto Bobbio, *Liberalism and Democracy*, trans. Martin Ryle and Kate Soper, London: Verso; Norberto Bobbio, *Il futurodellademocrazia* (Einaudi, 1995, 3rd ed.; English ed. Richard Bellamy, London: Polity Press, 1987).
5. Norberto Bobbio, "Il future dellademocrazia", pp. 6-7.
6. Richard W. Krouse (1982), "Polyarchy and Participation: The Changing Democratic Theory of Robert Dahl", Polity, vol.14, no.3, pp. 441-463.
7. Robert Dahl, "Democracy and its critics", p. 323.
8. "Political Parties in Conflict-Prone Societies: Regulation, Engineering and Democratic Development", ed. by Benjamin Reilly and Per Norduland. Centre for Democratic Institutions (CDI), International Institute for Democracy and Electoral Assistance (IDEA), and United Nations University (UNU), 2008, United Nations University Press, at http://www.idea.int/publications/ppcps/upload/Political-Parties-in-Conflict-Prone-Situations.pdf (accessed on 28 October 2014).
9. Peter Burnell, "Building Better Democracies, Why Political Parties Matter?" National Democratic Institute, U.S., 2004, at http://www.cdi.anu.edu.au/featured_articles/featured articles_dowloads/CDI.News_FEB_MAR_06_FA_1.pdf(accessed on 28 October 2014).
10. General Election Commission of Mongolia, 1990.
11. For the full text of the Constitution, See *The Constitution of Mongolia*, Ulaanbaatar, 1992.
12. Ibid.
13. Ibid.
14. General Election Commission of Mongolia, 1992.
15. G. Bayantur (2005), "Democratic Transition and Electoral Process in Mongolia",Degree of Master's Thesis Submitted to the University of Saskatchewan Saskatoon, at http://

www.collectionscanada.gc.ca/obj/s4/f2/dsk3/SSU/TC-SSU-04082008161438.pdf(accessed on 29 October 2014).

16. Sharad K Soni (2008), "Democratic Transition in Mongolia: Achievements and Challenges ahead of 2008 Elections", *Bimonthly Journal of Mongolian and Tibetan Current Situation* (Taipei), vol.17, no.1, p. 40.
17 . These seven parties are MPRP (Mongolian's People Revolutionary Party), Democracy Coalition, RP (Republican Party), MPNU (Mongolian Party of National Unity), MUCP (Mongolian United Conservative Party), MLP (Mongolian Liberal Party) and MGP (Mongolian Green Party).
18. Kerry Dumbaugh and Wayne M. Morrison (2006), "Mongolia: Political and Economic Status", *CRS Report for Congress*, at http:// digital.library.unt.edu/govdocs/crs//data/2006/ upl-meta pcc1156153190knordstr_nt104619_unt/RS21155_2006May03.pdf pg-8 (accessed on 15 November 2014).
19 Mary Kaldor (1998), "Democracy and Globalization", 1998, at http:// www.global.asc.upenn.edu/docs/CSY08ch2_mkaldor.pdf (accessed on 28 October 2014).
20. Verena Fritz (2008), "Mongolia: The Rise and Travails of a Deviant Democracy", *Democratization*, vol.15, no. 4, pp. 766-788

CHAPTER 8

Civil Society in Contemporary Mongolia

Santosh Kumar Jha

The Soviet collapse in 1991 provided Mongolia with a historic opportunity to launch democratic political and economic reforms by dismantling its communist regime and command economy. Mongolia's democratic transformation expressly indicates that Mongolia has attained remarkable achievements in reaching this goal. Today, Mongolian democracy meets the criteria for a liberal democracy and goes through consolidation. Mongolia's parliamentary democracy has had a leading role in building democracy and market economy in which a matured civil society has been playing a significant role. In the post-1991 period, democratic transition was a major policy shift in Mongolia that brought the country on a new stage of development where democracy at work is visible not only in forming political parties but also institutionalizing the parliamentary democracy.[1] The adoption of a democratic constitution in 1992 guaranteeing human rights and freedoms resulted in a functioning government formed through regular free and fair elections, emergence of a multi-party system, NGO sector, independent media and religious organizations.[2] Civil society space does exist in contemporary Mongolia and its role in the overlapping areas, especially with the state, political society and economic society, are quite observable. In the absence of armed conflicts, elements of uncivil society appear to be under control. The Mongolian case establishes that only democratic government provides more space for civic activities than the totalitarian and authoritarian regimes do. It is in this context that this article examines the state of civil society in today's Mongolia.

Understanding the Concept of Civil Society in Mongolia

The term 'Civil Society' has begun to be used since the late twentieth century, though the concept and meaning of civil society goes back to at least the time of Hobbes and Locke.[3] Quoting the London School of Economics Centre for Civil Society Vandangombo defines the civil society in the following words: "Civil Society refers to the arena of uncorked collective action around shared interests, purposes and values." In theory, its institutional forms are distinct from those of the state, family and market, though in practice, the boundaries between state, civil society, family and market are often complex, blurred and negotiated. Civil society commonly embraces a diversity of spaces, actors and institutional forms, varying in their degree of formality, autonomy and power."[4] The Mongolian term for civil society is "citizens' society." As such, it is fundamentally political as it asserts the primacy of the citizen's well-being, his/her rights and interests over the interests of the State and describes a society wherein this principle is a reality. It is in this sense that the term was used in the 1992 democratic Constitution of Mongolia, which states in the preamble that the supreme objective of the people of Mongolia is "building a humane, civil and democratic society in the country."[5]

The Civil Society Review stresses the importance of understanding civil society in a broader, more systemic sense and paying careful attention to the nature of power relations between the state and citizens, their organizations and activities. In order to bring further clarity to the use of the concept of civil society in Mongolia, there are three levels of understanding which have been elaborated by the Civil Society Review participants in the following manner:[6] Firstly, in the broadest (constitutional) sense, "civil society" is to be understood as a society that is based on democratic principles, wherein 1) citizens are able to make their State institutions to serve them according to the will of the people, 2) citizens are able to check the State's arbitrary power and protect their own and other fellow citizens' human rights and freedoms, 3) citizens deeply understand and value human rights and freedoms and other democratic principles and 4) citizens have equal access to political power and are provided with equal opportunities to benefit from economic and socio-cultural development.

Secondly, "civil society" is to be understood as citizens' activities that are independent of the State, which contribute to developing horizontal networking schemes and help check the State's abuse of its monopoly of coercive force and create an environment in which citizens can solve their issues with each other without the intervention of the State. This definition would encompass all independent of the State civic action, whether or not it is conducted by a formally institutionalized NGO. And thirdly, "civil society" is to be understood as formal institutions, which may include NGOs, religious groups, media organizations and political parties, depending on the nature of their actions and agenda. These organizations are to be de facto independent of the State and are to be, in principle, supporting democratic values and principles. The development of these formal institutions bears strategic importance for promoting the establishment of "civil society" in its constitutional sense. Thus, along with focusing on, for instance, NGO sector development, activists and their supporters must constantly check if their programs are in fact resulting in the empowerment of citizens at all levels, particularly at the grassroots, vis-à-vis their governing institutions and other components of the society.

In Mongolia, the democratic Constitution and Law on Non-Governmental Organisations (NGOs) opened up a legitimate ground for NGOs. In particular, after the Law on NGOs (1997), the number of NGOs registered to the Ministry of Justice and Home Affairs has boomed and reached over 5000.[7] The law guarantees the right of Mongolian citizens to freely establish NGOs on the basis of their interests and opinions without any state or other parties' intervention.[8] However, the Mongolian NGOs sector is still in its embryonic stage. The sector faces numerous challenges ranging from their internal issues to their broader influences on society for allowing the democratization process. The Civil Society Index 2005, developed by the International Civil Society Forum for Democracy, explains that the political, economic and social environments of Mongolia, underdeveloped internal capacities and weak external cooperation are the major difficulties for the development of NGOs.[9] Yet, these organizations did fulfill many civil society functions, such as developing citizens' capacity to organize and interact in the public sphere, collect and distribute information, though with an ideological tilt and relate to the institutions of the modern state. Many of these skills as well as some of the mass organizations that helped motivate them, contributed to the growth of citizen-initiated movements and organizations in the transition period.[10]

The broad definition of "civil society" was further elaborated at the 2003 Civil Society Review round table discussion, in contradiction to the 'imported' meaning of the term "civil society," which has been used interchangeably with the term "NGOs" and "NGO Sector" since the late 1990s.[11] Until then, the operational term for citizens' independent and voluntary organizations and activities was the term "NGO," which emphasized the independence from the State in the context of the overarching task of promoting democratization and increasing pluralism. This term came to be used in Mongolia in the early 1990s with the inflow of donor support for the development of non-governmental organizations as part of the democratization process, replacing the term "mass organizations" that was used in the socialist period.[12]

However, following the 1996 peaceful transition of power through the parliamentary election, international donors shifted their focus to Mongolia's economic development and socio-economic functions of NGOs. In the late 1990s, donor organizations began to actively use the term "civil society." The term was translated into Mongolian identically with the constitutional term of "civil society" but was not clearly defined as it was not clearly distinguished from the term "NGOs" and became widely used interchangeably, without bringing more clarity to the understanding of state-society relations. Such a conceptual confusion failed to make the distinction between the new breed of independent voluntary organizations and nominally non-governmental organizations that have functioned largely as an extension of the State machinery.[13] This situation undermined the strengthening of more politically-oriented human rights, policy advocacy and government oversight NGOs, especially in the context of greater emphasis put on social service-delivery functions of NGOs by important international organizations such as the World Bank, ADB and UNDP and the Mongolian Government during 2000-2004 period.[14]

Classification of Civil Society under CSI's Definition

Unlike previous repressive regimes, today the democratic regime in Mongolia provides more space for the civil society. Since the state has no systemic control, manipulation, and intimidation over civil society space and people's lives, any attempts to impose regulations over civil society space encounter serious scrutiny from the media, CSOs, and the public. Moreover, civil liberties (freedom of expression, assembly, association, movement, and religion) and human rights are recognized by the Constitution and adhered to by the state institutions. Significantly, international organizations, Western governments, and human rights watch groups have acknowledged Mongolia as a "free" democratic country since democratic governance started. Thus, civil society space does exist in contemporary Mongolia despite occasional incidents which remain under the control of law enforcement. The civil society in Mongolia under the definition of the Civil Society Index (CSI) includes the following groups:

1. **Non-governmental organizations (NGOs)**: These are registered with the Ministry of Justice and Home Affairs (MJHA) under the 1997 Law on Non-State Organizations (NGO Law). The number of NGOs is based on the registration at the MJHA of Mongolia.[15] Article 4 of the Law on NGOs sets out two types of NGOs: Public Benefit NGO and a Member Benefit NGO. The charitable activities for the promotion of arts, culture and education, protection of nature and environment, support of human rights and community development are defined as the public benefit. A public benefit organization is defined as the one that makes the main purpose of its charter its engagement in public benefit or charitable activities. A mutual benefit organization is an NGO that operates primarily to serve the legitimate interests of its members.[16]

2. **Trade Unions:** These are registered with the MJHA under the 1991 Law on Trade Unions, which include inherited structures and fewer new unions formed in the context of market economy. This is one of the best structured sectors of civil society with provincial and district Trade Unions' Councils in all areas and the Mongolian Trade Unions' Federation at the national level.[17]

3. **Chambers of Commerce:** It is registered with the MJHA under the 1995 Law on Chambers of Trade and Industry, which stipulates that there may only be one National Chamber of Trade and Industry (NCTI) and one chamber per province or for two to three provinces. The existing NCTI regularly organises consultation meetings with business representatives and has close ties with the Government.[18]

4. **Political Parties:** These are registered with the Supreme Court under the 1990 Law on Political Parties.[19] In 2003, there were 18 political parties registered.[20] However, the main competition is between the MPRP and Mongolian Democratic Party (MDP), the only parties that have truly national memberships. The Mongolian New Social Democratic Party, the Civil Courage-Republican Party and the Mongolian Republican Party have won few seats in the parliament since 2004 elections.[21]

5. **Religious organizations:** These are founded to help fulfil the religious and spiritual needs of the believers and conduct religious rituals and teachings.

These organizations are registered with the MJHA under the 1993 Law on State and Monastery/Church Relations, after a review by provincial and capital city legislatures.[22]

6. **Apartment Owners' Unions (AOUs)**: These are registered with district and sum administrations under the 2003 Law on the Legal Status of Apartment Owners' Unions and Common Property of Apartment Buildings.[23]

7. **Association of Mongolian Advocates' (Defence Attorneys)**: It is registered with the Ministry of Justice and governed by the 2002 Law on Legal Defence (Advocacy). The Association was first formed in 1934 as the Mongolian Advocates' Committee, a part of the unitary Party-State structure. In 1990, it was renamed as the Mongolian Advocates' Association and was granted a monopoly right to represent all defence attorneys in the 9-member Specialization Committee that determines lawyers' eligibility to act as defence attorneys by the Law on Legal Defence.[24] The Association claims a membership of over 1000 defence attorneys and is by law declared to be a non-governmental professional organization with the main aim of defending defence lawyers' rights.[25]

8. **Non-profit Media**: These are few in number due mainly to financial obstacles. Most publications are produced by public education NGOs such as the Political Education Academy (PEA), Oyuntulkhuur Foundation, and National Centre against Violence (NCAV), Women for Social Progress Movement (WSP), Democracy Education Centre (DEMO Centre) and Mongolian Women's Federation (MWF). A number of FM radio stations were set up with the assistance of the Mongolian Open Society Institute (MOSI), UNDP and other donors in rural areas, significantly strengthening this sector of civil society.[26]

Civil Society in Post-Cold War Period

Over a period of time a variety of citizens' organizations has been experienced by Mongolia such as[27] (1) mass resistance, led by feudal lords to overthrow the Manchu yoke in the pre-socialist period before 1921, (2) quasi-governmental mass organizations intended to transform Mongolian people into 'homo socialisticus' during the socialist period from 1924 to 1989, and finally (3) pro-democracy mass movements and small-size issue-oriented Western-style voluntary organizations, which emerged in the late 1980s and later and after 1990. However, most of the scholars consider the transition to democracy in 1989 and 1990 as the beginning of the development of Mongolia's civil society.

The development of democracy and civil society in Mongolia that is going ahead in the past 25 years, have seen substantial achievements. The theory and practice of promoting democracy and civil society have today become important topics of discussion in the country ever since Mongolia embarked on its grand objective of constructing "a humane, civil and democratic society"[28] as declared in the 1992 Constitution. The adoption of the democratic constitution in 1992 and the holding of the first free and fair parliamentary elections in the same year provided further impetus for the emergence of a new type of citizen's organization: Western-style issue-oriented, office-based, more professionalized advocacy and oversight non-governmental organizations (NGOs) aimed at influencing public policy and holding the government accountable. Some of the most active pro-democracy and pro-development NGOs are formed by the politically active women who were affiliated with political parties.[29]

In the 1990s, initially NGOs were supported financially and technically by a number of foreign and international organizations, such as The Asia Foundation (USA), Konrad Adenauer Foundation (Germany), USAID, UNDP, NED, AusAID and the Global Fund for Women. This support was essential for the adoption of the NGO Law in 1997, which further facilitated the formation of new NGOs in accordance with the law. Towards the late 1990s, however, donor support became less focused on political aspects of democratization. Rather it began playing a socio-economic support role in the emerging non-governmental sector, "emphasizing service-delivery functions of NGOs over their advocacy and monitoring roles."[30]

At the same time, mass organizations, inherited from the socialist period, sought to restructure themselves and redefine their mission and relationship with the former communist party MPRP and the Mongolian State. To a large extent, however, these organizations with extensive national networks have maintained close ties with the State through their largely unbroken ties with the MPRP that was in power in 1992-1996 and 2000-2004, controlling 72 out of 76 parliamentary seats during these two terms.[31] These organizations include women's, children's, youth and pensioners' associations to peace and friendship associations, chambers of commerce, the Mongolian Red Cross Association and traditional trade unions. Independent women's organizations were the most successful in breaking the monopoly of the Mongolian Women's Federation largely due to extensive donor support for women's rights programmes, whereas in other sectors the inherited umbrella organizations are still hegemonic.[32]

A few independent trade unions remain weak such as the Mongolian Federation of Trade Unions and until very recently the Mongolian Pensioners' Association had monopolized the right to represent the elderly. The Free Pensioners' Association was formed in 2005 and captured public attention through its bold and consistent struggle for an equitable pension system and most recently, through the active role it played in anti-corruption and pro-democracy mass protests and demonstrations.[33] Self-organized community groups barely existed during socialist period as the Party-State and its subsidiary organizations held the monopoly of citizens' organization. However, in the post-socialist period, such groups began to emerge, mobilizing actively against the encroachment on their living environments by construction and mining companies. In addition, herders' groups also began to emerge, with support from environmental protection projects funded by international organizations, bonding around alternative and supplementary income-generation projects and developing grassroots democracy.[34]

Social movements that played a vital role in bringing about the democratic changes in the country have re-emerged very strongly after 2000. Wide-spread social discontent over the lack of improvement of the majority's living conditions, continued high poverty rates, increasing crime and most importantly, increasing corruption among public officials has been channelled into the formation of a number of mass movements, which have invoked intensive series of public protests and demonstrations demanding the restitution of justice, government accountability and drastic anti-corruption measures.[35] The activities of the movements grew stronger following the 2004 parliamentary elections that ended the MPRP's near-monopoly of political power by more evenly distributing the seats between the MPRP and other democratic parties. This significantly helped expand the political space for independent citizen action and more balanced and timely reporting on current events by the independent media.[36]

Major challenges that Mongolian Civil Society Organisations are facing today are lack of adequate government support or required cooperation with the government, lack of an effective legislation or tax policy that would support the CSOs and their activities, weak civil society infrastructure, concentration of most CSOs activities in the capital city of Ulaanbaatar and some other cities, as well as lack of experience and financial resources. Also, there is a weak understanding of the importance and support of civil society activities within the society at large.[37] Hence, there is a need to strengthen civil society by consolidating it as an important part of the Mongolian democratic society and promoting it through CSO-Government and CSO-private sector cooperation.

Conclusion

The Mongolian people have actively embraced democratic transition and reforms in political and economic fields. In the last 25 years, the country has made impressive progress, especially by adopting a democratic Constitution and based on it hundreds of laws as well as setting up the required democratic institutions. Since the domestic reforms require a vigorous civil society, the rule of law and the effective freedom of the press, Mongolia has done a lot to achieve that. In particular, the civil society has come a long way since its emergence in the early 1990s. While the field of civil society is broad and defies generalizations, the human rights, women's rights and pro-democracy advocacy NGOs have matured substantially. They have clearly articulated their values and principles by maintaining ethical practice, effectively building new forms of democratic structures and organizations, fostering solidarity and movement building for progressive social change.[38] More importantly, they have been able to sustain their work in a largely unfavourable political, economic and cultural environment without having adequate support from either the government or international community. Today, the Mongolian civil society plays a crucial role to empower citizens and communities to rise against corruption and human rights violations, to hold government and private sector accountable and plan more reasonable path of development.

Notes and References

1. Sharad K Soni (2013), "Evaluating Mongolia's Experience of Democratization: Post-Soviet Scenario", *The Mongolian Journal of International Affairs*, p. 34.
2. "State of Civil Society in Mongolia (2004-2005)", *CIVICUS Civil Society Index Report for Mongolia*, atwww.civicus.org/new/media/csipdf (accessed on 25 September 2014).
3. D. Robertson (2006), The Penguin Dictionary of Politics, London: Penguin, p.223.
4. Danaasuren Vandangombo, "NGOs As Accountability Promoters: In the Mongolian Case", at http://apira2010.econ.usyd.edu.au/conference_proceedings/APIRA-2010-166-vanDanGombo-NGOS-as-accountability-promoters-Mongolia.pdf (accessed on 25 September 2014).
5. See Preamble, Constitution of Mongolia (1992),http://www.con.gov.mn(accessed on 20 July 2014).
6. "State of Civil Society in Mongolia" (2004-2005), *CIVICUS Civil Society Index Report for Mongolia*, at www.civicus.org/new/media/csipdf(accessed on 19 August 2014).

7. Open Society Forum (2005), "NGOs in Mongolia", Report, at http://www.opensocity foundations.orgpdf(accessed on 19 August 2014).
8. The State Great Khural of Mongolia (1997), cited in Vandangombo Danaasuren (2010), "NGOs as Accountability Promoters: In the Mongolian Case", pp.8-9, at http://apira2010.econ.usyd.edu.au/conference_proceedings/APIRA-2010-166-vanDanGombo-NGOS-as-accountability-promoters-Mongolia.pdf (accessed on 25 September 2014).
9. UNDP in Mongolia (2006), at www.mn.undp.org.pdf
10. Danaasuren, "NGOs as Accountability Promoters".
11. "State of Civil Society in Mongolia (2004-2005)", *CIVICUS Civil Society Index Report for Mongolia*, at http://www.civicus.org/new/media/CSI_Mongolia_Country_Report.pdf (accessed on 25 September 2014).
12. *Ibid.*
13. *Ibid.*
14. *Ibid.*
15. Open Society Forum (2005), "NGOs in Mongolia".
16. *Ibid,* p. 6
17. "State of Civil Society in Mongolia (2004-2005)",
18. *Ibid*
19. *Ibid.*
20. Supreme Court data quoted in The Asia Foundation (2004), *Legal Empowerment in Mongolia. Research Report,* Ulaanbaatar, p. 7.
21. "State of Civil Society in Mongolia (2004-2005)".
22. Law on State and Monastery/Church Relations of Mongolia (1993), Section 3, Article 6
23. *Ibid.*
24. *Law on Legal Defense (Advocacy) of Mongolia*(2002).
25. *Ibid.*
26. "State of Civil Society in Mongolia (2004-2005)".
27. *Ibid.*
28. Jargalsaikhan Enkhsaikhan, *Promotion of Democracy and Civil Society in Northeast Asia*, at http://r-cube.ritsumei.ac.jp/bitstream/10367/948/1/7-RJAPS26_Promotion%20of%20Democracy%20and%20Civil%20Society%20in%20Northeast%20Asia.pdf (accessed on 24 December 2014).
29. "State of Civil Society in Mongolia (2004-2005)".
30. *Ibid.*
31. *Ibid.*
32. Open Society Forum (2005), "NGOs in Mongolia".
33. *Ibid.*
34. "State of Civil Society in Mongolia (2004-2005)".
35. *Ibid.*
36. *Ibid.*
37. Enkhsaikhan, *Promotion of Democracy and Civil Society in Northeast Asia.*
38. T. Undary (2013), "State of Civil Society Development in Mongolia", *The Mongolian Journal of International Affairs*, no.18, p.68. For more detailed analysis on the state of civil society in Mongolia, see pp. 52-68.

CHAPTER 9

Human Security in Mongolia

Renu Sain

Security is not 'a new concept', it is an old concept existing since the human being started living in the groups. The concept of security is very dynamic and broad. In the traditional model, security means the interaction among the states which used to be the main focus. But modern concept of security has rejected traditional security model and started focussing on security of the state instead of security of the individual. After the Second World War, establishment of the UN system was in real term aimed at protecting security of the people. The UN principle for security was initially focused on ways in which the structures and practices of the modern state might address threats to its sovereignty.[1] Security is the protection of a state, person, property and organization from any type of attacks. It is the degree of protection against danger, damage, loss, and criminal activity. It is also a structure and processes that provide or improve security as a condition. It includes state security, regional security, social security and human security etc.[2]

Human Security in Theoretical Perspective

Human security is security of human being from any type of threat. The concept of human security is not a new concept in the domain of international relations. But formally it was mentioned in the 1994 UNDP report. The 1994 UNDP report originally argued that human security requires attention to both freedoms from fear and freedom from want.[3] Human security does not have specific borderlines. Anything, which affects the security of individual and collective existence, may come under human security. Human security has gone through three stages: Pre-Cold War era, Cold War era and Post-Cold War era. In the Pre-Cold War era, there was traditional type of security. It was about how states used force to manage threats to their territorial integrity, their autonomy and their domestic political order primarily from other states. In the Cold War era, newly independent countries emerged with a new set of problems like extreme poverty, population, under nutrition, industrial backwardness, civil war, ethnic conflicts, epidemics etc.[4] Newly independent states were not enough to address these problems. Therefore, in this context, a group of development theorists including Samir Amin, Gunder Frank and Franz Fennen, put forward alternative approaches to development, focusing on equal distribution of resources and income.[5] In the post-cold war period, the development of human security emerged through two different streams, 'Freedom for Fear' and 'Freedom of Want'.[6]

Today the notion of human security is gaining worldwide acceptance, especially after the end of the bi-polar world system. Kofi Annan argues that human security, in its broadest sense, "embraces far more than the absence of violent conflict. It focusses on human rights, good governance, access to education and health care, and ensuring that each individual has opportunities and choices to fulfill his or her potential."[7] He further states that "every step in this direction is also a step towards reducing poverty, achieving economic growth and preventing conflict." At the beginning of the 21st century, the globalization of inequality at the inter-state, intra-state and private company levels seems to be entrenched. This may affect security ranging from the human to the intra-state, inter-state, regional and ultimately global levels. The globalisation process is resulting in highly uneven distribution of gains and without concerted action inequality may deepen further with all its attendant implications, and therefore alternative pathways for the pursuit of human security must be explored.[8]

The 1994 Human Development Report (HDR) defines human security as including "safety from such chronic threats as hunger, disease and repression and protection from sudden and hurtful disruptions in the patterns of daily lives, whether in homes, jobs or communities". It has been observed that "Human security is a 'people centered' approach that focusses jointly on 'freedom from fear and freedom from want'. So, human security is ... people centered, multi-dimensional, inter-connected, universal concept".[9] Mahbubul Haq first drew global attention to the concept of human security in the

UNDP's *1994 Human Development Report.* According the report, the scope of global security should be expanded to include threats in seven areas: economy security, food security, health security, environment security, person security, community security, and political security.[10] The idea of human security can be clearly delineated in relation to the dominant, neo-realist conception of security and that its elements can be presented compactly enough for further refinement'.[11]

Describing human security as a "promotion of basic human freedoms and grass-roots economic growth", Sen argues that "we do need an integrated understanding of human freedom and security. Human freedom is the mean, in which not just political freedom and personal liberties, but also societal concern with food, medical attention, basic education, and other elementary ingredients of human lives comes".[12] He says that "richness of human life is more important, rather than the richness of the economy in which human beings live which is only a part of the human security." Buzan further argues that the bottom line of security is survival, but it also reasonably includes a substantial range of concern about the condition of existence.[13] The idea of human security can be clearly explained in relation to the dominant, neo-realist conception of security and that its elements can be presented compactly enough for further refinement. Human security does not just pertain to situations of extreme violence like the Iraq conflict. It is more inclusive and extends to all conditions which have forced millions to live in extreme insecurity such as war, poverty, disease, and natural disasters. Furthermore, human security emphasizes how security is established as much as its establishment.[14] For example, Kaldor endorsed NATO's intervention in the Kosovo conflict but questioned its use of air strikes.

The realist view of security looks at security in terms of 'power.' This view could be considered relevant during the period of world war, where state seemed to be in the struggle for power. According to realism, "security of state is main point, because in the international system there is anarchy, so the security of state comes first, others security comes under state security. If state is not secured than how other thing like human security can be secure there".[15] Hans Morgenthau is considered to be one of the founding fathers of the realist school in the 20th century. This school of thought holds that nation-states are the main actors in international relations and that the main concern of the field is the study of power. Morgenthau stressed on the importance of national interest. In his book *Politics Among Nations,* he stated that "the main signpost that helps political realism to find its way through the landscape of international politics is the concept of interest defined in terms of power".[16] On the other hand, neorealism was developed to reformulate the classical realist tradition of E.H. Carr and others. The neo-realist approach of human security has been advocated by the structural or neorealist such as Barry Buzan in "*people state and fear.*" Buzan argues that the straitjacket militaristic approach to the security that dominated discourse during the Cold War led to the underdevelopment of the concept.[17] Liberal theorist focuses on the security of individual. This theory owes its origin to John Locke. It argues that it would be security of life, liberty and property which is more important and also they envisages the creation of a liberal democratic political system. Liberal theory believes in the innate goodness of mankind to conduct peace keeping relation in the international system.

As stated earlier the core of liberalism is individual. The liberalism theory of security management consists of two key methods: collective security and arms control.[18] Social constructivists highlight the impact of social values in the construction of human identity. It may be recalled that the issue of human security is closely intertwined with other forms of security which is gaining importance in recent year. Constructivists argue that through processes of *accommodation* and *assimilation*, individuals construct new knowledge from their experiences. They incorporate the new experience into an already existing framework without changing that framework.[19] Green theory and environmentalism talk about environmental security. Environmental degradation caused by human activity has a long and complex history. At the present time global warming and other environmental degradation are main challenges for the humanity. Other theorists like feminist also talk about the human security and focusses on the issue related to women security, women rights. It opposes the patriarchal structure and calls each policy area into question from a critical perspective, positing that the global system is created and based around a male dominated agenda.[20]

Human Security in Mongolia: The Food Security Issue

The disintegration of the former Soviet Union and end of Mongolia's special relations and of the political, economic and social system modeled after the Soviets brought about many radical changes. With the collapse of the economic system, the social guarantees of the people also collapsed. In early 1990s, production fell, inflation skyrocketed, unemployment appeared as a novel social and economic phenomenon and the living standard of the people fell, bringing about the rise in poverty. Street children, prostitution and other social ills become part of the present day reality.[21] The new geopolitical, economic and social realities of the post-Soviet period and national security are closely related to the human security. However, today the global food crisis, hunger and malnutrition has become one of the most important and crucial issues. Nowadays hundreds of people in the world are dying from starvation and suffering because of food shortage.

Mongolia has broad and wide territory which covers an area of 1.6 million square kilometers and a dense population of 2.7 million people. The environmental security and human security are closely related to each other. The climate of the country is a deciding factor for the food security, because the production of agricultural products is decided by the climate. The Mongolian climate is continental with four seasons a year. While discussing Mongolian food supply, two main sectors can be discussed: Agriculture and Animal husbandry. There are five strategic products of Mongolia, which come from the above sources: wheat, meat, potato, milk and vegetable. In 1990s, Mongolia was self-sufficient in wheat and an occasional exporter. Wheat production has declined steady since 1994 and commercial imports, food aid of wheat have increased. Wheat is the main crop in the country and wheat flour is the major food staple, covering approximately 59 percent and 52 percent of the daily caloric intake in urban and rural areas respectively.[22] In particular, wheat flour is essential in the diets of the extreme poor populations of the cities who could not afford to buy meat and milk products. Since animal husbandry is a traditional custom of Mongolian life, the main livelihood source and the wealth is livestock. The main foundation of Mongolia's economy is pasturing livestock husbandry which still plays an important role in the country's economy, employment and export revenues.[23] Around 50% of Mongolians work as herders but only around 10% of land is suited to agriculture. In 2005, the worst wheat crop on record forced Mongolia to increase expensive imports further to ensure enough food was available.[24]

Some 70 percent of Mongolia's food is imported from China and the rising Chinese currency and costs of transporting food are making it much more expensive for parents to feed their children. Children are already facing challenges of malnutrition in Mongolia. Around 13% of them are underweight and many suffer from other nutrition-based conditions such as skin disease and rickets. The impact of rising food costs can be seen not only in increased malnutrition of children and their parents, but also in decisions made at a family level which affect children, for instance taking them out of school or sending them into exploitative labour. Mongolia has seen several consecutive years of unprecedented extreme climate conditions, with harsh winters (called "dzüüd"), followed by dry summers. This has had a devastating impact on the country's cattle population, thus depriving the rural population of its food security. This has, in turn, resulted in domestic migration from the rural areas to the already deprived urban areas that are incapable of catering for the excluded. Countless cattle-breeders who have lost their livelihoods are trying to settle in the towns and the country is not at all prepared for natural disasters".[25]

Mongolia's natural resources are fragile and stressed by human activity, harsh winters, hot summers, and low rainfall. For more than two decades, the country has been making the transition from a centrally planned to an open market economy. During this transition, its natural resources have been heavily exploited. For example, deforestation rates have risen since the mid-1990s from around 40,000 ha annually to around 60,000 ha. Now only 12.4 million ha of closed forest remain. Urbanization has also accelerated rapidly, but environmental infrastructure, regulation and enforcement have not kept pace. The result is significant urban environmental degradation. Urban air quality is deteriorating due to increasing pollution from household heating, power generation, industry, and transport. High levels of particulates and other pollutants pose serious health risks, as indicated by the increasing number of young children with respiratory diseases. Sewerage coverage is one of the lowest in Asia, causing widespread contamination of surface and groundwater, both in Ulaanbataar and secondary cities. Waste collection and management covers very little of the waste stream. The county's deteriorating environmental situation is exacerbated by irresponsible vested interests, inadequate monitoring of natural resource conditions and weak enforcement of environmental regulations.[26]

Poverty and Food Insecurity in Mongolia

There is very close connection between poverty and food insecurity. Poverty is a recent reality in Mongolia. Until about 1990 there were virtually no poor people in rural areas. Poverty has been a direct consequence of the transition to a market economy. Privatization of industry and state farms brought high levels of unemployment. Presently, one in three people in Mongolia are poor, and the number of poor people grows as the income gap widens. Poverty is becoming entrenched not only in urban centers but also in rural areas, where about half of the country's poor people live. Poverty is more likely to affect women than men. In 2002, more than 55,000 households in Mongolia were headed by women, 250 per cent more than in 1990. One in four of these families have six or more children. People tend to move their herds closer to *soums* so that they can have easier access to health and education services and basic supplies. Most rural poor people are herders. Although livestock production is still the principal source of livelihood for rural people, the number of livestock per herder is decreasing dramatically. It shrank by more than half between 1990 and 2000.[27]

After recovering quickly from a brief but difficult period in 2008-09, Mongolia's economy is growing at a fast pace. Driven by the mining sector, the economy grew at more than 16% in the first quarter of 2012 and on average has grown at more than 9% in the last decade. With the expected launch of new large-scale mining projects, Mongolia is likely to witness rapid growth. It is imperative for Mongolia to diversify its economy and create alternative employment sources, especially for the youth. The overall unemployment rate is around 10% but nearly one in four youths (15-24 years) are unemployed. The country is affected by serious ecosystem degradation, including that of pastureland, forest and water and loss of biodiversity and air pollution in urban areas. The growing mining sector and the impacts of climate change pose new challenges to Mongolia's environment. There is a lack of adequate water and sanitation.[28]

Measures for Human and Food Security

Article 14 of the Mongolian Constitution says that all the citizens of Mongolia are equal before the law and the court, and no person shall be discriminated against on the basis of ethnic origin, language, race, age, sex, social origin and status, property, occupation and post, religion, opinion or education.[29] Article 16 says that the citizens of Mongolia shall be guaranteed to right to life. Deprivation of human life shall be strictly prohibited unless capital punishment is imposed by due judgment of the court for the most serious crimes, constructed by Mongolian Penal Law. The Constitution also provides for right to healthy and safe environment and to be protected against environmental pollution and ecological imbalance, in addition to right to the protection of health and medical care. According to the Constitution, men and women have equal rights in political, economic, social, cultural fields and in family affairs. Article 19 clearly defines that the State shall be responsible to the citizens for the creation of economic, social, legal and other guarantees for ensuring human rights and freedoms, and to fight against violation of human rights and freedoms.[30]

The humanitarian aid organization, Action against Hunger ACF International, which has been working in Mongolia since October 2001, is aiming to reduce the nutritional impact of poverty in Ulaanbaatar and providing cattle-breeders in the far western province of the country with resources to enable them to cope with the risk of extreme climate conditions and natural disaster in order to halt the rural exodus. Action against Hunger is involved in opening soup kitchens for the marginalized parts of the population, such as the homeless, street children, the unemployed and the retired, with 300 to 600 hot meals served every day. This is being done in order to diversify the range of food supplies and to generate a small income to cater for the basic needs of this population. At the same time, Action against Hunger runs porridge distributions all year round to fight against malnutrition in children. In the rural areas, particularly in the Western part of the country, a programme has been put in place in order to increase the ability of cattle-breeders to cope with the harsh winter conditions, by building up emergency fodder supplies and constructing cattle shelters.[31]

On its part, the Government of Mongolia approved the National Food Security Programme (NFSP) for the period 2009-2016. The overall goal of the programme is to provide the entire nation with stable supplies of accessible, nutritious and safe food to create healthy livelihoods and high labour productivity. The programme emphasizes the participation of the people, the government, and the public and private sectors. The IFAD-funded Rural Poverty Reduction Programme was involved in the preparation of the national programme, especially with respect to the programme's experience in improving food security and its household support for cultivating potatoes and vegetables in rural areas. The first national food security programme (NFSP), from 2001-2007, was an ambitious endeavor to address weaknesses in the food supply chain to provide Mongolians with sufficient, safe and nutritious food and to mitigate the risk posed by over-reliance on imported food staples. Today, Mongolia is experiencing a price escalation of food staples and serious food safety incidents. Some of the key lessons learned during the first programme were as follows: (a) The current food law failed to provide adequate clarity to regulators, industry and consumers; (b) Too many organizations have over-lapping responsibilities for food security, and (c) The programme had too many objectives, sub-programmes and activities to be able to be implemented efficiently.[32]

The second NFSP for the period 2009-2016 promotes a more pro-active, pro-poor approach to further reduce poverty and uses a more targeted strategy in partnership with the private sector. The design of the second programme factors in Mongolia's unique situation related to food security, in particular traditional nomadic pastoral systems in rural areas, extreme vulnerability of herders and farmers, isolation of many rural households and communities, unique food consumption patterns and seasonality, and high concentration of urban population. The NFSP comprises four priority areas or pillars covering the following elements:[33]

1. *The enabling environment:* This pillar includes, building capacity to make necessary reforms in food policy and institutional frameworks to meet modern needs, promoting food research, information and monitoring and evaluation, developing innovative financing and credit schemes for the agricultural investments such as the Agricultural Development Fund.
2. *Food security:* This pillar focuses on two aspects. Firstly, it addresses commercial agriculture to increase national food production and generate incremental incomes in rural areas. Secondly, it supports food-insecure rural households in intensifying and diversifying their agriculture production and, in urban area, assuring their access to adequate and affordable food.
3. *Food safety:* This pillar focuses on modernizing and expanding food processing and on rationalizing the food control management system into a modern, pro-active, cost-efficient structure.
4. *Nutrition:* This pillar includes, increasing public awareness, managing research and information, preventing micro-nutrient deficiency, supporting food fortification, reducing non-communicable diseases, promoting clean water supplies.

To address environmental challenges, the Government of Mongolia has enacted a series of environmental laws, expanded its system of nature reserves, and started to invest in energy-efficient technologies and pollution abatement schemes. In addition, it is trying to mainstream environmental concerns into development, and is working with international organizations and civil society to promote environmental awareness. The transition to a free market economy may have brought prices closer to the market equilibrium, but challenges in addressing market failures remain and are dependent on design and implementation of effective environmental regulations. The World Bank is collaborating with WHO on air pollution/health analysis and produces annual Environment Monitors, the first of which focused on the overall environment, the second on land resource management and the third on urban environment services. The World Bank is also providing technical assistance to the Ministry of Nature and Environment on environmental assessment, regulation and enforcement. Besides, the World Bank is helping to raise herder productivity by improving animal production and marketing systems, reforming pasture land management systems, and establishing a livestock insurance system.[34] Mongolia has also joined many environment-related UN Conventions and International Treaties and passed more than 30 environmental laws and reforming many other laws.[35]

Conclusion

Human security is a broad and old concept. In recent years, it has gained worldwide acceptance due to the rapidity of globalization as well as emergence of non-traditional threats, welfare state and democracy, all are working for one center point that is human security. All other systems, institutions and principles are in the periphery of the center point. In the 1994 UNDP report, there are seven types of human security in which environmental security, food security and health security are closely interrelated. Today environmental degradation is the major challenge facing the world and its effects are visible on food production and health. The role of the food supply and demand is tightly related to the sustainable development of the Mongolian agricultural sector. Even though Mongolia suffered hard times in the agricultural sector after the 1990s when the economic and social transformation occurred, the country is optimistic about its food security because there are various kinds of possibilities to improve it in the future in order to ensure human security.

Notes and References

1. Richard Jolly and Deepayan Basu Ray (2006), *National Human Development Reports and the Human Security Framework: A Review of Analysis and Experience*, New York: The Human Development Report Office (UNDP).
2. D. Lieberman (2010), What is Security?, at https://www.infosecisland.com/blogview/9564-What-is-Security.html (accessed on 19 March 2014).
3. UNDP (1994), *Human Development Report 1994*, New York: Oxford University Press, p. 22.
4. Sudha Menon (2007), "Human security: Concept and Practice", MPRA Paper presented on 31 March 2007 at ICFAI Business School, Ahmadabad.
5. Ibid.
6. Ibid.
7. Kofi Annan (2000), *We the Peoples: The Role of the United Nations in the 21st Century*, at

http://www.un.org/en/events/pastevents/pdfs/We_The_Peoples.pdf (accessed on 19 March 2014).

8. Carolin Thomas (2001), "Global governance, development and human security: exploring the links," *Third World Quarterly,* 22(2):159-175.
9. Sabina Alkire (2008), "A Conceptual Framework for Human Security", *Minerva Citizens For Global Solutions World Federalist Institute* 33:7.
10. UNDP (1994), *Human Development Report 1994*, p. 22
11. Kanti Bajpai (2000), "The Idea of Human Security", *International Studies* 40(3): 195-228.
12. Amartya Sen (2000), "Why Human Security?",Paper at the International Symposium on Human Security, Tokyo, 28 July.
13. Barry Buzan (1991), "New Patterns of Global Security in the twenty first century," *International Affairs,* 67 (3): 431-451.
14. Mary Kaldor (2006), *New and old war organized violence in the globalised era,* Cambridge: Polity Press.
15. Buzan, "New Patterns of Global Security".
16. Hans J. Morgenthau (1978), *Politics among Nations: The Struggle for Power and Peace,* New York: Alfred A. Knopf publisher.
17. Buzan, "New Patterns of Global Security".
18. Morgenthau, *Politics among Nations.*
19. Jean Piaget (1967), "Cognitive Theory of Constructivism", athttp://www.community independentschool.org/pdfs/Constructivism.pdf (accessed on 25 January 2011).
20. Barry John (2007), *Environment and Social Theory,* New York: Routledge.
21. J. Enkhsaikhan (2000), "Human security factor in Mongolia's national security concept", The*Mongolian Journal of International Affairs,* no.7, pp. 26-36.
22. Enkhbayar Tumurtogoo (2009), "Food Demand and Supply of Mongolia" Mongolian State University of Agriculture, at http://www.nodai.ac.jp/cip/iss/english/9th_iss/fullpaper/1-2-4msua-enkhbayar.pdf (assessed on 2 May 2014).
23. Ibid.
24. For more details see, FAO/UNICEF/UNDP Report, April 2007, Joint Food Security Assessment Mission to Mongolia, Ulaanbaatar, at http://www.fao.org/docrep/010/j9883e/j9883e00.HTM (assessed on 2 May 2014).
25. Action Against Hunger (2003) "Action Against Hunger warns of poor food security in Mongolia", at http://www.actionagainsthunger.org/blog/action-against-hunger-warns-poor-food-security mongolia (accessed on 2 May 2014).
26. The World Bank (2013) "Mongolia Environment", at http://web.worldbank.org/WBSITE/EXTERNAL/COUNTRIES/EASTASIAPACIFICEXT/EXTEAPREGTOP ENVIRON MENT/0,,contentMDK:20266325~menuPK:537827~pagePK: 34004173~piPK: 34003707~theSitePK:502886,00.html#institutional_capacity (assessed on 5 February 2014).
27. "Rural poverty in Mongolia", at http://www.ruralpovertyportal.org/country/home/tags/mongolia (accessed on 10 May 2014).
28. UNDP in Mongolia (2013), "About Mongolia", at http://www.mn.undp.org/content/mongolia/en/home/countryinfo/ (accessed on 7 May 2014).
29. *Constitution of Mongolia* (1992), at http://engconstitution.files.wordpress.com/2013/04/the-constitution-of-mongolia.pdf (accessed on 11 May 2014).
30. Ibid.

31. "Action Against Hunger warns of poor food security in Mongolia".
32. Gun-Uyanga Soninbayar (2010), "Improving food self-reliance in Mongolia: The National Food Security Program", *The APR Newsletter 'Making a Difference in Asia and the Pacific'*, Issue 30, January/February.
33. Ibid.
34. The World Bank, "Mongolia Environment".
35. UNDP in Mongolia, "About Mongolia".

CHAPTER 10

Mongolia's Security Policy: An Overview

Anurag Tripathi

> "In the post-Cold War era, the world experienced dramatic changes in many areas of International life. Globalization has made the world unimaginably interdependent. Mongolia is no more an isolated country from International life."
>
> **M. Batchimeg,** *Former National Security Policy Advisor to the President of Mongolia*

The study of security has developed within International Relations as a gateway for understanding driving forces within international politics. Increasingly global and catastrophic conflict makes the study of security central to policy makers and academics seeking to understand, and predict, behaviour in global politics.[1] Political analysts agree that international security is the most important contemporary global issue. Other concerns include global inequality, disease control, the effectiveness of international treaties, economic expansion, environmentalism, and so on. However, the focal concern for all states is security.[2] State interest that implies independence, sovereignty and territorial integrity has always been one of the major security concerns for a small state like Mongolia.[3] After the disintegration of Union of Soviet Socialist Republics (USSR), Mongolia lost its twentieth century protector, and has had to navigate Asian and global politics at a time when China is becoming a dominant economic and military power in the region. The security environment of Mongolia is directly related to global and regional political, economic, social and army processes, and furthermore, the activities of foreign policies, their internal society, political life, bilateral relations and cooperation of the two neighbouring countries, namely the Russian Federation and the People's Republic of China.[4] Chinese economic and demographic expansion may directly impact Mongolia and the precedent of the signification of Inner Mongolia demonstrates new challenges to the isolated Mongolian Republic.[5]

Since 1990s or more precisely since the post-Cold War period, Mongolia redefined its priority directions in the domestic and foreign policies because not only state interest but also social and civilian interests came to the forefront as the overall national security concerns. As such, it became clear that national security of Mongolia could be ensured not only in terms of preserving independence, sovereignty and territorial integrity but also achieving a sustainable socio-economic development with guarantee of human rights and freedom to civilians. It was more so because in today's context, "security is defined not by a country's self-defence capacity but by its capacity to survive and compete".[6] In that perspective relations with outside world often play key roles in ensuring a country's overall national security.

Theoretical Approach to Security

In the field of international politics, various theories has been developed to explain events that take place around us, such theories include: Realism, Neo-Realism, Idealism, Liberalism, Neo-Liberalism, Marxism and so on. Neo-realist theory has long been at the centre of the debate about security within the discipline and the discourse is heavily influenced by it. From its origins in Machiavelli and Hobbes, to Morgenthau and classical realism, neo realism continues to be popular within the discipline, with thinkers such as Waltz and Mearsheimer offering seminal texts that discuss security from a neo-realist perspective in some depth[7]. After the disintegration of the USSR, events within the international system have challenged but neo-realist theory seems to be relevant within current International Scenario.

Neo-realist shuns classical realism's use of often essentialist concepts such as "human nature" to explain international politics. Instead, neo-realist thinkers developed a theory that privileges structural constraints over agents' strategies and motivations. According to Neo-realist approach, International system is anarchic system, there is no central authority in International system. This system is composed of formally equal sovereign states. These states act according to the logic of self-help states seek their own interest and will not subordinate their interest to another's. States are assumed at a minimum to want to ensure their own survival as this is a prerequisite to pursue other goals. This driving force of survival is the primary factor influencing their behavior and in turn ensures states develop offensive military capabilities, for foreign interventionism and as a means to increase their relative power. Because states can never be certain of other states' future intentions, there is a lack of trust between states which requires them to be on guard against relative losses of power which could enable other states to threaten their survival. It also gives rise to the "security dilemma" that all nations face. There are two ways in which states balance power: internal balancing and external balancing. Internal balancing occurs as states grow their own capabilities by increasing economic growth and/or increasing military spending. External balancing occurs as states enter into alliances to check the power of more powerful states or alliances.[8] Neo realist thinkers believe that the state is the key actor when it comes to security, and that due to the anarchic nature of the international system, states will pursue some sort of offensive military capability in order to defend themselves or expand.[9] The security policy of Mongolia in this regard is following neo-realist approach.

Moreover, energy security and climate change are, for example, becoming increasingly important as without energy a state's economy would grind to a halt and it certainly could not even think about running a military. As energy demands continue to increase, states can now use energy as a method of hard diplomacy and to gain power. So it is clear that neo-realism fails to effectively deal with many security issues in International Relations, however the Neo-Realist approach gives a broader picture of Security by which any state can form its Policy. Other theory which is important to mention here is Neo-Liberal theory of International Relations. Neo-Liberals Keohane and Nye's theory of complex interdependence is a theory which tries to give an opposing view to the realist theories which have dominated world politics since the turn of the century. At the time of writing the cold war was dominating the contemporary world arena. Complex interdependence is a liberal theory, it is my view that the arena we see today falls in the middle ground between the realist's "soldiers and diplomats" and Keohane and Nye's ideal type of international system. The vital point of disagreement between Keohane and Nye's view and realist views is that they believe that military force does not take priority over other issues due to the costs involved. "Complex interdependence refers to a situation among a number of countries in which multiple channels of contact connect societies; there is no hierarchy of issues and military force is not used by governments towards one another."

The Current situation and development trend of international relations automatically involves Mongolia into globalisation and resulting interconnected and interdependent relationships. In this case, the policy of ensuring national security will be politically defined by the strategy of 'having a third neighbour', as well as in economic development on the basis of democracy.[10] This is provided in the concepts of national security and external policy of Mongolia with the aims and activities to ensure strategic stability in Asia-Pacific region, especially North East and Central Asia, to strengthen peace, to make a coherent security system policy, to not possess nuclear weapons in Central Asia; to gain confidence in the military sector, to participate in joint activities of regional security, to develop joint cooperation and good neighbourly relationship with the Russian Federation and the People's Republic of China in whole sustainability; to raise economic and other interests of the United States of America, Japan, the Republic of Korea and India towards Mongolia, and to reach appropriate and sustainable level therein. Therefore, it aims to work for country's development in politics, economic and social sectors. But, in terms of the security space and military action theatre, Mongolia is a country that has significant location and wide strategic capacity and may be easily affected by another country's political-military intentions. The political-military environment surrounding Mongolia is defined on the one side by strategic partnership with the Russian Federation and countries of Central Asia and on the other hand the People's Republic of China. Mongolia's political-military relationships are also defined by ties with the countries of North East Asia. One of the important multilateral measures for ensuring security of Mongolia is to create an environment of friendly relations, co-operation and mutual confidence around the state frontiers and to guarantee the security by political and diplomatic means. As a result of the changes in negative and positive factors affecting the external security environment, prior notions of foreign army risks and aggression are now reduced when compared to the period known as the "Cold War". Nevertheless, geo-economical issues such as economic crisis, weak infrastructure development, natural disasters and catastrophes, poverty, unemployment and crimes are becoming relevant issues of today's time.

Security Challenges for Mongolia

Mongolia faces no immediate external or internal military threats as long as it keeps friendly relations with Russia and China. As the margin between security and development has been narrowed, for a small and underdeveloped country like Mongolia, development challenges indeed constitute the biggest security challenges. There are two immediate security challenges, economic and political:[11] Managing the fast growing economy and Balancing interests of big powers.

Over the past years, the external and internal environments of the national security of Mongolia have rapidly changed, while the nature and sources of threats have become multifaceted and intricate. There have been big changes in relations and balance of power between and among big powers—the main factors to determine the world order. Furthermore, rivalry in political, economic and military sectors has intensified and there have emerged new non-traditional threats at international level. At national level as well, dramatic changes have taken place many new issues have arisen relating to refining capacity of government and administration, ensuring economic security, creating healthy and safe living condition of our citizens, and protecting the environment, traditions and customs.

Mongolia's Security Approach

The first democratic National Security Concept of Mongolia was adopted by the Parliament of Mongolia twenty years ago. The concept strengthened the views of the new Constitution of Mongolia and for the first time declared the ideal of supremacy of basic national interests in policies and actions to ensure national security. Moreover, the Concepts provided for the comprehensiveness of national security and have become the vital leverage of the state policy to realize national security.[12] Emergence of new geopolitical situation as well as impact of domestic political reforms and economic restructuring particularly during 1990-1992 compelled Mongolia to consider its future development and security issues in the framework of new realities. As such, a major review of its foreign and security policy was undertaken which, in June 1994, resulted in the formulation of three very important documents i.e., Concept of National Security, Concept of Foreign Policy and Military Doctrine.[13] Mongolia's national security has been defined on quite a new basis in terms of a number of primary areas of concern such as security of the existence of Mongolia, security of the social order and state system, security of citizens' rights and freedoms, economic security, scientific and technological security, security of information, security of Mongolian civilization, security of the population and its gene pool, and ecological security.

So, any policy with regard to Mongolia's security concerns revolves around its national interests in the first place, depending upon how constructively the policy and strategy can achieve the defined goals.

The National Security Concept further suggests that in its foreign relations Mongolia shall exercise "political realism and consistently principled approach, accord top priority to vital national interests and other national considerations, seek to secure many partners in its international relations and promote a non-aligned policy so long as it does not threaten the country's vital interests." Following this comprehensive approach Mongolia is now pursuing an open foreign policy with a commitment to "promote the policy of consultation with influential countries on issues of strengthening world peace and security, of developing international cooperation, of enhancing the country's strategic significance and fostering strategic interests of major powers in Mongolia." Furthermore, in its relations with developing and land locked countries, Mongolia follows the line of jointly defending and promoting the shared interests on the international field. Mongolia is also committed to ensure the security of its existence by strictly observing the policy of not allowing the use of the country's territory against other States; ensuring its Nuclear-Weapon-Free status at the international level and making it an important element of strengthening the country's security by political means.

In implementing its foreign policy, Mongolia shall be guided by the following:[14]

1. Maintaining friendly relations with the Russian Federation, People's Republic of China shall be priority directions of Mongolia's foreign policy.
2. Developing friendly relations with highly developed countries of the West and East such as the United States of America, Japan and the Federal Republic of Germany. At the same time it will also pursue a policy aimed at promoting friendly relations with such countries as India, the Republic of Korea, Thailand, Singapore, Turkey, Denmark, the Netherlands, Finland, Austria, Sweden, Switzerland and at creating and bringing to an appropriate level their economic and other interests in Mongolia.
3. Strengthening its position in Asia and securing a constructive participation in the political and economic integration process in the region. Within the framework of this objective, greater attention shall be given to Asia and the Pacific region, in particular to North-East

and Central Asia. Mongolia shall take an active part in the process of initiating dialogues and negotiations on the issues of strengthening regional security and creating a collective security mechanism. It will strive to become a member of the Asia, Pacific Economic Cooperation (APEC) forum. Prerequisites for participating in regional integration shall be created primarily through expanding and promoting bilateral relations with the countries of the region.

4. Promoting cooperation with the United Nations Organization and its specialized agencies, and with international financial and economic organizations, including the International Monetary Fund, the World Bank and the Asian Development Bank.
5. Developing friendly relations with countries of the former socialist community, as well as the newly independent states. When developing relations with these countries, a flexible approach will be adopted, reinforcing the positive legacy of our past relations while at the same time taking into account the potential of promoting relations in conformity with the new circumstances. Particular attention will be given to promoting relations with Poland, Hungary and the Czech Republic in Eastern Europe as well as with Kazakhstan, the Ukraine, Belarus, Kyrgyzstan and Uzbekistan.
6. Developing friendly relations with developing countries and cooperating with them, as much as possible, in the solution of common objectives. Beyond the framework of bilateral relations with these countries, this task will be realized mainly through cooperation within the framework of international organizations and movements, such as the United Nations, the Group of 77 and the Non-Aligned Movement.

The third document, which became the guiding principles of preserving the country's strategic interest, is the Military Doctrine. It was adopted at a time when Mongolian leadership acknowledged that although the prospects for mutual understanding, trust and partnership came to be prevailed in international relations with the end of the Cold War, the danger of war and armed conflicts had not been fully eliminated and a collective security system had not yet been formed either at the global or regional level. Mongolia, thus, needed a guiding principle, which has been enshrined in this military doctrine to avoid any kind of danger militarily. Significantly, the document asserts that

Mongolia's international relations had "shifted from predominantly political and military fields to economic, scientific-technological and informational fields, in other words, from geopolitics to geo-economics." Mongolia has pledged that it would never engage in a conflict except if invaded and that the country would never enter into any military bloc so long as its independence and sovereignty were not threatened.[15] In sum, the military doctrine has been formulated on the basis of broader security issues particularly in the Asia-Pacific region, and hence the objective of Mongolia's defence policy aims at participating in the creation of collective security systems. Though Mongolia has engaged itself in various dialogues on broader regional security issues in order to find a worthy place in the regional cooperation, it still has to do much. Nevertheless, Mongolia's foreign policy and national security interests are undoubtedly a reflection of both the internal politics as well as regional dynamics, and therefore, relations with the outside world have significant roles to play.

In the year 2010, new National Security Concept was adopted by State Great Hural (SGH), the parliament of Mongolia. This document included the national security environment and stated goals and objectives of national security policy including the defence policy. Military should "take active participation in international peace support operations" as a leverage of political strategy to "continuously develop bilateral and multilateral security and Defence relations and cooperation with its two neighbours Russia and China, the United States, NATO member nations, the European Union, and nations of the Asia-Pacific.[16] The year 2011 eventually became the year of starting point of the security sector reform. At least seventy laws have been amended to achieve the goals stated in the National Security Concept. As a part of this, the Ministry of Defence submitted the draft of Basics of National Military Policy (BNMP) to the Government cabinet (Defence Minister's Speech, 2011). Two main themes of this document have been managing rapid economic growth and balancing of big powers.[17]

Securing Relations with World Community

Mongolia's foreign policy in the political field is an important instrument for ensuring and strengthening its security. Thus its results are to be measured first and foremost by how the country's security and independence interests are met, and to what extent its international position has been strengthened and its prestige enhanced. In developing its relations with other countries, Mongolia has committed itself to be guided by universally recognized principles and norms of international law as defined in the Charter of the United Nations, including mutual respect for each other's sovereignty, territorial integrity and inviolability of frontiers, right to self-determination, non-interference in internal affairs, non-use of force, settlement of disputes by peaceful means, respect for human rights and freedoms, and equal and mutually beneficial cooperation.[18]

In its foreign policy Mongolia tries to uphold peace, strive to avoid confrontation with other countries and pursue a multi-base policy. While always championing its national interests, it will at the same time respect the legitimate interests of other countries and its partners. Mongolia will not interfere in the disputes between its two neighbouring countries unless the disputes affect Mongolia's national interests. It shall pursue a policy of refraining from joining any military alliance or grouping, allowing the use of its territory or air space against any other country, and the stationing of foreign troops or weapons, including nuclear or any other type of mass destruction weapons in its territory. Mongolia also seeks to guarantee its interests in the international arena through bilateral and multilateral treaties and agreements. Mongolia respects and observes international law, and tries to fulfil in good faith its obligations under international treaties. As a member of the world community Mongolia also strives to make active contribution to the common cause of settling pressing regional and international issues. In doing so, it is again guided primarily by its national interests, values and fundamental principles.

Mongolia-China Relations

After the disintegration of USSR, Mongolia and China both have taken major steps to normalize their relationship.[19] In 1994, Chinese Premier Li Peng signed a treaty of friendship and cooperation with Mongolia. The most important clause of this Treaty was their understanding that neither of them "will take part in any military-political alliance directed against each other and will not conclude any treaty and agreement with a third country that may adversely affect the state sovereignty and security of the other Party." Mongolia and China also decided that they will not "allow a third country to use its territory which may adversely affect the state sovereignty and security of the other Party."[20] China offered to allow the use of its Tianjin port to give Mongolia and its goods access to trade with the Asia Pacific region.[21] China also expanded its investments in Mongolia's mining industries, giving it access to the country's natural resources. Mongolia and China have stepped up cooperation on fighting terrorism and bolstering regional security. China is likely to support Mongolia's membership in to the Asia Cooperation Dialogue (ACD), Asia-Pacific Economic Cooperation (APEC) and granting it observer status in the Shanghai Cooperation Organization.[22]

Recently on October 16, 2014, Mongolia and China have continuously advanced relations and strengthened cooperation in various fields since the establishment of diplomatic ties 65 years ago. Mongolian Prime Minister Norov Altankhuyag said, "Mongolia is one of the first countries that established diplomatic relations with new China...According to the fundamental documents of traditional friendly relations and cooperation, our two countries mutually respect their independence, sovereignty and territorial integrity, and resolutely adhere to the principles of equality, mutual benefit and peaceful coexistence, as well as of mutual respect of the development paths they have chosen...China's commitment to exchanging development experience has contributed not only to Mongolia-China relations, but also to regional cooperation."[23] Significantly, both sides have announced the year 2014 as the Year of China-Mongolia Friendly Exchanges.

Mongolia-Russia Relations

After the disintegration of the former USSR, Mongolia's trade with Russia declined by 80% and China's relations and influence over Mongolia increased.[24] However, Russia has sought to rebuild strong relations with Mongolia in recent years to enhance its standing as a regional power. In 2000, the Russian President Vladimir Putin made a landmark visit to Mongolia the first by a Russian head of state since Leonid Brezhnev in 1974 and one of the first of Putin's presidency and renewed a major bilateral treaty. The visit and improvement in bilateral relations was popularly welcomed in Mongolia as countering China's influence. Russia lowered prices of oil and energy exports to Mongolia and enhanced cross-border trade. The Russian government wrote off 98% of Mongolia's state debt and an agreement was signed to build an oil pipeline from Russia to China through Mongolia.[25] This visit also marked by endorsing a military pact committing to a peaceful future between the two sides. The pact, among other things, also signifies impending closer security relationship between Ulaanbaatar and Moscow.[26]

On September 3, 2014, Russian President Vladimir Putin oversaw the signing of a series of agreements with Mongolia on a whistle-stop visit. He and his Mongolian counterpart Tsakhia Elbegdorj watched as officials signed 15 deals covering transport and infrastructure, mining, education, and communications. Both countries are rich in resources—while Mongolia has huge coal and copper deposits, Russia provides most of its fuel and electricity supplies—and Putin has periodically moved to reaffirm Russia's interests in Asia and the Pacific. China is by far Mongolia's biggest economic partner. Two-way trade between Mongolia and Russia was worth more than US $1.6 billion in 2013 but with China it was four times higher, accounting for more than half of Mongolia's commerce. However, the current level of Mongolia-Russia relations can be gauged from the fact that cooperation in trade and economic sphere has been developing very calmly despite some negative tendency that helps Russia to remain still the second largest trade partner for Mongolia after China.[27]

Mongolia-U.S. Relations

The United States established diplomatic relations with Mongolia in 1987. The two countries have signed a cultural accord, a Peace Corps accord, and a consular convention. U.S. and Mongolian legislators participate in exchange programs in which Mongolian and U.S. participants share information and experiences about democracy and institutional reforms. Mongolia deployed troops to Iraq from 2003 through October 2008, and now has approximately 350 troops in Afghanistan supporting Coalition operations.

Just over a decade ago, the Mongolian economy barely exceeded US $1 billion, with a national budget of US $400 million, direct foreign investment of US $43 million, and total annual foreign aid of approximately US $300 million. By contrast, nominal 2012 GDP was US $10 billion, the national budget was nearly US $5 billion, direct foreign investment amounted to US $2 billion, and foreign aid remained at US $300 million (thereby declining to approximately three percent of nominal GDP). Businesses have been a part of the story of Mongolia's economic expansion. U.S. exports to Mongolia grew from just over US $40 million in 2009 to over US $650 million in 2012, although 2013 saw a decline to US $285 million due to the conditions cited above. The United States and Mongolia have signed a Bilateral Transparency Agreement in 2013 which has been ratified by the Mongolian Parliament in 2014. Besides, a Bilateral Investment Treaty and Trade and Investment Framework Agreement have also been signed between the two countries.[28]

Mongolia's Membership in International Organizations

Mongolia belongs to a number of the international organizations, including the United Nations, ASEAN Regional Forum, International Monetary Fund, World Bank, and World Trade Organization. Mongolia also is an observer at the Shanghai Cooperation Organisation (SCO) apart from being a participating state in the Organization for Security and Cooperation in Europe (OSCE) as well as a NATO Partner Nation. From 2011 to 2013, Mongolia was the Chair of the Community of Democracies, a group of democratic nations focussing on strengthening democratic institutions globally. S. Oyun, Minister of Environment and Green Development, has been elected chair of the UN Environmental Assembly, and in 2015, Mongolia will be the Chair of the Freedom Online Coalition.[29]

Conclusion

As an advantage of the geostrategic position, Mongolia enjoyed the two big buffers of Russia and China and will remain the same way as long as the balance of power between them is kept. Mongolia feels no immediate military threat so far, but the location has its own disadvantage of isolation from the rest of the world and global development. Development challenges constitute political and economic risks for the national security of Mongolia. An immediate problem Ulaanbaatar faces is managing the fast economic growth along with balancing strategic interests of big powers on the natural resource deposits. There should be an effective mechanism that ensures fair distribution of the mineral resources in a balanced way of the big powers' interests, which should eventually become the guarantee of national security of Mongolia.

2011 was a significant year for the Mongolian Defence sector in two ways: reviewing national Defence policy and investing in weapon purchases. Defence modernization of Mongolia will impact the regional balance of power, especially the balance of power between Russia and China. Mongolia is keen to maintain a friendly relationship with the U.S. and China, a new US-China-Mongolia triangle is born. Maintaining good neighbourly and balanced relations with both Russia and China seems to be in the best interests of the country to take maximum benefits for ensuring its overall security. For the foreseeable future Mongolia will have to rely much on its diplomatic initiatives to safeguard its security and foreign policy concerns for maintaining not only the country's sovereignty and territorial integrity, but also achieving the socio-economic security. Understandably, Mongolia cannot escape from the fact that due to the problem of its landlocked geographical position, the state of its relations with Russia and China would always be of vital importance.

Notes and References

1. Emily Tripp (2013), "Realism: The Domination of Security Studies", at http://www.e-ir.info/2013/06/14/realism-the-domination-of-security-studies/ (accessed on August 10, 2014).
2. Saleha Faruque, "Liberal and Realist Theory Perspectives on International Security", at http://suite.io/saleha-faruque/4r5124n (accessed on August 20, 2014).
3. Sharad K. Soni (2006), "Mongolia's Security Thinking and Outside World: A Reappraisal", *Bimonthly Journal of Mongolian and Tibetan Current Situation* (Taipei), vol. 15, no. 6, November 2006, p. 27, at http://www.mtac.gov.tw/mtacbook/upload/09511/0202/2.pdf (accessed on August 15, 2014).
4. A. Tuvshintugs, and Z. Boldbaatar, "Mongolian Civil Security Environment", at http://www.dcaf.ch/content/download/36647/528511/file/5Tuvshintugs_Boldbaatar.pdf (accessed on August 15, 2014).
5. Robert E. Bedeski (2005), "Mongolia in Northeast Asia: Issues of Security Survival and Diplomacy: Mongolia's place in Asia Today", *The Mongolian Journal of International Affairs*, no.12.
6. R. Bold (2000), *The Security of Small State: Option for Mongolia*, Ulaanbaatar: The Institute for Strategic Studies, p.36, cited in Soni (2006), "Mongolia's Security Thinking and Outside World", p.27.
7. Charles L Glaser (2010), "Realism", in Alan Collins, ed. (2010), *Contemporary Security Studies*, Oxford: Oxford University Press.
8. "Neorealism", at http://www.princeton.edu/~achaney/tmve/wiki100k/docs/Neorealism_(international_relations).html (accessed on September 15, 2014).
9. John Mearsheimer (2010), "*Structural Realism in* Dunne", Tim. Kurki, Milja and Smith Steve.(2010), *International Relations Theories. Discipline and Diversity.* Oxford University Press, Oxford
10. A Tuvshintugs and Z. Boldbaatar, "Mongolian Civil Security Environment",file:///C:/Users/vcpl/Downloads/5Tuvshintugs_Boldbaatar%20(2).pdf(accessed on August 15, 2014).
11. Otgonbayar Sarlagtay Mashbat, "Mongolia's Immediate Security Challenges: Implication to Defence Sector and The Regional Cooperation", pp.104-5, http://www.nids.go.jp/english/publication/joint_research/series7/pdf/08.pdf (accessed on October 1, 2014).
12. Ch. Sumiyabazar (2010), "Renewed National Security Concepts of Mongolia Passed", http://www.smhric.org/SMW_69.htm (accessed on October 10, 2014).
13. Soni, "Mongolia's Security Thinking and Outside World", p. 28.
14. While analysing the foreign policy of new Mongolia Batbayar and Soni have highlighted the guidelines to be taken into considerations while implementing the foreign policy objectives. For more details, see Ts. Batbayar and Sharad K Soni (2007), *Mongolia: A Concise History*, New Delhi: Pentagon, pp.121-123 ; Embassy of Mongolia, http://www.embassyofmongolia.co.uk/index.php?option=com_content&view= article&id= 59%3Aconcept-of-foreign-plocy-of-mongolia&catid=36%3Arelation&Itemid=76&lang=en (accessed on October 2, 2014).
15. Soni, "Mongolia's Security Thinking and Outside World", p. 31.
16. Mashbat, "Mongolia's Immediate Security Challenges".
17. Ibid.
18. Embassy of Mongolia.http://www.embassyofmongolia.co.uk/index.php?option=com_

content&view=article&id=59%3Aconcept-of-foreign-plocy-of-mongolia&catid=36%3Arelation&Itemid=76&lang=en (accessed on October 2, 2014).

19. In fact, normalization of Mongolia-China relations was the result of a series of events in the middle and late 1980s that led to Sino-Soviet rapprochement following a radical shift in Moscow's China policy. See Sharad K Soni (2005), "Mongolia-China Relations: Post-Cold War Scenario", in Mahavir Singh, ed., *Asia Annual 2004*, Delhi: Shipra & MAKAIAS, pp. 221-225.
20. Soni, "Mongolia's Security Thinking and Outside World", p. 34.
21. Wei-fang Wang (2005), "Pan-Mongolism and U.S.-China-Mongolia relations",*China Brief*, vol.5, Issue 10, 5 May, *TheJamestown Foundation*, http://www.jamestown.org/programs/chinabrief/single/?tx_ttnews%5Btt_news%5D=3856&tx_ttnews%5BbackPid%5D=195&no_cache=1#.VOEMbvmUckA (accessed on 7 April 2013).
22. Ibid.
23. "Mongolian PM hails development of relations with China" *Xinhua News Agency*, 16 October 2014.
24. Nomin Lhagvasuren (2000), "Russia Seeks to Restore Position in Mongolia As Most Favored Neighbor", Eurasianet.org, 16 November, http://www.eurasianet.org/departments/insight/articles/eav111700.shtml (accessed on 7 December 2014).
25. Sergei Blagov (2005). "Mongolia Drifts Away From Russia toward China", *China Brief*, vol.5, Issue 10, 5 May, The Jamestown Foundation, http://www.jamestown.org/single/?tx_ttnews%5Btt_news%5D=3855 (accessed on 7 April 2013).
26. Soni, "Mongolia's Security Thinking and Outside World", p. 34.
27. "Mongolia-Russia relations: A new page in the history of cooperation", *Voice of Russia UK*, 3 September 2014.
28. US Department of State, "U.S. Relations with Mongolia", 3 September 2014.
29. Ibid.

CHAPTER 11

Contours of Mongolia's Foreign Policy

Subhash Kumar Baitha

The foreign policy of a state can be termed as a strategy to deal with external environment in order to not only safeguard their national interest but also survive in the ongoing international system. However, due to the globalization and transnational activities, particularly in the post-cold war period, foreign policy changes have been noticed in several states worldwide to suit the interest of the nation. Mongolia is an example of such foreign policy changes through high-level decision-making processes ever since the country opted for reforms in its internal and external affairs taking into consideration the national interest. It all started after the collapse of the former Soviet Union in 1991, though the seeds were sown in 1986 when the then Soviet leader Gorbachev disclosed afresh initiative in Moscow's foreign affairs in a speech on Asian security delivered in Vladivostok. He indicated Soviet interest in improving Moscow-Beijing relations, and declared a plan to withdraw Soviet troops from Mongolia, a major factor in Soviet diplomatic initiatives designed to meet China's conditions for normalization of relations. At the same time, the Soviet Union did not appear to be overlooking the interests of its ally Mongolia while making its overtures to China. In another speech delivered on September 16, 1988, at the southeastern Siberian city of Krasnoyarsk, Gorbachev presented a seven-point programme designed to enhance security in the Asia-Pacific region and to promote his view of a multipolar approach to resolve issues in foreign relations. The Krasnoyarsk initiative was considered as reassuring Mongolian leaders that Soviet proposals of involving China were not to threaten Mongolian national security.

The challenge for Mongolia's foreign policy makers was whether to comply with Soviet initiatives about which they had little choice, or formulate the policy in a manner that could suggest that Mongolia was acting as an independent country and its foreign policy was to serve its national interests.[1] The task became easy after the Soviet collapse and the end of the cold war which "altered the geopolitical environment of Mongolia and left it in a great power vacuum".[2] However, democratic reforms gave the country its first post-cold war constitution which, in turn, helped frame Mongolia's security and foreign policy to suit the new geopolitical environment and enhance the country's image on the world map. It is in this background that this paper examines the contours of Mongolia's foreign policy and highlights its implications for relations with major countries that include both the immediate as well as distant neighbours.

Emergence of Mongolia's Foreign Policy

As part of democratic reform process domestic and external setting experienced a sweeping change which also resulted in Mongolia's security and foreign policy objectives coming into head among the country's policy makers.[3] In this process, a new constitution was adopted in 1992 by replacing the 1960 constitution, which made extensive changes to Mongolia's political system as well as foreign policy. It was then assumed that Mongolia's national security could only be guaranteed through unilateral, bilateral and multilateral measures. Soon Mongolia conducted a major review of its foreign and security policy. In June 1994, it came out with its own independent documents entitled "Concept of Foreign Policy" and "Concept of National Security" as well as the Military Doctrine, which were endorsed by the Mongolian Parliament.[4] The overall concerns for Mongolia's security aimed at realizing favourable internal and external conditions for protecting vital national interests, which include the existence of the Mongolia people and their civilization, the country's independence, sovereignty, territorial integrity, inviolability of state frontiers, relative economic independence, sustainable ecological development and national unity.[5] Similarly, the post-Soviet foreign policy described as a "multi-pillar" foreign policy was aimed, first of all, at developing long-term, stable and good neighbourly relations with Mongolia's neighbours, particularly Russia and China. The policy core was not to adopt the line of either of these two neighbours but maintain a "balanced" relationship with both of them.

Another important development in the modern Mongolian history due to revamping of domestic and foreign policy occurred in June 1996, when the third multi-party elections for the Parliament were held. The majority of voters desired the opposition democrats over the communists who had won the preceding two elections held in 1991 and 1992. Shortly afterwards, the democrats occupied the power for the first time in the history by gaining two thirds of the votes. The reform process, which was initiated in 1986, became visible during and after the election campaigns. The 1996 election validated that Mongolia was undergoing democratic changes, not only for the sake of politics but also for the entire society that wished to broaden the country's outlook in the international arena. Hence, the new government of democrats began focussing on implementing the newly adopted foreign policy objectives as outlined in the "1994 Concept of Mongolia's Foreign Policy" to attract more foreign partners that could be a reliable partner in international affairs apart from helping to put Mongolian economy on the right track through investments in major sectors.

Mongolian foreign policy also emerged due to the necessity of its alignment with international institutions. As such the foreign policy also focuses on Mongolia's participation in the regional and international forums. Mongolia has thus been actively participating in regional forums in the Asia-Pacific, Northeast Asia and Central Asia, as well as in international organizations such as the UN, IMF, WB and ADB. One of the key directions of Mongolia's foreign policy has been to keep up a continued dialogue with other developing countries through mediums such as the G77, UN, and Non-Aligned Movement. Mongolia fundamentally seeks to maintain good relations on a global scale, while continuing to develop its own culture, language, and tradition. The Ministry of Foreign Affairs, at that time, declared that Mongolia's membership in various international institutions and the United Nations has been "the most viable guarantee of its independence and sovereignty. If Mongolia ever faces a threat and decides to refer the matter to the UN Security Council, the U.S. along with other members of the security council would consider appropriate steps to be taken." This is a clear indication that this threat of action should act as a deterrent to any country directly threatening to Mongolia's territory. Mongolia actively participates in UN processes and actions, most notably the UN sponsored peacekeeping activities, in particular the contribution of its military personnel to assist with reconstruction in Iraq,[6] Afghanistan and other places.

Not only the international institutions but also individual nations are important in Mongolia's foreign policy. In developing its relations with other countries Mongolia has followed universally recognized principles and norms of international law as defined in the Charter of the United Nations. Mongolia's foreign policy is based on mutual respect for sovereignty, territorial integrity and inviolability of frontiers, right to self-determination, non-interference in internal affairs, non-use of force, settlement of disputes by peaceful means, respect for human rights and freedoms, and equal and mutually beneficial cooperation with other countries. While pursuing its multi-pillar foreign policy, Mongolia upholds peace and tries to avoid confrontation with other countries keeping in mind its national interests first and foremost. At the same time, it is committed to respect the legitimate interests of other countries and its partners. Besides, as per the directions of its foreign policy, it also ensures itself not to interfere in the disputes between its two neighboring countries unless the disputes affect Mongolia's national interests.[7] A number of scholars are of the view that Mongolia has "aggressively courted" Europe, US and Asia in the search for a "third neighbour"[8] to guarantee national security. Initially there was optimism that the US or Japan might prove to be such a 'neighbour', however "political realism" set in and authors such as Ginsberg (1999)[9] and Bruun and Odgaard (1997)[10] concluded that "it is the international community as a whole that guarantees Mongolia's security and survival, rather than one individual nation". With such imperatives in mind Mongolian policy makers gave the country a fresh foreign policy concept in 1994 which was revised in 2011.

The "Third Neighbour" Objective of Mongolia's Foreign Policy

Independent and sovereign Mongolia, in terms of its state structure, is a unitary State upholding rights, freedoms and free economy. In political and geographical respects, it is a developing country in Asia, landlocked between two great powers—Russia and China. Mongolia's foreign policy is based on its national interests as defined in its Constitution. However, one may find that the country's specific external and internal situation constitutes the basis for determining its foreign policy objectives, principles and priorities. In practical terms, Mongolia's foreign policy objectives reside "in ensuring its independence and sovereignty by following the trends of human society's advancement, maintaining friendly relations with all countries, strengthening its position in the international community and forming with influential countries in the region and in the world a network of relationships based on the interdependence of political, economic and other interests."[11] The priority of the foreign policy focusses on safeguarding of Mongolia's security and vital national interests by political and diplomatic means and creating a favourable external environment for its economic, scientific and technological development and, hence, its foreign relations are considered within the political, economic, scientific, technological, cultural and humanitarian fields of foreign policy.[12]

The domestic influence on Mongolia's foreign policy is most visible in securing sovereignty and identity. This is more so because ethnically Mongolia is a homogenous nation comprised of 86 per cent of Khalakh Mongols and a small Kazakh minority. Its culture is very distinct from both the Chinese and Russian cultures. Traditionally a nomadic society, there is a conflict in foreign policy making between those who see Mongolia's future in embracing this traditional identity and forging closer ties to Central Asia with its similar culture, Soviet history and economic ties and those who believe nomadism to be uneconomic in a modern market economy that Mongolia is trying to become[13] and as such ties with Northeast Asia should be encouraged. At the same time, despite the greater potential for investment, trade and security, scholars are of the opinion that "tying itself mainly to Northeast Asia will not work economically and militarily, because Russia and China are the main developing economies which overwhelmingly attract investment money and trade",[14] and, therefore, Mongolia should reinforce its links with more viable Central Asia. So the relative importance accorded to Mongolia's different identities, both modern and traditional, impacts the priority it places on relations with neighbouring regions. The "Concept of Foreign Policy" indicates that in reality the priority is given to the whole Asia Pacific region rather than only Central Asia. Further evidences have confirmed that there are higher levels of diplomacy and trade with this region and interestingly there are plans to 'Latinize' the Russian 'Cyrillic' alphabet[15] which will end a significant common link between Mongolia, Russia and much of Central Asia.

As cited elsewhere one of the main objectives of Mongolia's foreign policy has been to find out its "third neighbours." Since the country shares borders only with Russia and China, such strategy aims at forging special ties with more distant countries that may like to invest and support Mongolia's efforts of development, democratization and security, both economic and territorial. Today, "Mongolian diplomacy is indeed characterized by the 'Third Neighbour' policy."[16] Even Mongolia's revised National Security Concept of 2010 makes it clear that "the third neighbour policy is aimed at developing bilateral and multilateral cooperation with highly developed democracies in the areas of politics, economy, culture and humanitarian affairs."[17] It is clear that Mongolia's third neighbour policy, in fact, calls for reaching out to states that could balance its two neighbours—China and Russia. And this is often cited as the rationale behind its engagement with the U.S.

This policy, however, no longer carries the same strategic weight in Ulaanbaatar as it once did. The failure of "third neighbour" partnerships to balance against China has led a number of Mongolian politicians and diplomats to view the policy as a failure. Rather than just depending on the third neighbour policy, Mongolia is now focused on developing domestic means to deal with China's influence. For example, some of the clauses in the 2010 National Security Concept limit the amount of FDI Mongolia accepts from each source, and also new legislation limits the state-owned companies from gaining control of strategic assets."[18] Hence, there is a big difference between the 1994 Concept of Foreign Policy and the 2011 Concept of Foreign Policy with regard to the third neighbour policy. Experts point out that while the 1994 Concept of Foreign Policy emphasizes on balancing the two neighbours, the 2011 Concept of Foreign Policy focusses more on "balance of influence" between the two neighbours.[19] In addition, the 2011 Concept of Foreign Policy identifies the United States, Japan, the European Union, India, South Korea and Turkey as Mongolia's preferred third neighbour partners. Even so, "one crucial challenge faced by the Mongolian leadership is to achieve a balance of influence between the two neighbours-Russia and China by building on the strong economic and political competition in which they engage in Mongolia."[20]

Foreign Policy Implications for External Ties

The implications of Mongolia's foreign policy are largely geopolitical. Therefore, one needs to examine Mongolia's external ties with important individual countries.

Mongolia-Russia Relations

Soon after the election in May 1990, President Punsalmaagiyn Ochirbat went to Moscow for a meeting with the Soviet President Gorbachev. Mongolian and Soviet leaders agreed to review all treaties and contracts signed by the two sides since the Mongolian revolution of 1921, but Moscow could not be persuaded to reduce Mongolia's 9.5 billion rouble debts to the Soviet Union. In September 1990, Prime Minister Dashiyn Byambasuren made it clear that Mongolia wanted more talks with a view to recalculating the debt. "Some of the Soviet projects in Mongolia cost too much and are very inefficient", he said after January 1991, the upkeep of Soviet technical advisers in Mongolia had fallen within two years by almost 50% to just over 18,500, plus some 6,300 dependents.[21] While coming back from Washington in January 1991 through Moscow, President Orchirbat and President Gorbachev agreed that their Prime Ministers would meet to stimulate action on trade, joint ventures, construction projects and geological prospecting. At a meeting with Soviet Premier Valntin Pavlov in February 1991, Byambasuren called for greater efficiency and the 'balancing' of economic ties. Byambasuren also had talks with Russian Premier Ivan Silayev and signed Mongolia's first inter-governmental agreement with Russian on economic co-operation, trade and joint ventures.[22]

After the collapse of the USSR at the end of 1991, the declaration of friendship and good-neighbourly cooperation (1991) between Russia and Mongolia was the first affirmation of their equality as sovereign states. Later in January 1993, a Treaty of Friendly Relations and Cooperation was signed between Mongolia and Russia during President Orchirbat's visit to Moscow. Replacing the 1966 Mongolian Soviet friendship treaty, it provided a new legal basis for the associated inter-governmental agreement on economic co-operation concluded during the visits. In a joint communiqué, Ochirbat and Russian President Boris Yeltsin expressed deep regret for Mongolian victims of Stalinist repression and the harm this had done to relations between the two countries. Mongolia and Russia also took steps to ease tensions on Mongolia's border with the Republic of Tuva, where large-scale smuggling and cattle-rustling had led to shooting incidents.[23] But during 1990s Russia was in "a weak position vis-à-vis the Mongolian economy, unable to promote economic cooperation by providing substantial aid, loans, and investment".[24] Trade with Mongolia had significantly fallen, aid was insignificant and there had been little military cooperation because 'neither side had sufficient incentive or resources to foster a cooperation regime'.[25] The only sector Russia retained any influence over was the energy sector because it was a 'key supplier' of oil and electricity.[26]

Since Mongolia is of strategic importance to Russia as a buffer between itself and China, today it is a matter of Russian pride to retain influence over its protégé. After Putin's (President of Russia) first visit to Mongolia at the end of 2000 relations between the two sides began to refresh. This is important to note that now Russia has come up again in Mongolia in matters of bilateral and multilateral relationship, and a Russia in agreement would be far more likely to push its interests in Mongolian foreign policy decisions.[27]

Mongolia-China Relations

In May 1990, President Ochirbat paid a short official visit to Peking, the first by a Mongolian President. In November, he had what Chinese sources called a 'cordial' meeting with President Yang Shangkun during another short visit following consultations in Tokyo with Prime Minister Toshiki Kaiju.[28] In February 1991, Gombojavyn Ochirbat, the then MPRP Chairman met Chinese Communist Party General-Secretary Jiang Zemin in Peking, the first meeting between leaders of the two parties for 30 years. In June, Mongolian and Chinese officials signed agreement on the opening of eight new border crossing points. In August, President Yang Shangkun paid a state visit to Mongolia, first by a Chinese head of state. At that time President Ochirbat said that they shared identical views on expanding cooperation between the two countries.[29] He made special mention of new agreements signed on the transit of Mongolian goods through China via Tianjin, and on postponing Mongolia's debt repayment to China.

In April 1994, when the Chinese Prime Minister Li Peng visited Mongolia, he defined China's five point policy towards Mongolia: adherence to the five principles of peaceful coexistence; respect for Mongolia's independence, sovereignty and territorial integrity; development of trade and economic cooperation on the basis of equality; support for Mongolia's policy of being free from nuclear weapons and foreign troops; and a preparedness to see Mongolia develop relations with other countries. During this visit, a new Mongolian-Chinese Treaty of Friendly Relations and Cooperation signed between the two countries underlined regular consultation and non-interference in each other's internal affairs.[30] The two parties also signed agreements on cooperation on border-water protection, animal quarantine, trade-goods standards and joint economic and technical projects.

During the 1990s and afterwards Mongolian-Chinese relations drastically improved from a state of virtually non-existent to one of mutual cooperation, based on the Treaty on Friendship and Cooperation signed in 1994.[31] This can be attributed to the improvement in Sino-Soviet relations, the removal of Soviet troops from Mongolia and the collapse of the USSR. China's interest in Mongolia is also strategic, and forms part of a policy of expanding its influence throughout Asia.[32] In comparison to Russia, China's influence over Mongolia is increasing. 'In recent years, Chinese aid has become significant annually going upward of 50 million Yuan.[33] China is also the biggest investor in Mongolia accounting for over 50% of Mongolia's total FDI. It appears that China is using its economic influence more prominently than its military one. This provides a strong position for the Chinese to negotiate and influence potential issues of conflict, of which there are several.

However the most important issue from the Mongolian perspective is a fear of Chinese expansion. The 'Concept of National Security' and 'Concept of Foreign Policy' both identify "massive inflows of migrants from a neighbouring state" as a real threat to Mongolian national interests. There is also a fear that increases in Chinese investments will lead to economic if not physical control over Mongolia.[34] In this respect "the Chinese have to tread carefully as actual incursions into Mongolia would probably result in at the least, outcry from the international community."[35]

Mongolia-U.S. Relations

The most important country to play a significant role in influencing Mongolian foreign policy decisions is the U.S. In 1986, Soviet foreign minister Shevardnadze gave Mongolia the "green light" to establish diplomatic relations with the U.S. Finally, in January 1987, the two sides did so to ensure Mongolia's security in the absence of Soviet like protection.[36] The Mongolian Foreign Policy Blue Book states that "the relationship with the two immediate neighbours remains a top priority in Mongolia's foreign policy, however from the country's development and national security perspective, the expansion of the relations with highly developed countries is also a top priority agenda".[37] So, development of relations with the US is fully consistent with the national interests of Mongolia.

Possibly, at first glance, Mongolia would not look like a country of strategic importance outside of Russia and China, however as Kaplan says, "we live in an era when anyplace can turn out to be strategic and after September 11 Central Asia, including Mongolia, became strategic to the US."[38] The USAID website states that US interests in Mongolia "center largely on its strategic location between Russia and China, two traditional rivals that are also nuclear powers and important global players". China's rapid growth both militarily and economically is of great concern to the US who wish to remain world hegemon, but "if we look beyond the present conflagrations in the Middle East, China looms as the greatest challenge to American power."[39] In addition to its own strategic interests, the US sees a stable Mongolia as important for regional stability as a whole.

As regards the extent of America's military influence, most of Mongolia's foreign military training and assistance come from the U.S., and in the 2004 joint statement between the two sides, the U.S. states its intention to "further increase" its military assistance.[40] In addition to military support the U.S. assists the Mongolian Government in policy making, by providing a full-time American policy adviser in the Prime Minister's office. According to the US Department of State (2004), this advisor "has worked closely with the Government of Mongolia to set the policy agenda and provides policy advice and expert technical assistance for the government's major reform initiatives".[41]

The extent that Mongolia is compliant with American wishes is a reflection of its third neighbour policy apart from its need for overseas financial assistance. There are historical reasons to see international aid as coinciding with larger geopolitical interests. Over the years the sequence of Russian and Chinese aid reflected delicate balances between the superpowers to which Mongolia had once to submit but today its survival as an independent nation owes much to the U.S. without which it will be difficult to replace China and Russia.

Mongolia-India Relations

Relations between Mongolia and India have entered into a new stage since the beginning of 1990s when Mongolia embarked the uneasy road of multi-party democracy and a market oriented economy. India was the first country among the non-socialist world to establish diplomatic relations with Mongolia in 1955. The 1992 visit of India's Vice-President Dr. Shankar Dayal Sharma to Mongolia can be considered as an Indian support of Mongolia's firm commitment to choose a democracy and a market-oriented economy. The Vice-President of India pledged to increase technical assistance to Mongolia, i.e. training of Mongolia technicians through Indian programme. Further, in 1994 when the then President of Mongolia P. Ochirbat paid an official visit to India, a Treaty on Friendly Relations and Cooperation was signed. In 2001, the President of Mongolia N. Bagabandi paid a state visit to India. During his visit both sides noted the relevance of the 1994 treaty of friendly relations and cooperation and also signed a number of agreements. These agreements formed a solid basis for further development of bilateral relations between the two countries.[42]

Today Mongolia attaches great importance to trade and economic relations with India. The government of India in 2001 decided to give Mongolia for the first time a soft loan of 50 million Rupees (US$ 1.7 million) which was used for financing the construction of a factory of vegetable oil. A new loan from India was used to finance a small-scale hydro energy projects in the western part of Mongolia. Mongolia has consistently been expressing its interest in import of Indian drugs, tea, coffee, and industrial equipment. On the other side, India is interested in coking coal, fluorspar, copper, uranium, and other minerals. At this stage transportation of goods becomes a major hindrance for trade promotion. In January 2001, the Mongolian President Natsagiin Bagabandi visited India. During this visit, a Joint Declaration was issued in addition to signing of six important agreements to promote cooperation in the fields of Information Technology, Investment Promotion and Protection and mutual legal assistance in civil, criminal and commercial matters.

The Mongolian Prime Minister Nambaryn Enkhbayar visited India in January 2004. During this visit, three agreements were signed in order to promote mutual cooperation in the fields of Animal Health and Dairy, Space Science and biotechnology. Enkhbayar laid the foundation stone for a Mongolian-run Buddhist monastery in the historic city of Bodh Gaya. India offered a soft loan of US$ 25 million to improve its infrastructure. Proposals for an Atal Bihari Vajpayee Centre for Excellence in Information Technology and Communication Technology in the Mongolian capital Ulaanbaatar were formalized during this visit, and now this Centre is running successfully.

Recently on 17 May 2015, Narendra Modi, the first Indian Prime Minister to visit Mongolia, held wide ranging talks with his counterpart Chimed Saikhanbileg. During this visit the two sides signed 14 agreements covering defence, cyber security, agriculture, renewable energy and health sector. India also extended a US $1 billion credit line to Mongolia as they decided to upgrade their relationship from comprehensive to "strategic partnership."[43] Modi also laid the foundation of an IT Center in Mongolia. As a third neighbour of Mongolia India has been paying great attention to the development of Mongolia. On its part, Mongolia has always conveyed its support to India's bid to become a permanent member of the United Nations Security Council and also indicated its support for India's peace efforts with Pakistan.

Conclusion

Sovereignty and economic independence are Mongolia's main national interests. Today, more than ever before in recent history, Mongolia is secure as a sovereign nation in her own right by pursuing its external ties on the basis of its foreign policy, particularly the third neighbour policy. However, the need to secure financial assistance and the interests of countries (in particular China, Russia and the US) compromise Mongolia's ability to make fully independent foreign policy decisions. The influences on Mongolian Foreign Policy are unique, but it is a case that illustrates a problem for all small developing countries in strategic positions: the need to walk the line between sovereignty and independence, securing economic development and giving in to the interests of more powerful nations. Even so, since the development of political pluralism and transition to democracy and market economy, Mongolia has been pursuing a peaceful, open, independent and multi-pillared foreign policy. Today the country maintains diplomatic relations with 184 countries which include its two physical neighbours, third neighbours and many western and eastern countries. Due to its pragmatic foreign policy Mongolia's participation has increased in multilateral regional activities which have led to strengthen its reputation in international arena.

Notes and References

1. Sharad K. Soni (2006), "India's New Role in East Asia: Implications For Mongolia", *The Mongolian Journal of International Affairs*, pp. 32-41.
2. Ibid.
3. Ibid, pp.27-39.
4. Sharad K Soni (2001), "Mongolia's Foreign Policy Priorities", *Himalayan and Central Asian Studies*, vol.5, no.1, p. 57.
5. Concept of National Security of Mongolia, 1996, p. 173.
6. G. Tumurchuluun (1999), "Mongolia's Foreign Policy Revisited: Relations with Russia and the PRC into the 1990s", in S. Kotkin, and B. Elleman, eds. Mongolia in the Twentieth Century, Landlocked Cosmopolitan, New York: M.E. Sharpe, pp. 277-289.
7. Sharad K Soni (2013), "Evaluating Mongolia's Experience of Democratization: The Post-Soviet Scenario", The Mongol Journal of International Affairs (Ulaanbaatar), vol.18, 2013, p. 40.
8. The view that Mongolia must find a nation or group of nations to counterbalance the traditional monopoly of China and Russia began dominating Mongolia's foreign relations. For more on this aspect of Mongolia's foreign policy, see Alicia Campi (2003), "Mongolia as a Bridge to Central Asia", *The Geopolitical Relations between Contemporary Mongolia and Neighboring Asian Countries: Democracy, Economy and Security*, Taipei: Mongolian and Tibetan Affairs, p. 30.
9. T. Ginsburg (1999) "Nationalism, Elites and Mongolia's Rapid Transformation", in S. Kotkin and B. Elleman, eds., *Mongolia in the Twentieth Century, Landlocked Cosmopolitan*, New York: M.E. Sharpe, pp. 250.
10. O. Bruun and O. Odgaard (1997), "Consolidating Independence", in O. Bruun and O. Odgaard, eds., *Mongolia in Transition: Old Patterns, New Challenges*, Routledge Curzon, pp. 253-254.

11. Mongolia's Foreign policy objectives have been taken from *Concept of Mongolia's Foreign Policy*, Ulaanbaatar, 1999:36-46.
12. Ibid.
13. Ts. Batbayar (2002), "Mongolia's Foreign Policy in the 1990s: New Identity and New Challenges", *Regional Security Issues and Mongolia*, vol, 17, Ulaanbaatar: Institute for Strategic Studies.
14. Alicia Campi (2003). "Mongolia as a Bridge to Central Asia", in *The Geopolitical Relations between Contemporary Mongolia and Neighboring Asian Countries: Democracy, Economy and Security*, Taipei: Mongolian and Tibetan Affairs, p.48.
15. See *UB Post*, 25 July 2003.
16. Sharad K Soni (2012), "Looking beyond Geographic Neighbours: Post-Soviet Mongolia's Third Neighbour policy", in Suchandana Chatterjee, Anita Sengupta and Sushmita Bhattacharya (eds), *Eurasia: Twenty years After*, Delhi: Shipra Publications, p. 489.
17. For more detailed analysis, see Sharad K Soni (2009), "Indo-Mongolian Ties: Implications for Regional Cooperation in North East Asia", in Sudhir Kumar Singh (ed.),*Post 9/11 Indian Foreign Policy: Challenges & Opportunities,* New Delhi: Pentagon Press, pp. 190-199.
18. Jeffrey Reeves (2012), "Mongolia's Strategic Calculus", *The Diplomat,* 15 October.
19. Sharad K. Soni (2015), "The 'Third Neighbour' Approach of Mongolia's Diplomacy of External Relations: Effects on Relations between India and Mongolia", India Quarterly, vol. 71, no.1, January-March 2015, p. 42.
20. Ibid, p.44.
21. "Mongolia", *Asia 1991 Yearbook Review*, Hong Kong, 1991.
22. William R.Heaton (1992), "Mongolia in 1991: The Uneasy Transition", *Asian Survey*, vol. 32, no.1, pp. 50-55.
23. Sharad K. Soni (2004) "Mongolia-China Relations: Post-Cold War Scenario", in Mahavir Singh, ed., *Asia Annual 2004,* Delhi: Shipra Publications, 2005.
24. Batbayar, "Mongolia's Foreign Policy in the 1990s".
25. Ibid.
26. Alicia Campi (2004), "Modern Mongolian-Chinese Strategic Relations: Challenges for the New Century", U.S.-Mongolia Advisory Group.
27. Sarah Telford (2004), "To What Extent does Post-1990 Mongolia Pursue an Independent Foreign Policy?",*UNISCI Discussion Papers*, October, p. 7.
28. Sharad K. Soni (2007), "Towards Confidence Building: Sino-Mongolian Relations in the Post-Cold War Era", *The Asia Scholar*, E-journal, issue no. 4, at http://www.asianscholarship.org/asf/ejourn/articles/Sharad%20K%20Soni2.pdf (accessed on 12 April 2014).
29. Heaton, "Mongolia in 1991", pp. 50-55.
30. Soni, "Towards Confidence Building".
31. It is interesting to note that, although the PRC has recognised Mongolia as sovereign since 1950, the Kuomintang (KMT) Government on Taiwan did not recognize Mongolia as an independent nation until as recently as February 2002.
32. Ts. Batbayar (2002), "Mongolia's New Identity and Security Dilemmas", *The Mongolian Journal of International Affairs*, nos. 8-9, pp. 3-11.
33. Campi,"Modern Mongolian-Chinese Strategic Relations".
34. R.D. Kaplan (2004), "The Man Who Would be Khan", *The Atlantic Monthly*, March, at

http://www.theatlantic.com/magazine/archive/2004/03/the-man-who-would-be-khan/302899/ (accessed on 23 May 2014).

35. Ibid.
36. Batbayar, "Mongolia's New Identity and Security Dilemmas", pp. 3-11.
37. *The Mongolian Foreign Policy Blue Book*, 2000, p. 23.
38. R.D. Kaplan (2003), "Supremacy by Stealth", *The Atlantic Monthly*, July/August, at http://www.theatlantic.com/magazine/archive/2003/07/supremacy-by-stealth/302760/ (accessed on 22 March 2014).
39. Kaplan, "The Man Who Would be Khan".
40. US Department of State (2004), *Joint Statement on Bilateral and Regional Cooperation between Mongolia and the United States of America*, 31 January 2004, at http://www.state.gov/p/eap/rls/prs/2004/29143.htm (accessed on 11 March 2014).
41. Ibid.
42. OidovNyamdavaa (2003), *Mongolia-India Relations*, New Delhi: Pentagon Press, p. 128.
43. Sharad K. Soni (2009), "India-Mongolia Relations: Implications for Regional Cooperation in North East Asia",http://www.mtac.gov.tw/mtac_quarterly/quarterly_e/2/1249109132.pdf (accessed 24 January 2013)
44. *Press Trust of India*, New Delhi, 17 May 2015.

CHAPTER 12

Energy Resource Management in Mongolia

Ritesh Rai

Having huge natural resources Mongolia has now become increasingly urbanized, with 62.6 percent of the population currently living in urban areas, mostly in the capital city of Ulaanbaatar.[1] In recent years, Mongolia has experienced a rapid economic transition, from socialism to market oriented economy and democracy, which has been driven mainly by growth in the mining industry accounting for 22.5 per cent of Gross Domestic Product (GDP) and 60 per cent of total exports.[2] At the same time, there has been a tectonic shift in Mongolia's international relations as observed by Soni (2010), "Mongolia's international relations shifted from predominantly political and military fields to economic, scientific-technological and information sectors, in the other words from geopolitics to geo-economics."[3] The country attracts many international investors due to its wealth of natural resources including the energy one. The mining boom has pushed the country to be one of the fastest growing economies in the world, with an economic growth rate over 12 per cent annually since 2013.[4] With the expected launch of new large mining projects, GDP is likely to double by 2015.[5]

In addition, Mongolia is also one of the top 10 most energy intensive countries in the world as listed by the US Energy Information Administration. However, an efficient and sustainable energy resource management is crucial for ensuring long term energy security in any country including Mongolia. Energy resource management involves not only conservation and sustainable uses of energy resources but also entails to efficiency and process of monitoring and controlling. It also intends accounting of the natural resources which facilitates sustainable planning and development. As threats of climate change loom large, growing environmental concerns are key challenges to planning and development process and energy issue is the mainstay in the process. Clean and renewable sources of energy are essential for reducing the greenhouse gas emissions. In addition, energy efficiency is important to energy resource management because it optimizes the uses of energy resources and reduces the waste of energy. This helps in conservation of energy as well as enhancing the energy security. Energy management strategies for better utilization of energy is necessary for most of the formal and informal sector and improving energy efficiency is not considered as means but as an end. The four major components of energy management are demand, supply, regulation, and environment. These are the important principles and concepts for the successful energy resource management. It is in this context that this paper assesses Mongolia's efforts for Energy Resource Management.

Energy Situation in Mongolia

Energy security is indispensable prerequisite for the economic and social development of a country. It has been the driving force for the human civilization since time immemorial. Today, energy security is primarily determined by the several national and international factors. Management of energy resources has become crucial element for the energy security. It ensures domestic supply of energy resources as well as attracts foreign investment in a country. However, Natural resources management requires well-articulated policy, effective and efficient institutions, good governance, adequate capital, advance technology, and so on. As energy plays very important role in the developmental processes of the country, management of energy resource is a critical issue, particularly for the developing countries. This also applies to Mongolia which is a developing country with scarce of energy and most of the resources are untapped and unexplored. Coal-burning thermal and electric power stations were main supplier of energy in Mongolia before 1991. Hydroelectric power, wood, and imported gas and diesel fuel were other sources of energy supplies in the country. Although growth in power generation increased in Mongolia in 1990s, it faced the problems of energy shortages because of reliance on the former Soviet Union. Shortage of electricity was detrimental for economic and social development in the country.

It has forced Mongolia to take initiatives for energy resource management in order to achieve sustainability of resources to fulfill country's demands.

Companies that produce, transmit and distribute electricity and heat or in other words public utilities are one of the most significant parts of the infrastructure. They are also the power house on which the development of national economy is based. The utilities are large, capital intensive entities. They have not been a subject of competition among contributors historically. However, considering their critical role in the economy, they are considered to be strategic in the Mongolian economy too. It is also being argued that for a long time now Mongolia needed to frame and implement a comprehensive energy policy to ensure energy security because it is surrounded by two great powers (Russia and China) and it is also a landlocked country. The issues related to the energy resources safety are, therefore, required to be solved within the conceptual frameworks of the internationally accepted policies, as well as within the law on national security and foreign policy of Mongolia. Yet, there has been no formal mandated agency delegated to develop and implement the national and spectral energy efficiency policies and programmes. Various ministries and some other organizations are engaged in a number of activities. But the activities between different stakeholders are not coordinated and no information is available for what has already been initiated or implemented in certain areas.[6]

However, Mongolia has made many strides in upgrading and restructuring its energy resources supply system over the last decade. Due to these improvements, attention has been given to energy demand issues. This trend is likely to increase in future.[7] Use of Energy resources in Mongolia has both intensive and inefficient. In parts of the country which experience extreme climates and have very sparse population, transport facilities need to transport people and goods to great distances in which energy is used very extensively. The inefficient use of energy can be explained by artificially low prices, the central energy planning's focus on output maximization rather than input minimization and out dated technologies and equipment used in energy generation and consumption. At this juncture, improvement in energy efficiency management throughout the economy is very essential to bring about cost reductions which will help make Mongolian industry more competitive internationally. This in turn may go a long way in improving the living standards of Mongolian consumers.

Of late, Mongolia has actively been trying to develop necessary legal, institutional and operational framework for promoting and implementing programmes and measures which could facilitate energy conservation and improve energy efficiency within the country.[8] Through these programmes, the idea has been to improve efficiency for energy use as well as an increase in the energy resource savings which could eventually benefit the national economy, protect the environment and ensure that energy conservation is a priority for all energy consumers. The energy resource management involves the long term planning for energy security of a country. Mongolia too has created an institutional mechanism that draws on the global standards for rules and regulations and is based on an overall energy resource strategy and long term strategic planning. The main objectives of energy resource management are to introduce competition among companies, to increase private sector participation, to open the energy sector, to create open access to transmission and distribution segment for new entrants, and to create an independent regulatory body for licensing, pricing and monitoring.

Theories on natural resource management have been based on the concept of regulating user's access through control and implementation of statutory policies. Privatisation is one way of controlling access to natural resources. This is triggered by the 'tragedy of the commons' metaphor, which states that free access to natural resources under communal management results in over exploitation, leading to tragedy.[9] Yet, empirically, it is widely acknowledged that communal natural resource management can be successful and success can be achieved in many ways other than privatisation or government control.[10] McCay and James (1990) relate the success of communal resource management to community traditional management, particularly customary communal rules and regulations and case of the existence of conflicting uses. Communal management, therefore, is still justified as an effective form of resource management in many places.[11]

Institutional Mechanism for Energy Resource Management

Considering the importance of energy resources management, Mongolia has taken a number of initiatives for proper management of resources. These initiatives include establishing the institutions for policy making and implementation, mainstreaming energy issues in the agenda of external relations. The key institutions involved in policymaking, managing and operating the energy sector according to the Energy Law of 2001 are as follows:[12]

- The State *Ikh Khural* (Parliament) formulate state policy on energy and makes decisions regarding the construction of nuclear power plants;

- The Ministry of Mineral Resources and Energy (MMRE), formerly Ministry of Fuel and Energy, is in charge of the development of policy, including the development of energy resources, energy use, import and export of energy, construction of power plants, transmission lines and networks, energy conservation, use of renewable sources, regulation and international cooperation.
- The Energy Regulatory Authority is in charge of issuing licenses, approving tariffs and protecting the rights of consumers and licensees. Previously, all state-owned power enterprises operated under the management of the Energy Agency within a centralized vertical management structure. Under the 2001 Energy Law, this structure was separated and independent companies were created to deal with generation, transmission, distribution and supply. The core policy areas of responsibility lie with the MMRE. The MMRE is in charge of policy development on use of energy and energy resources and its Energy policy department is responsible for the development of energy resources, energy use, import and export of energy, construction of power plants, lines and networks, energy conservation, use of renewable energy, monitoring the sector, approving rules and regulations for the sector, and international cooperation.[13] According to Law on Renewable Energy, MMRE have the following full powers with regard to renewable energy sector:[14]
- To develop and implement strategy documents for renewable energy sector.
- To develop research, investment and feasibility studies for constructing renewable energy power sources to be financed by public investments funds.
- To develop and have approved the maintenance, safety, and operation standard of renewable energy equipment in compliance with relevant procedures.
- To develop a policy on renewable energy human resources, to organize implementations of this policy in collaboration with the State Central Administration Authority in charge of education.
- To develop and have approved regulation on implementation of Renewable Energy Law.

The Energy Regulatory Authority (ERA) of Mongolia has taken steps towards the management of the energy resources in the country. It was established as an independent regulatory organisation in July 2001 to implement the Petroleum Law of Mongolia related to the generation of energy. The institution is the main body concerned with the regulation of the generation of energy, transmission, dispatch and distribution and supply of energy. Its main duties include issuing of licenses to energy companies and other organisations operating in the sector. It also reviews, approves and regulates energy tariffs through the length and breadth of the country. Besides, it is currently an implementing agency under the MMRE. The ERA is also responsible for the organisation of research for utilisation of energy resources, project and program implementation, conducting feasibility studies, research for energy efficiency, renewable energy resources assessment, and technical monitoring of construction of energy facilities in the country. Scheme of strategic management of the Energy Regulatory Authority has been shown in figure 1.

Figure 1: Institutional Framework for Energy Resource Management[15]

Since energy conservation practice and energy efficiency improvement measures were carried out on voluntary basis, the Energy Law of Mongolia came into force in 2001 which provided the legal framework to allow the energy sector to be restructured from being centrally planned to a market based system. This law authorized the creation of an independent energy regulator and gave powers and responsibilities to key institutions involved in managing and operating the energy sector (Article 38).[16] Further, the Government of Mongolia passed a "Resolution no. 164" on 9 July 2001, which was the first step in corporatizing existing state-owned enterprises in the energy sector. By adopting the resolution, the Government unbundled large state owned enterprises into 18 joint stock companies covering each stage of the energy cycle, including generation, transmission and distribution. Further in 2002, Mongolia developed and approved its Sustainable Energy Sector Strategy which focussed on changing the energy sector from being a drain on the national economy to one that would become a dynamic engine of growth.[17] The adoption of both the Energy Law as well as Sustainable Energy Sector Strategy provided not only the much needed bulwark to the proper management of Mongolia's energy resources but also gave direction to the sustainable development of the entire energy sector.

Mongolia's Strategy for Sustainable Development of the Energy Sector (2002-2010) was approved by the cabinet in July 2001 and revised in 2004. Its aim is to bring sustainable development of the energy sector, reduce poverty and increase involvement of the private sector and public interest in the sector through a more secure energy supply.[18] Moreover, within the regional context also Mongolia's energy sector should be developed, but this must be achieved taking advantage of new technologies and sources of energy that might further promote economic efficiency and at the same time not leaving behind the questions of environmental sustainability. The strategy focuses on the following main principles:

- Financial sustainability to transform the sector from a drain on state finances to a net contributor to economic growth.
- Restructuring to foster commercialisation and private sector participation.
- Capacity building to ensure success of market transformation.
- Energy access and affordability to ensure that poor and rural areas benefit from reforms.
- Energy conservation to promote efficiency, consumer choice, and environmental sustainability.

Management of Renewable Source of Energy

During the initial period of industrialisation, not much attention was given to the use of non-polluting and clean fuels and renewable sources of energy. Fossil fuels, like coal, oil, and natural gas were found extensively and were cheap. Hence, they were exploited as much as possible. This helped the world's wealthy nations to grow fast. In present scenario developing nations are transforming into major industrial power-houses of the world. In such a scenario, many experts are aware of the fact that these newly developed nations adopt policy promoting the use of renewable energy resources which is fast gaining ground. As added benefits use of renewable energy side by side to preventing more greenhouse gases from being added in the fast deteriorating atmosphere is more efficient which saves a lot of money too. Therefore, renewable sources have become major resources around the world. Mongolia is a case study that has been exploring sustainable energy resource for quite sometimes now.

Creation of necessary institutional framework for the facilitative development of renewable energy is being undertaken seriously in Mongolia in order to improve the efficiency in the energy sector. Steps are being taken to attract private sector participation (PSP) as well as to accelerate the commercialisation of public sector energy firms and gradually privatise them. A strong legal, institutional and regulatory framework as believed by the government is required to reduce the risks faced by the investors. This will also pave the way for their long term commitment to being independent power producers (IPP). Power purchasing agreement (PPA) is, thus, necessary to bring the private sector in building new capacities, developing power links, introducing energy efficient technologies, and promoting the use of renewable energy sources etc. In line with this idea, in 2001, the State *Great Khural* (Parliament) adopted the "Mongolia Integrated Power System" (MIPS) programme. The programme aims at contributing to energy access development and helping to reduce operational expenses to create favourable socio-economic conditions for regional development as well as creating reliable electricity supply. The ultimate goal of MIPS programme is to create a unified power grid connecting Central Energy System (CES) of Mongolia with the Western and Eastern systems thus creating a network which could improve the reliability and cost effectiveness.[19]

During 1996-2000, state involvement in the energy sector was implemented through two agencies: the State Property Committee and the Energy Authority. The Energy Authority (EA) was established in 1965,[20] and since then it served as the implementing agency which was responsible for implementation of Government's policies for utilisation of energy and related resources. For all aspects concerning property issues, such as profitability, the return on equity and increasing dividends on state equity the State Property Committee was responsible.[21] Similarly, for all technical and professional aspects in the energy sector, such as licensing and technical expertise, establishing rules and regulations of operations and service of networks and power plants, maintenance and supervision of services the Energy Authority is responsible. Considering the detrimental effects of unregulated development on environment, contemporary world has become more concerned about greenhouse gases. Most of the countries of the world began to switch to renewable energy from non-renewable to make the development sustainable. With vast coal deposits Mongolia has made a remarkable attempt to incorporate wind-powered energy to supply electricity to its citizens because it has a high potential for wind generated power. Coal is used for 80 percent of Mongolia's energy needs because it is abundant and cheap, though wind power is more sustainable way to produce energy.[22]

In order to manage renewable source of energy the National Renewable Energy Corporation (NREC) was established in 1987 by the Mongolian government.[23] Sustainable development of energy in the country is one the major concerns of the NREC since its inception. The main aim of NREC is to offer clean alternative energy sources in rural areas of the country. Though the NREC has placed FORTIS and PROVEN small-scale wind turbines in rural Mongolia,[24] it has struggled in the past to create dependable and safe turbines. Most of these equipments are inefficient and costly but to a large extent they remain reliable. A study by the NREC finds that renewable energy has increased the standard of living of the Mongolians.[25] The NREC has been playing a positive role to ensure sustainable, smooth and balanced economic and energy resource development through utilization of ecologically clean renewable energy. Providing electricity to the people living far away from the centralized electricity grid is also one of the key concerns of the NREC that is being fulfilled by renewable energy generation. It is important to note that the NREC also promotes hybrid energy systems which combine wind, solar and diesel generators as these have an advantage of uninterrupted power supply.

The Asian Development Bank (ADB) and the NREC of Mongolia have together started a programme called "Promotion of Renewable Energy, Energy Efficiency, and Greenhouse Gas Abatement" (PREGA) to promote the use of renewable energy.[26] In this programme, they found that the Gobi desert and plain regions of Mongolia abound in wind. Mongolia as a whole produces 836.8 billion kWh of wind, which is usable 3.5 to 4.6 thousand hours per year.[27] A Wind Energy Atlas has been produced for Mongolia. Areas totaling over 160,000 km^2 were found to have good-to-excellent wind potential for utility scale applications. Such areas amount to about 10 percent of the total land in Mongolia. According to estimates, up to 1,100,000 MW of energy can be produced from these areas alone using large scale wind farms. In addition, rural and small-scale wind turbines can be used in 50 percent of Mongolian land with an estimated potential of 4,300,000 MW of energy.[28] At present, in the remote rural areas, wind turbines are used to generate energy since they cost lesser than diesel generators as they are more efficient and input cost is negligible. Under the aegis of the NREC and the Mongolian Ministry of Fuel and Energy (MMFE) six major projects were launched to produce wind power since 1989.[29] The NREC working with other organizations, is persistently pursuing its aim to establish wind energy as a key source of energy in the Mongolian energy scenario.

The major strengths of Mongolian institutional mechanism for managing the country's energy resources are that it adheres to most of the international best practices. However, lack of coordination among the State Professional Supervision Administration, inter-governmental regulatory and information management and the local administrative bodies pose a grave challenge to the existing system.[30] The country also lacks public education, local community participation and information mechanisms to manage energy resources sustainably.

Conclusion

Over the years Mongolia has taken initiatives for managing its energy resources by adopting various institutional and legal mechanisms. However, its institutional framework for managing energy resources seems to be weak in the enforcement of regulations related to the procedures for local governments to issue land user permissions/contracts, for governors to approve of environmental notifications, and for enforcement of sanctions for license violations. Coordination between the ministries of nature and environment, finance, and the state professional supervision administration as well as between inter-governmental regulatory and information management activities and local administrative bodies is inherently poor. Despite all these problems, Mongolia has been trying its best to ensure an appropriate level of public participation, public education and information disclosure, particularly at the local level.

Ever since Energy Law was adopted its in 2001, enforcement and compliance of existing provisions are functioning well. The government has been maintaining the stability with the help of the available procedural mechanisms. As a result, management of energy resources has improved to the extent of helping the government in accelerating mine production, generating long-term mineral revenues and attracting foreign and domestic investments in the energy and mineral sectors. However, there is still a need to speed up reforms in the energy sector to overcome inefficiency in the energy supply and develop the plan to increase efficiency in accordance with the government action plans. Viable energy resource management techniques are highly desirable to ensure the efficiency of the energy sector.

Notes and References

1. Cited in UNESCO Country Programming Document for Mongolia, 2012-2016, p.2. http://unesdoc.unesco.org/images/0022/002212/221215e.pdf (accessed 22/07/2014).
2. Ibid.
3. K. Warikoo and Sharad K Soni (2010), *Mongolia in the 21st Century: Society, Culture and International Relations,* New Delhi: Pentagon Press, p. viii.
4. Sharad K Soni (2013), "Evaluating Mongolia's Experience of Democratization: The Post-Soviet Scenario", The Mongol Journal of International Affairs (Ulaanbaatar), vol.18, 2013, p.31.
5. For more about how Mongolia has managed a comprehensive post-Soviet economic and political reforms, see World Bank, Mongolia Quarterly Economic Update, October, 2011. http://www-wds.worldbank.org/external/default/WDSContentServer/WDSP/IB/2011/11/14/000356161_20111114031157/Rendered/PDF/655050WP00PUBL00Economic0Update0Oct.pdf (accessed 22/07/2014).
6. Energy Charter Secretariat (2011), *In-Depth Review of Energy Efficiency Polices and Programmes: Mongolia*, p.15. http://www.encharter.org/fileadmin/user_upload/Publications/Mongolia_EE_2011_ENG.pdf (accessed 19/07/2014).
7. USAID (2002), *Contributions to Mongolia's Sustainable Energy Strategy,* Report prepared by James P. Rizer and Garry Vollans. http://pdf.usaid.gov/pdf_docs/PNADB440.pdf (accessed 18/07/2014).
8. Ibid.
9. Garrett, Hardin (1968), "The Tragedy of the Commons", *Science,* vol.162, no.1, p.1244.
10. Berkes, et al. (1989), "The Benefits of the Common", *Nature,* vol.340, no.1, pp.91-93.
11. Bonnie J. McCay and James M. Acheson (1990), *The Questions of the Commons: The Culture and Ecology of Communal Resources,* Tucson: University of Arizona, pp.384-85.
12. Energy Charter Secretariat, *In-Depth Review of Energy Efficiency Polices and Programmes,* p. 51.
13. Ibid, p.52.
14. Karl, F. Lenz (2012), "Mongolian Renewable Feed-in Tariff Law". http://k.lenz.name/LB/2012/03/17/mongolian-renewable-feed-in-tariff-law/ (accessed 05/07/ 2014).
15. UNESCAP (2009), *Mongolia Renewable Energy Report,* prepared by Iderbat Lkhagvadorj.

http://recap.apctt.org/download.php?p=Admin/Country/Report/8.pdf (accessed 22/07/2014).

16. Energy Charter Secretariat, *In-Depth Review of Energy Efficiency Polices and Programmes,* p. 14.
17. USAID, *Contributions to Mongolia's Sustainable Energy Strategy,* p.177.
18. Energy Charter Secretariat, *In-Depth Review of Energy Efficiency Polices and Programmes,* p.14.
19. Tumentsogt Tsevegmid (2007), "Mongolian Energy Strategy: Current Status and Programs", *The Economic Research Institute for Northeast Asia,* vol.77, September, p.15.
20. Energy Authority is establishing and operating an effective energy regulatory body for the energy sector of Mongolia. The Energy Authority had the authority to supervise and monitor all professional activities regarding power production, dispatching, transmission and distribution, see USAID (2002), p. 175.
21. Ibid, pp.175-77.
22. International Resource Management (2010), *Organizations Working in Mongolia to Assess and Produce Wind Generated Power,* Report prepared by Kristin Mroz, p.22. http://www.uwsp.edu/forestry/StuJournals/Documents/IRM/kmroz.pdf (accessed 19/07/2014).
23. Energy Charter Secretariat, *In-Depth Review of Energy Efficiency Polices and Programmes,* p.58.
24. In recent times, the small-scale wind turbine is going popular for renewable energy resources. These two (FORTIS and PROVEN) are uses for small wind turbines that account for the vast majority of sales. FORTIS is the world leader in design and manufacturing of high performance stand alone and grid connected wind turbines in the range from 1400 Watt up to 10 kilowatt (kW) and PROVEN wind turbines provides low maintenance small scale wind turbines.
25. International Resource Management, *Organizations Working in Mongolia,* p.2.
26. Mongolia has now become one of the fastest growing countries in the world, and finds itself on the threshold of prosperity. While Asian Development Bank is playing an integral role in the National Development Strategy of Mongolia, ADB focusses in Mongolia on inclusive social development, natural resource management, and private sector development and in regional cooperation.
27. ADB (2006), *Clean Energy Applications in Asia and the Pacific,* Report prepared by Bindu N. Lohani. http://www.unpei.org/sites/default/files/PDF/policyandprogrammes/Clean-energy-applications.pdf (accessed 10/06/2014).
28. International Resource Management, *Organizations Working in Mongolia,* p.9.
29. Cited in Ibid.
30. World Bank (2004), *Mongolia Mining Sector Sources of Growth Study,* Report prepared by Edward Elgar. http://www-wds.worldbank.org/external/default/WDSContentServer/WDSP/IB/2005/06/06/000011823_20050606180057/Rendered/INDEX/29999.txt (accessed 11/07/2014).

PART III

Assessing External Linkages

CHAPTER 13

Mongolia's Relations with Russia: Security Dimension

Vaishali Krishna

The term "Security" can be defined as the degree of resistance to, or protection from harm that can be applied to any vulnerable and valuable asset, such as a person, dwelling, community, nation, or organization. In other words, "Security" means freedom from threats but over the years the term has been evolved as a concept with different meanings: It has been broadened to include political, economic, societal, and environmental as well as military aspects.[1] Hoffman, on the other hand, defines security or more precisely "national security" as the "protection of a nation from physical attack and safeguarding its economic activities from devastating outside blows".[2] National security fundamentally is the ability of a nation to maintain its identity and its constitutional set up though the meaning and nature of security differs from nation to nation as each nation is different in its position and size. In that sense, geographical, historical, and political factors also shape the process of securitization. Nevertheless, today economic security has become more dominant than the military security as the security not only encompasses the political and strategic but also the social, economic, environmental and cultural realms of a society.[3] Yet, this paper remains confined to military security and focusses more on defence related issues in order to examine the extent of security relationship between Mongolia and Russia.

Post-Soviet Security Strategy of Mongolia

While explaining the security concerns of Mongolian policy makers Soni (2012) stresses that "Mongolia's national security could only be ensured by securing international guarantees through a combination of unilateral, bilateral and multilateral measures."[4] Geographically, Mongolia is located at an important geostrategic position on a crossroad of geopolitical and geo-economic interests of great powers as well as at conjunction point of the world's main religions in terms of cultural interest both within and outside. During the Cold War period, conflicts between the great powers competing to maintain their influence in Asia made strong impact on relations between Russia and China, the two neighbouring countries of Mongolia that sometimes led to tragic events. But Soviet collapse changed the whole geostrategic scenario surrounding Mongolia and the emergence of new geopolitical realities demanded for strengthening of democracy and market economy as well as an ideal definition of security policy taking into account the existing geostrategic environment and internal situation of the country. This was required because substantial military-political changes occurred in the geostrategic environment of Mongolia, and a number of new factors affecting Mongolia's regional security emerged. The main content of the new geostrategic situation was that the super powers, instead of confronting each other, started to seek for mutual understanding, cooperation and joint efforts to fight against common threats thus preventing global wars.

On its part, what Mongolia needed was to create an integrated security system as part of its defence policy that could also help upgrade the capability of the armed forces in terms of meeting modern demands for fighting against traditional and non-traditional threats. The content of defence policy, i.e., the security strategy of every nation is defined by the state external and internal policy, its social, political and economic system, geographical location, specifics of possible military threats, the country's defence capability as well as by level of its scientific and industrial development, and some other factors.[5] Keeping this fact in mind, in the post-1991 period, "Mongolia's security concerns are aimed at achieving favourable internal and external conditions for ensuring national interests".[6] The adoption of the National Security Concept in 1992 thus was a landmark event that brought "a fundamental change in Mongolia's post-Communist security thinking as well." According to this Concept, "the vital national interests of Mongolia consist in the existence of the Mongolian people and their civilization, in the country's independence, sovereignty, territorial integrity, inviolability of State frontiers, relative economic independence, sustainable ecological development and national unity."[7]

However, the Concept of National Security of Mongolia with regard to country's foreign relations insists that Mongolia will exercise "political realism and consistently principled approach, accord top priority to vital national interests and other national considerations, seek to secure many partners in its international relations and promote a non-aligned policy so long as it does not threaten the country's vital interests."[8] Soni (2002) argues that by pursuing an open foreign policy Mongolia is committed to "promote the policy of consultation with influential countries on issues of strengthening world peace and security, of developing international cooperation, of enhancing the country's strategic significance and fostering strategic interests of major powers in Mongolia".[9]

In fact, Mongolia has been able to clear itself of the mentality of a politically differentiated approach towards its neighbours and has built up its relations with them on the principle of a balance approach.[10]

One of the major procedures for implementing the Concept of National Security has been the State defence policy. In line with the major changes in the political, social, and economic systems, the defence policy of Mongolia has been formulated on quite a new basis in conformity to the new conditions of democracy, market economy and international relations brought about since the 1990s. The creation of a unified political, economic, social, legal, and military system to ensure the defence of the country; the modernization of the armed forces and other troops aimed at making them professionally-oriented, compact and efficient; the strengthening of the border troops; and the prioritization of political and diplomatic means in the defence policy of the country constitute the fundamentals of the defence policy of Mongolia reflected in the Action Program of the Government of Mongolia for the years 1996-2000.[11]

In 1993, the Mongolian Parliament adopted the Law on the Defence of Mongolia in order to facilitate establishment of an integrated defence system, determine the structure, organization, and functions of the armed forces, and regulate relations rising from implementation of the state defence policy.[12] According to the Law on the Defence of Mongolia, the defence of Mongolia forms part of the activities to ensure the national security through complex political, economic, social, legal and military measures to defend the people, independence, sovereignty, and territorial integrity of Mongolia against foreign armed incursion and aggression. Activities directed toward ensuring the inviolability of the state frontiers of Mongolia and defending its population against natural disasters and weapons of mass destruction are a component of the state defence system. In other words, the safeguarding of state frontiers and civilian defence are included in the notion of "defence".[13]

The most important document on defence policy adopted in 1994 by the Mongolian Parliament is the "Fundamentals of the Military Doctrine of Mongolia" which was of great significance. It formulated the main directions of foreign and domestic policies in relation to a legal basis for implementing military reforms and ensuring military security. By abandoning the military policy of being part of the community of socialist countries and its obligations to defend its eastern frontiers by military means, the new military doctrine of Mongolia declared that priority shall be given to political and diplomatic means in ensuring the security of the country. The document stipulated that, "Mongolia shall develop all round, friendly relations and cooperation with the countries of the world, particularly with neighboring states, and work to bring about military trust, refrain from and/or prevent any activity that may adversely affect its vital national interests, and thereby eliminate grounds for and causes of external military threat".[14]

Mongolia pledged that it would never engage in a conflict except if invaded and that the country would never enter into any military bloc so long as its independence and sovereignty were not threatened.[15] In sum, the military doctrine has been formulated on the basis of broader security issues particularly in the Asia-Pacific region, and hence the objective of Mongolia's defence policy aims at participating in the creation of collective security systems. Given the fact that Mongolia set its defence objectives on its own, and framed its military doctrine in accordance with the post-Cold War international situation, it can be attributed to the needs imposed by the state and social changes that took place in the early 1990s. Mongolia-Russia security relationship is part of such needs that requires to be examined.

Mongolia-Russia Security Ties

In the Soviet days in terms of equipment, the Mongolian military remained almost entirely dependent on Soviet arms.[16] However, the Mongolian military's equipment system has already begun to change, and this will inevitably bring about the transformation of its construction, ideas on warfare and even military strategies. Due to its geo-strategic importance, in the post-1991 period, Mongolia became the object of a multinational power struggle between the

United States, Russia, China, Japan, Korea, the EU and others. In addition to striving to merge with the West, Mongolia had two possible choices: first, relying once again on its traditional ally, Russia; second, strengthening its strategic links with China. But instead, Mongolia pursued a balanced relationship with Russia and China.[17]

However, shrinking bilateral cooperation between Mongolia and Russia in the defence and military spheres during 1990s caused anxiety in Moscow, though the signing of the Treaty of Friendly Relations and Cooperation in 1993 provided scope for the re-emergence of good neighbourly, equal and mutually beneficial ties between the two countries.[18] The Treaty which was concluded on the basis of equal terms stipulated that Russia would respect Mongolia's policy of denying foreign troops to be stationed or pass through its territory, besides making it clear that neither party would participate in any military or political alliance that would be detriment to the interests of the other. Unlike the 1966 Treaty, the 1993 Treaty was more democratic as although it envisaged wide ranging collaboration, it did not "provide for any form of military alliance and allowed both states to develop relations in accordance with their own national interests".[19]

Simultaneously, Moscow continued to watch with growing nervousness the increasing diversification of Mongolia's military and defence contacts with other countries—China, the United States, South Korea, Japan, India, and Germany. These contacts have been intensified since 1996, especially with the United States. In that year, Ulaanbaatar and Washington signed an agreement on military exchanges and visits that covered diverse areas, including civil-military relations, civil defence, disaster relief, and humanitarian aid. Meanwhile, Russia began taking initiative in restoring relations with Mongolia, and strengthening cooperation in the political and security realms. Moscow's goal was quite clear: to persuade Mongolia to cast off US military influence in order to guarantee both the Siberian region's security and Russia's influence on Central Asian countries. If Mongolia falls completely under the influence of the United States or China, the strategic situation for Russia on the Eurasian continent would present a dilemma with no easy solutions.[20]

Overall, in its foreign relations, the defence sector of Mongolia is guided by the basic principles of being multi-pillar, active, equal, and consistent with the national interests as directed by the Government. One of the prominent elements in the centuries-long, comprehensive, and neighborly relationship between Mongolia and Russia was the defence cooperation between them. Initially, defence cooperation between the two sides was based on the

"Agreement on military cooperation between the Ministry of Defence of Mongolia and the Ministry of Defence of the Russian Federation" concluded during the visit of the Chief of the General Staff of the Russian Armed Forces to Mongolia in 1993, and on the "Agreement on military and technical cooperation between the Governments of the Russian Federation and Mongolia" signed during the visit of the Russian Deputy Minister for Foreign Economic Relations of in the same year. These two agreements serve as the legal basis for post-1991 defence relations and cooperation between Mongolia and the Russia.

Though on the ground level nothing concrete could be witnessed in defence ties between Mongolia and Russia during the 1990s, at least the two sides planned several things to carry out. Mongolia, on its part, tried to develop friendly relations in the defence sector with Russia based on the principles of mutual benefit, balance, and consistency with national interests which would contribute to the strengthening of Mongolia's national interests and security in the Asia-Pacific region. Significantly, an official visit to Russia by high-ranking military officials, headed by the Defence Minister of Mongolia in early 1997, was considered as a step towards propelling defence relations between the two neighbors to new heights. During the visit, a considerable amount of work was planned to invigorate defence relations between the two countries and an agreement was reached to conduct cooperation on an annual plan basis. However, no tangible results could be seen in the two countries' defence ties.

Russia had been counting on the weight of economic, military, and cultural factors to make certain that it would remain the leading power in Mongolian affairs. But it remained unsuccessful to achieve that objective, because it "lacked the economic wherewithal and remained wedded to a narrow, outdated, geostrategic conception of political influence."[21] Though the visit of Mongolian President N. Bagabandi to Russia in 1999 provided optimism to cooperate on security issues, it was, in fact, in the year 2000 that the issue of bilateral military cooperation was given prominence in the Ulaanbaatar Declaration. The two sides affirmed the importance of reviving cooperation in the military and defence-equipment spheres.

Watershed in Security Relationship

The visit of the Russian President Vladimir Putin to Mongolia in 2000 turned the tide of Mongolia-Russia security relationship, which was the direct result of an all out effort by both Mongolia and Russia to cooperate in several key areas, including the military one. Putin's visit marked the signing of a 25-point memorandum of cooperation termed as Ulaanbaatar Declaration. It was a document, which determined the principles of directions of extending and developing Mongolia-Russia relations in the 21st century.[22] The declaration displayed that "in many cases both countries see eye to eye on the most important aspects of the global situation, and sets forth the willingness of Moscow and Ulaanbaatar to closely coordinate their policy in international affairs on a wide range of issues".[23] As stated in the Ulaanbaatar Declaration, both Mongolia and Russia expressed their satisfaction at the strengthening of cooperation between the National Security Council of Mongolia and the Security Council of the Russian Federation. They were in favour of continuing their joint efforts and of coordinating their activities in the field of national and international security on the basis of the Protocol on cooperation between the Security Councils of the two countries. On the issue of strategic partnership, the Ulaanbaatar Declaration recognized that Mongolia and Russia emphasized the importance of resuming military and military technical cooperation, and of collaborating in the training of career personnel.[24]

Putin's Ulaanbaatar visit also marked the endorsing of a military pact committing to a peaceful future between the two sides.[25] The pact, among other things, also points to develop the impending closer security relationship between Ulaanbaatar and Moscow.[26] Russia, on its part, agreed to provide aid for the training of Mongolian military specialists in addition to launching military cooperation in other areas. At the same time, an agreement to help build a Mongolian nuclear power plant was signed. High officials of the Mongolian National Security Council and their Russian counterparts exchanged visits in April and September 2000, respectively.[27] Anatolii Kwashnin, Chairman of the Russian General Staff, followed up with a visit to Ulaanbaatar in October 2000, the result of which was the signing of documents regarding military cooperation between the Mongolian and Russian armed forces. Bilateral contacts related to border troops and civil defence were also resumed.

Since the issue of bilateral military cooperation was given prominence in the Ulaanbaatar Declaration, the two sides affirmed the importance of reviving cooperation in the military and defence-equipment spheres. Russian General Kwashnin's visit to Mongolia in October 2000 underlined the importance of these matters. Negotiations finally led to agreements to resume the training of Mongolian officers in Russian military colleges and for Russia to assist in repairing and modernizing Russian-made defence equipment, which had long been used by the Mongolian military.[28] In April 2001, Russian Defence Minister Sergei Ivanov declared that Moscow was preparing to help Mongolia upgrade their defence systems and troop training. In January 2004, when Russia's Minister for Foreign Affairs Igor Ivanov paid an official visit to Mongolia a joint Russia-Mongolia statement was issued in which both sides advocated reinforcing security and cooperation in the Asia-Pacific Region, particularly, in the North East Asia.[29] Both sides also reaffirmed their commitment to the development of multilateral cooperative approaches towards resolution of existing problems in the interest of safeguarding regional stability and security by politico-diplomatic means. It appears that after Putin's visit to Mongolia while the two sides were restoring and developing their conventional bilateral ties in the economic realm, they were also working hard to expand their cooperation in the military field.[30]

New Developments in Security Relationship

In the decade of 2000 especially after the 9/11 event, the nature and sources of threats became multifaceted and intricate and there have been great changes in relations and balance of power between and among big powers, the main factors to determine the world order. The impact of such changes was felt in Mongolia's security environment also. Thus, the Mongolian President Ts. Elbegdorj issued a decree in November 2009 to renew the 1994 National Security Concept. On 15 July 2010, Mongolian Parliament passed the renewed National Security Concept at its plenary session.[31] The 2010 National Security Concept identifies seven major national security "concepts" to speed up Mongolia's political, economic and military development: Preservation of liberal democracy by replacing the present presidential model of government of Mongolia with a parliamentary democracy; enactment of a national security strategy; assurance of the country's territorial integrity; limiting foreign firms' investment to one-third of their total products' market value; balancing investments from neighbouring countries to preclude Mongolia becoming a "subsidiary" to other countries and seek greater diversification among foreign country investments and business in Mongolia; and conducting all financial transactions in Mongolian currency (tugrik).[32] From the military security point of view, the National Security Concept stipulates that assurance of Mongolia's independence, sovereignty, inviolability of borders, territorial integrity, and security of Mongolian civilization, population and genetic uniqueness shall constitute a foundation for the security of its existence.[33] Basically, the National

Security Concept set important norms to be complied in some of the vital security concerns.

The creation of a unified political, economic, social, legal, and military system to ensure the defence of the country; the modernization of the armed forces and other troops aimed at making them professionally-oriented, compact and efficient; the strengthening of the border troops; and the prioritization of political and diplomatic means in the defence policy of the country constitute the fundamentals of the defence policy of Mongolia reflected in the Action Program of the Government of Mongolia for the years 1996-2000. The Action Plan of the Government of Mongolia for the years 2008-2012 and 2012-2016 set the key objectives and activities to be carried out while implementing the country's defense policy in a more constructive manner. Activities under this policy include deepening of the reforms in the Armed Forces and taking the sector to a new development stage which is characterized by professionalism and competency. The Action Plan says that "this shall be achieved through strengthening the unified structure that is able to safeguard the country, taking active part in operations to keep security in the international and regional levels with aims to deepen trusts between various armed forces personnel, and implementing long and midterm programs and projects."[34]

Earlier, the year 2006 brought a new approach in Mongolia-Russia security relationship when the two sides agreed to move from "traditionally good-neighborly partnership" to "strategic partnership".[35] Such a development meant only to strengthen the existing defence cooperation through various other means. The 2008 visit of Russian Defence Minister, A.E. Serdjukov to Mongolia is further evidence of growing defence and security ties between the two sides. The visit followed agreements reached in January 2008 in Moscow between the Chiefs of the Joint Staffs of the two countries which gave a clear signal of a possibility to revive the elapsed relations by rendering the Russian technical help for modernization and maintenance of Mongolian arms and military technology for the sum of 60 million dollars. A joint Russian-Mongolian military training called "Darkhan-1" also took place at the same time to teach Mongolian military experts to repair and restore military equipment in field conditions.[36] The training was organized on the bases of two military units of Armed Forces of Mongolia deployed in Darkhan and Erdenet.

Further in August-September 2009, "Darkhan-2", the joint Russian-Mongolian military training in the form of military exercise took place which was a matter of great satisfaction for both sides. Noticeably in 2010, bilateral security ties, in particular the military one, further expanded with the two sides agreeing on continuing the joint military training like the 'Darkhan-2' exercise and holding of 'Selenga' anti-terrorist training exercise in 2011 as well as Russia's pledge of multimillion dollar military assistance to Mongolia in the form of weapons and training.[37] On 3-10 September 2011, Russia and Mongolia staged the Selenga 2011 anti-terrorist exercise in northern Mongolia, involving 500 servicemen on both sides and 200 pieces of military hardware and specialist equipment.[38] Further, the Russian-Mongolian Selenga 2012 military exercise took place from 21 to 29 September 2012 at the training range Burduny near the city of Kyakhta in Russia's Buryatia Republic.[39] The Mongolian side was represented by motorized infantry and tank units as well as an AD and a mortar battery, while Russia was represented by motorized infantry and tank units as well as batteries of the Grad multiple-launch rocket system and Gvozdika (Carnation) self-propelled gun mounts.

During Selenga 2011 the Russian-Mongolian combined force, which included about 250 Mongolian military and about 300 military of the Russian Eastern Military District, carried out an imaginary antiterrorist operation in an underpopulated mountain-woody area and worked out methods to settle a crisis situation to ensure security in the region. For the first time, the two countries' servicemen employed attack aircraft during the joint exercise besides practicing the tactics of evacuating civilians from a militant-infested area. In February 2013, a military delegation from Mongolia led by the country's Defense Minister Dashdemberel Bat-Erdene paid a visit to Russia.[40] Over the last few months, Mongolia has participated in several multi-national military exercises including the one with Russia in an effort of advancing the Mongolian army's peacekeeping abilities as well as pursuing military-to-military ties as a "tool of diplomacy".[41] As such on 11-18 September 2013, about 300 military personnel of the Russian Eastern Military District along with 800 Mongolian troops participated jointly in the Selenge 2013 counter-terrorism tactical exercise which took place at Doityn Shar Nuur in Segelen*sum* of Mongolia's Tuv*aimag* (province).

In the post-Cold War period, Mongolia's military security strategy has specifically been designed with a particular focus given on distancing the state from Russian security dependency. Russia's role concerning Mongolia's military security vis-à-vis China is that it acts as a direct balancer. Having Russia as a potential ally while at the same time maintaining a distance to give the impression of not becoming aligned with Moscow is necessary for Mongolia to balance China. By pursuing such a policy, Mongolia's military relationship with Russia is considered to be strength in the sense that China will remain committed to competition over Mongolia's loyalties rather than attempt to force it to adopt a Chinese military alignment. According to Sarlagtay (2012), "Russia is the only state upon which Mongolia could rely for support in a ground war against China in addition to serving as an important balancer."[42]

Conclusion

The conclusion that can be drawn is that every state is constrained by circumstances and seeks security and the realization of national interests within a sea of ever-shifting limitations. A dominant influence on Mongolia's national security is geography and hence its security has, for the past six centuries, been intertwined in its relations with Russia and China and in their relations with one another.[43] After the conclusion of the Cold War, Mongolia abandoned its foreign policy of "leaning" towards the former Soviet Union, and instead established equidistant, friendly relations with both Russia and China, and at the same time, strengthened its relations with the United States, Japan, the EU, India and other so-called "third neighbours". It thus began pursuing an equidistant, nonaligned foreign policy. Since Mongolia is completely encircled by China and Russia, its traffic and communication with the outside world must pass through one of the two counties. If China or Russia refuses to open up airspace or seaports to Mongolia, then its multinational joint exercises with other countries and the successful arrival of the related personnel and equipment would be cut off.

Today, as in the past, only Russia has the potential capability and interests necessary to protect Mongolia from Chinese coercive bullying or military invasion, and only China is in a position to afford Mongolia similar protection against Russia. Under these conditions, as Magid and Mansbach (1998) argues, "Mongolia may seek to be one of two in a sphere of three, but the asymmetry in power between Mongolia and either of its potential 'protectors', China or Russia, is so great that the result once again would be to render Mongolia a dependent satellite."[44] However, as Soni (2005) opines that "it is also important to keep in mind that being a landlocked country any future external threat to Mongolia's security by whatever means it is, could be related directly or indirectly with either or both of its two neighbours—Russia and China."[45] Moreover, security relationship between Mongolia and Russia has always been based on geostrategic concerns paying much attention to improve the level of their defence cooperation. In recent years, Russia has shown keen interest to assist in the modernization of the Mongolian military without binding to a pro-Russian alignment or treaty. Bilateral defence cooperation, thus, is of great importance to both countries as they see the Northeast Asian region as increasingly unstable. And despite the fact that Mongolia has already cultivated defence relationships with other regional players such as Japan, South Korea and the United States, Russia would continue to be a significant strategic partner in matters of Mongolia's bilateral and multilateral security concerns.

Notes and References

1. Water Lippmann (1943), U.S. Foreign Policy: Shield of the Republic, Boston: Little Brown, p. 4.
2. Stanley Haffman (1981), "Security in the Age of Turbulences: Means of Response in Third World Conflict and International Security", *Adelphi Papers,* no. 167, pp. 4-5.
3. B. Buzan (1983), *People, States and Fear,* London: Harvester.
4. Sharad K Soni (2012), "Looking beyond Geographic Neighbours : Post-Soviet Mongolia's "Third Neighbour Policy", in Suchandana Chatterjee, Anita Sengupta and Sushmita Bhattacharya (eds.), *Eurasia: Twenty Years After,* Delhi: Shipra Publications, pp. 487-88.
5. D. Maygmar (2008), "New Geopolitical Situation and Defence Policy of Mongolia", *The Mongolian Journal of Strategic Studies,* no. 2, p.68.
6. Sharad K. Soni (2002), *Mongolia-Russia Relations: Kiakhta to Vladivostok,* Delhi: Shipra Publications, p.225.
7. See "Concept of National Security of Mongolia", Document, *Strategic Digest,* February 1996, vol. 26, no. 2, p.173.
8. Ibid, p. 177.
9. Ibid.
10. R. Bold (2000), *The Security of Small State: Option for Mongolia,* Ulaanbaatar: Institute of Strategic Studies, p.8.
11. Ministry of Defence (1998), *Mongolian Defence White Paper, 1997-1998* , Ulaanbaatar, p. 38.
12. For the full text of the Law on the Defence of Mongolia, see Government of Mongolia (1995), '*Resolution of the State Great Khural, Concept of National Security of Mongolia, Concept of Foreign policy of Mongolia and Fundamentals of Military Doctrine of Mongolia: Documents,* Ulaanbaatar.
13. Ministry of Defence (1998), Mongolian Defence White Paper, 1997-1998 , p.38.
14. Ibid.,p. 42.
15. See "The Fundamentals of the Military Doctrine of Mongolia," *Strategic Digest,* vol. 26, no. 2, p. 176.
16. Wang Peiran (2009), "Mongolia's Delicate Balancing Act", *China Security,* vol. 5, no. 2, p.36.
17. G. Tumurchuluun (1999), "Mongolia's Foreign Policy Revisited: Relations with Russia and PRC into the 1990s", in Stephen Kotkin and Bruce A. Elleman, eds., *Mongolia in the Twentieth Century: Landlocked Cosmopolitan,* Armonk, New York: M.E. Sharpe, p. 279.
18. For full text of the Russo-Mongolian1993 Treaty see, Ministry of Defence of Mongolia (1998), *Mongolian Defence White Paper, 1997-1998,* Ulaanbaatar, 87-92.

19. Galina Yaskina (1998), "Russian-Mongolian Relations: Reality and Outlook", *Far Eastern Affairs*, vol.5, p.37.
20. Peiran, "Mongolia's Delicate Balancing Act", p.36.
21. Morris Rossabi (2005), Modern Mongolia: From Khans to Commissars to Capitalists, Berkeley: University of California Press, p.204.
22. Soni, *Mongolia-Russia Relations*, p.227.
23. Leonid Moiseev (2001), "Relations Between Russia and Mongolia Are Warming", *Far Eastern Affairs*, no.1, p.12.
24. United Nations General Assembly (2000), *The Ulaanbaatar Declaration issued upon the official visit of Mr. V. V. Putin, President of the Russian Federation on 13 and 14 November 2000 to Mongolia,* A/55/644, 24 November, New York.
25. *Independent* (Dhaka), 15 November 2000, cited in Soni, *Mongolia-Russia Relations*, p.227.
26. Sharad K. Soni (2001), "Mongolia's Foreign Policy Priorities," *Himalayan and Central Asian Studies*, vol. 5, no.1, p.61.
27. Ts. Batbayar (2003), "Mongolian-Russian Relations in the Past Decade," *Asian Survey*, vol. 43, no. 6, p.965.
28. Ibid, p.968.
29. See *The Joint Russian-Mongolian Statement*, 14 January 2004, at http://www.extmin.mn/UBTunhaglaleng.htm(accessed 29January 2014).
30. *BBC News* (2001), "Russia-Mongolia Military Deal", April 20, at http://news.bbc.co.uk/1/hi/world/europe/1287127.stm(accessed 29 January 2014).
31. The Office of the President of Mongolia (2010), "Renewed National Security Concepts of Mongolia Passed", 19 July, at http://www.president.mn/eng/newsCenter/viewNews.php?newsId=301 (accessed 18 February 2014).
32. Alicia J Campi (2012), Mongolia's Strategic Views on the Roles of Russia and China in its Future Development", *Mongolian & Tibetan Quarterly*, vol. 21, no.2, p.91.
33. Ministry of Foreign Affairs, Mongolia (2009), "Concept of National Security", 21 December, at http://www.mfa.gov.mn/index.php?option= com_content&view=article&id=66%3Aiii-&catid=35%3A2009-12-20-21-51-32&Itemid=54&lang=en(accessed 18 February 2014).
34. Government of Mongolia (2012), "Government Action Plan (2012-2016)", Unofficial Translation, at http://www.wpro.who.int/countries/mng/mongolia_government_ action_ plan_2012-16.pdf (accessed 11 March 2013).
35. See Remarks by Batbold Sukhbaatar, Minister of Foreign Affairs and Trade of Mongolia on "Mongolia's Relations with Russia and China and Its third neighbor policy: Relations with U.S, Japan", Hudson Institute, Washington DC, 8 June 2009, p.3.
36. Sharad K. Soni (2011), "Russia and Mongolia: Recent Upsurge in Ties", *Defence & Security Alert*, vol. 2, Issue 5, p.49.
37. R. McDermott (2011), "Russian-Mongolian Defence Cooperation and Selenga 2011", *Eurasia Daily Monitor*, 8 (172), 20 September, at http://www.jamestown.org/single/?no_cache=1&tx_ttnews%5Btt_news%5D=38426&tx_ttnews%5BbackPid%5D=512#.UdQWVUbibmQ (accessed 23 January 2013).
38. Ibid.
39. Itar-Tass (2012), "Russian-Mongolian military exercise begins in Russian Buryatia", 21 September, at http://zeenews.india.com/news/world/russian-mongolian-military-exercise-begins-in-russian-buryatia_800918.html (accessed on 18 February 2014).

40. RIA Novosti (2013), "Mongolian Defense Delegation Visits Moscow", 17 February, at http://en.ria.ru/military_news/20130217/179518190.html (accessed on 18 February 2014).
41. Mendee (2013), "Mongolian Defense Diplomacy", *Mongolia Focus,* 9 October, athttp://blogs.ubc.ca/mongolia/2013/mongolian-defense-diplomacy/ (accessed on 18 February 2014).
42. Sarlagtay, Mashbat Otgonbayar (2012), "Mongolia's Immediate Security Challenges: Implication to Defense Sector and The Regional Cooperation", *Security Outlook of the Asia Pacific Countries and Its Implications for the Defense Sector,* NIDS Joint Research Series No.7, p. 114, at http://www.nids.go.jp/english/publication/joint_research/series7/pdf/08.pdf (accessed 27November 2013).
43. Allan M. Wachman (2009), *Mongolia's Geopolitical Gambit: Preserving a Precarious Independence While Resisting "Soft Colonialism"*, EAI Fellows Program Working Paper Series 18,Seoul: The East Asia Institute, p.5.
44. Alvin Magid and Richard W. Mansbach (1998), "Mongolian Security in the 21st Century: In Quest of Friends and Partners, not Allies", *The Mongolian Journal of International Affairs,* no. 5, pp. 10-25.
45. See Sharad K. Soni (2005), "Mongolia's Security Concerns in the Post-Cold War Period", in Mahavir Singh, ed., *Building a New Asia,* Delhi: Shipra Publications, pp.282-294.

CHAPTER 14

Mongolia's Engagements with the U.S.

Guntash Kaur

Today Mongolia and the U.S. share increasing list of interest, values and remarkable growth in their political, economic and strategic ties despite remaining separate by vast geographical distance. All this happened after the Soviet collapse in 1991 when Mongolia underwent a transition from communism to democracy. A whole lot of new policies came to the forefront which gave Mongolia a new birth to access its independence in a different way. In the process of radical changes the country adopted its National Security and Foreign Policy Concepts in addition to a Military Doctrine. One of the major features in Mongolia's foreign policy is its "Third Neighbour policy" which scholars often describe as "a deft diplomacy of Mongolia's external relations."[1] This policy calls for reaching out to states beyond its two giant neighbours—China and Russia, which has been cited as the rationale behind Mongolia's engagements with the U.S. in various areas of cooperation that helped deepen mutual trust on each other. It is in this perspective that this paper deals with the growing engagements between Mongolia and the U.S. in the contemporary times.

Evolution of Mongolia-U.S. Relations

Mongolia affirmed its independence from Qing (Manchu) dynasty of China in early twentieth century which gave Mongolia innovative options to emerge as an independent country and also to establish Mongol nationalism. It was during the proclamation of Mongolia's independence status that three attempts were made to establish linkages with the U.S. through major commercial exchanges. Earlier in 1907, an American company was created in the Mongolian capital of Da Khuree (Great Monastery), now called Ulaanbaatar (Red Hero)."[2] The Soviet Russians were not in favour of Mongolia establishing relations with the western countries. Though a direct relationship was never created between Mongolia and the United States until the late twentieth century, the two sides had never been completely cut off from each other which were visible in 1966 when flood in Tuul River created huge destruction to Mongolian people and damaged bridges and rail lines. Though the U.S. had congressional limitations on providing any kind of aid or assistance to the Soviet Union and its allies, they provided the aid through Red Cross. This was an indicator that despite having no direct linkages between Mongolia and the United States they had never seen a complete cut off between them.

In 1986 at Vladivostok, Soviet leader Mikhail Gorbachev unambiguously stated that the Soviet Union wanted to bring a "new approach" to the rapid advancement of Russia and whole of Asia. The two new approaches *Perestroika* (Restructuring) and *Glasnost* (Openness) launched by Gorbachev for better development of the Soviet Union both internally and externally also produced ripple effects on Mongolia's drive towards democratization.[3] As a result, Mongolia also carried its own process of reforms and restructuring through *Iltod* and *Orchilanbaigalalt* even before the breakup of the Soviet Union. These policies led to a new wave of democracy in Mongolia not only domestically but also on international fronts. Establishment of diplomatic relations between Mongolia and the U.S. in 1987 was part of this new wave of democracy which got strengthened after the Soviet collapse in 1991. But the post-Soviet survival of Mongolia was the major issue at that point of time because "dependence" and "dominance" were the two fundamental features that characterized the bilateral ties between Mongolia and the Soviet Union for long.[4] It now became more visible following the Soviet collapse that resulted in a bitter blow to Mongolian economy, though the best part in Mongolian history was that the country became "completely" independent so that it could forge its relationship with other foreign powers including the U.S., Japan, India and the two Koreas on mutually advantageous basis.[5] Mongolia-U.S. relationship developed slowly in the beginning as the U.S. valued Mongolia only as "a window on the Sino-Soviet relationship and on the new *glasnost* and *perestroika* policies spreading from Moscow to a loyal Soviet Satellite."[6] However, the U.S. perception changed as Mongolia started strengthening its democratic credentials.

After 1991, Mongolia completely changed its concerns towards communism and discarded it to move towards more liberal principles. On September 25, 1992 while addressing the 47th Session of UN general Assembly, Mongolian President P. Ochirbatstated that "Mongolia had declared its territory to be nuclear weapon free zone and that it would work for having that status recognized internationally."[7] Such declaration brought Mongolia acclaims at the international level.[8] This has since been recognized by the U.S. which understands that Mongolia's status as NWFZ can play in stabilizing the entire Northeast Asian region. On foreign affairs, Mongolia's foreign policy has been termed as "Multi-pillared" and "Multi-dimensional" and also a combination of "unilateral, bilateral and multilateral measures."[9] This provided the much needed boost for Mongolia's engagements with the U.S. Earlier, in 1989-1990 a cultural accord, a consular convention, and an Overseas Private

Major Agreements between Mongolia and the U.S. (1991-2014)

Year	Agreement	Aims and Objectives
1991	Trade Agreement between Mongolia and the U.S.	Mongolia was granted the status of most favoured nation (MFN) now referred to as Normal Trade Relations (NTR). U.S. granted permanent NTR status to Mongolia in 1999.
1994	Bilateral Investment Treaty	It was basically meant for free transfer of funds associated with investments; freedom of investments from performance requirements; fair, equitable, and most-favoured-nation treatment; and the investor's or investment's freedom to choose to resolve disputes with the host government through international arbitration.
2004	Trade and Investment Agreement	Provided the U.S. to make an effort to reduce and resolve trade differences and also to deepen trade and economic relationship with Mongolia.
2007	Agreement on implementing the US$ 285 million grant programme in Mongolia funded by Millennium Challenge Corporation (MCC)	The MCC grant was given to Mongolia to reduce poverty through economic growth. The MCC is an independent U.S. foreign aid providing large grants for 'country-led solutions for reducing poverty through sustainable economic growth".
2010	Memorandum of Understanding on the Peaceful Use of Nuclear Energy	MoU was signed to promote cooperation on the peaceful use of civil nuclear energy.
2013	Agreement on Transparency in Matters Related to International Trade and Investment	For Promoting transparency in policy making, cross-border trade in services, bilateral investment and facilitate exchanges and also Publish all laws and regulations adopted in English.
2014	Joint Vision Statement for the U.S.-Mongolia Security Relationship	It is based on the challenges faced by both the countries in dealing with common threats in the form of weapons of mass destruction (WMD) proliferation, terrorism, climate change, transnational crime, pandemic disease, mass migration, and cyber-attacks.

Source: Compiled by the author on the basis of data gathered from various sources.

Investment Corporation agreement was signed in addition to a USAID initiated programme of technical assistance and training. However, after 1990 when Mongolia departed from communism and boarded to economic shift and democratization, the United States earnestly reformed its objectives and started supporting Mongoliain its overall development.

U.S. Investment/Assistance in Mongolia

In the past decade, opening up Mongolia's natural resources sector to outside investment carries great prospects for the Mongolia-US relationship, chiefly in terms of escalating trade and economic cooperation. American investment in Mongolia is increasing slowly but progressively. Today, the U.S. is Mongolia's third largest foreign investor, fairly a change from the period following the Second World War when Mongolians' familiarity of the US was typically limited.[10] Significantly, since 1991 the U.S. has been providing aid to Mongolia through USAID assistance programme. It has provided US$ 150 million to Mongolia all in grant form.[11] The major aim of this aid was to instigate Mongolian economy towards more and more solidity and also to enhance the accountability of the government governance to become more responsible. Under the USAID programme U.S. tried to focus on the following three major aspects:[12] (a) The Economic Policy Reform and Competitiveness Project; (b) The Gobi initiative focused on rural business; and (c) The Ger Initiative that endeavours to encourage business growth in the *ger* districts adjoining Darkhan, Erdenet, and Ulaanbaatar.

All these programmes initiated by the U.S. were not only limited to the economic upliftment of Mongolia but also to develop the whole political system including judicial reform in order to bring and encourage professionalism in judiciary and also to bring changes in the parliamentary system, particularly in political parties structure of the country. In terms of trade, the U.S. is moderately behind the two immediate neighbours-Russia and China. But it can be noted here that since the establishment of Mongolia-U.S. diplomatic relations the economic and trade relations have been increasing, especially in the new millennium when the U.S. became the third largest trading partner of Mongolia in the year 2003. While in 2003 the total bilateral trade in goods between Mongolia and the U.S. amounted to US$ 204 million, in 2013 it has increased to reach at approximately US$ 300 million.[13] But in 2014, the trade figure showed a downward trend due to sharp decrease in metal prices and low investment in Mongolia's economic sector. With the adoption of new foreign investment law in Mongolia the

Mongolia-U.S. trade is expected to increase in the coming years. According to the U.S. Department of Commerce, the major capable sectors for improved U.S. exports to Mongolia include mining, construction, franchising, information technology, tourism, and meat processing.

Mongolia's Participation in the U.S. led Peace Missions

Mongolia today recognizes that participating with the U.S. in the peacekeeping missions would be an opportunity by which Mongolia's position can be maintained at international level. Over the years, Mongolian forces has participated and helped in various international peacekeeping activities in countries like Ethiopia/Eritrea, Afghanistan, Sierra Leone, Iraq, Liberia and Kosovo. The credit goes to the democratic practices maintained by Mongolia in the post-Cold War period. Due to the democratic efforts of the Mongolian government the U.S. has provided various kinds of assistance and also modernized the Mongolian army for many international peacekeeping programmes as part of Global Peace Operations Initiative.[14] Mongolia has effectively contributed to many peacekeeping missions. This became possible because the U.S. assistance played a vital role in encouraging Mongolia to actively participate in peacekeeping operations.

Since 1992 when Mongolia established its military relations with the U.S. the Mongolia government has benefitted from the U.S. military assistance in diverse ways. Firstly the U.S. has been providing training to Mongolian military personnel at graduate programmes and making them aware of multinational operations including peacekeeping. Secondly, the U.S. has arranged various workshops and seminars for both civil leaders and military personnel to understand the challenges of defence reinstitutionalization and discover new missions.[15] This has served as a fundamental forum among civil and military agencies in Mongolia. And thirdly, the U.S. has also supported Mongolia's participation in the Asia-Pacific region in multinational training events. The U.S. Pacific Command has facilitated Mongolia's participation in major multinational exercises such as Cobra Gold, Balikatan and other smaller scale peacekeeping exercises in Central Asia, South Asia and South East Asia and co-sponsored an annual peacekeeping exercise Khan Quest and other multilateral events in Mongolia. This indeed helped Mongolia to include peacekeeping as one of the goals of its defence sector in all government plans.

In one of its main defence policy documents "Fundamentals of State Military Policy" (1998), Mongolia endorsed peacekeeping as the political diplomatic means of its national security.[16] Later in 2002, this was made clearer by the Mongolian parliament by approving a "Law on Deployment of Military and Police Personnel to UN peacekeeping missions and other operations."[17] This legislation was regarded as a key legal framework for the Mongolian military to participate in the peace keeping operations. Mongolia is also seen as an early logistic advocator by providing its Mongolian army engineers and also the medical personnel. The U.S. led operation started in Iraq in 2003 and continued till 2008 in which Mongolian army personnel participated in accordance with the agreement signed between Mongolia and the U.S. In addition, Mongolia also supported the U.S. anti-terrorism policy by sending its troops to assist in reconstruction in Iraq and dispatching another contingent on January 23, 2005 to assist in training in Afghanistan.[18] What the U.S. really wanted was to make Mongolia to join the training base in the Asia Pacific joint peacekeeping force of the Pacific Combat Zone. Last year in 2014, both Mongolia and the U.S. conducted PAGANGEL which was based on humanitarian assistance given by the U.S. Air force. PACANGEL 2014 includes general health, dental, paediatrics, engineering programmes as well as various subject matter expert exchanges.

Earlier in 2011, a major Aviation programme the 5th aviation project in Mongolia was launched by the U.S. Trade and Development Agency (USTDA). On June 16, 2011, both USTDA and U.S. FAA (Federal Aviation Administration) signed an agreement with Mongolia for mutual cooperation between the two countries.[19] A decent example of Mongolia's participation in the U.S. led peace missions is the 'Khaan Quest' which is a multilateral peace keeping training exercises being organized annually in Mongolia since 2001 by the General Staff of the Mongolian armed Forces with the support of the US Pacific Command.[20] Khaan Quest is simply an additional footstep taken by Mongolia after the Cold War to adjust its military strategies and outspreading military cooperation.[21] On the other hand, to the U.S., Khaan Quest seems to be more similar to "strategic military exercise". The last "Khan Quest" has been conducted in July 2014 in which India also participated. It was focused on four components which include "Command Post exercise, Field Training Exercise, Engineering Civil Action, Programme projects and a Cooperative health exchange".[22]

Mongolia-U.S. Strategic Needs and Mutual Benefits

Earlier in the beginning of 20th century, Mongolia was not able to attain U.S. support fully but the end of the cold war and beginning of a new political scenario gave another chance to Mongolia to enhance its relations with the

U.S. by giving due respect to America's strategic interest in the region.[23] The U.S. support to Mongolia or the interest in Mongolia can be categorized under three broader frameworks: firstly, Mongolia could be proved very beneficial for moderating Asian politics because of its geographical position as it is placed very strategically between Russia and China. Secondly, Mongolia is an example of democracy in the Asia-Pacific Region, though the democratic reforms and economic transformation are very fragile. Thirdly, Mongolia has supported the U.S. on various international fronts principally on the issue of war against terrorism.[24] On the other side, the American experts advocated that Mongolia could act as a bridge between Central Asia and North East Asia. They also thought that in this way Mongolia could develop its cooperation in multilateral economic zone. The idea of a "green zone" of economic development was visualized in the framework of generating a "nuclear weapon free zone (NWFZ) corridor" which would include Central Asia along with Mongolia stretching up to the Korean peninsula till Japan and Canada.[25]

As far as Mongolian-U.S. strategic needs are concerned, Mongolia is more interested in developing bilateral relations with the U.S. to ensure its regional and global security as well as economic development. The "Third Neighbour" policy was taken as a strategic perception by Mongolia that would be helpful to Mongolia for counter balancing the role of Mongolia's immediate neighbours—Russia and China. In recent years, Mongolia has shown more interest in the U.S., Germany, India and Japan than for its political, military, cultural, and economic mechanism.[26] Ulaanbaatar's major concerns towards its security and independence since 1990s were to affirm its strength in looking for "balanced, equidistant relations with its two neighbours while seeking wider recognition and global interaction to the utmost possible degree."[27] Mongolia gave more and more preference to the U.S. among the third neighbours because it perceived that the U.S. will be proved beneficial for its security by extending support in the prevailing regional and international scenario.[28]

The major diplomacy chosen by the U.S. in its Asian policy was based alliance system till the end of cold war.[29] It implied that alliances were developed by different countries based on security relationship. An essential rationale of the U.S. regional strategy after the cold war has been a suitable stability based on the following three factors:

1. The constant expansion of U.S. political and economic interests in East Asia and the Pacific;
2. Regional potential that the United States will maintain a reliable presence in the region; and

3. The objectives of U.S. global military development.[30]

However, the U.S. policy in Asia after the disintegration of the Soviet Union and subsequently after the Cold War showed a shift which was a mixture of both security and economy. On the other hand, U.S. found that Mongolia is the best option in countering Russia because of its strategic geographical position.[31] Hence, U.S. support to Mongolia has been vital in the region while taking both Russia and China into consideration. Mongolia perceived China as the threat because of its cold war history as well as China's economic rise. Keeping a balance between Russia and China is, therefore, important for Mongolia to be stable that will also help both Mongolia and the U.S. to fulfil their strategic needs in the region. After the Color Revolution, the U.S. understood the need to protect its foothold in Central Asia, which made Mongolia even more important as a potential associate for anti-terrorism efforts of the U.S. Since the 9/11 incident, the U.S. and Mongolia have been considering more and more military cooperation that has been improved in the post-Color Revolution.[32] On the issue of stability in the Korean peninsula, since Mongolia is a Nuclear Weapon Free Zone and has good relationship with North Korea the U.S. with the help of Mongolia could hold discussion indirectly from the backdoor without opposing directly North Korea at international level. Mongolia-U.S. strategic needs could help in resolving nuclear weapon crises, countering terrorism and peacekeeping not only at the regional level but also at the global level.

Conclusion

Following the establishment of diplomatic relationship between Mongolia and the U.S. in 1987 both the countries have shown outstanding growth in all spheres of their engagements whether it is political, economic or strategic. Each year was seen as a step ahead in enhancing new approach to the relationship between the two countries. Despite the fact that both the countries are separated by the vast distance they still have rising list of benefits and values. The most significant feature in Mongolia's engagements with the U.S. is the understanding the two sides have on their strategic needs and mutual benefits as outlined in Mongolia's "third neighbour" foreign policy. Though the "third neighbour" policy is applied to all nations who wish to expand relations with Mongolia and balance the inclinations of Russia and China, the Mongolian government views the U.S. as its main priority among the third neighbours. The U.S. considers Mongolia's stability as vital for its own strategic interest in the Asia Pacific region. Especially after the 9/11 event, mutual concerns on several issues brought the two sides to engage with each other in an improved manner and work together to their strategic benefits. The U.S. approach has been to facilitate Mongolia to strengthen its democratic norms and have a stable free market which would be a success story for other former socialist nations who are trying to make a transition from communism to democracy. Given the extent of Mongolia's engagements with the U.S. the two sides have today widened the scope of their mutual beneficial cooperation in political, economic and strategic fields in which Mongolia's "third neighbour" policy has been working suitably.

Notes and References

1. Sharad K. Soni (2015), "The 'Third Neighbour' Approach of Mongolia's Diplomacy of External Relations: Effects on Relations between India and Mongolia", *India Quarterly*, vol. 71, no.1, p.41.
2. See Tsolmon, Davaagyn (1995), "An Historical Outline of Mongol-American Relations and American Studies in Mongolia", *American Studies International*, vol. 33, no. 2, pp.71-77.
3. Ts. Batbayar (2003), "Foreign Policy and Domestic Reform in Mongolia", *Central Asian Survey*,vol.22, no. 1, pp.45-59;Peter Boone (1994), "Grassroots Macroeconomic Reform in Mongolia," *Journal of Comparative Economics*, vol. 18, no. 3, pp. 329-356.
4. Sharad K. Soni (2002), *Mongolia-Russia Relations: Kiakhta to Vladivostok*, New Delhi: Shipra Publication, p.222.
5. Ibid.
6. Alicia Campi (2010), "U.S. Government Policies towards Mongolia in the last 20 years—A Review", *Mongolian & Tibetan Quarterly*, vol. 19, no.3, p.82.
7. See "Memorandum of the Government of Mongolia regarding the consolidation of its international security and nuclear-weapon-free status", NPT/CONF.2010/12, 22 March 2010, *2010 Review Conference of the Parties to the Treaty on the Non-Proliferation of Nuclear Weapons*, New York, 3-28 May 2010, p. 1, at http://www.mfa.gov.mn/en/images/dwfile/memorandum2010.pdf (accessed on 16 October 2014).
8. For more on Mongolia's declaration of NWFZ, see J. Enkhsaikhan (1995), "Mongolia's Security Policy: Regional and International Aspects", *The Mongol Messenger*, no. 18(210), 14 July.
9. Sharad K. Soni (2013), "Evaluating Mongolia's Experience of Democratization: The Post-Soviet Scenario", *The Mongolian Journal of International Affairs*,no.18, pp. 30-46.
10. Ravdan Bold (2004), "Mongolia-US Relations: Seeking Strategic Partnership Based on Democracy", *Ambassadors Review*, pp. 30-31, at http://www.amazonaws.com/caa-production/attachments/300/bold_29.pdf(accessed on 17 August 2014).
11. US Embassy at Ulaanbaatar (2004), *USAID in Mongolia: Program Summary*, May, p.1.
12. E. John Endicott (2005), "A Mongol-U.S. Comprehensive Relationship", *Heritage Foundation*, Washington D.C., 28 February, p.8, at http://www.learningace.com/doc/6549565/0343c322d777d67ec7c93fe36d69eb61/u-s-_mongolial28_feb_05(accessed on 16 October 2014).
13. For more on Mongolia-U.S. bilateral trade, see United States Census Bureau, US

Department of Commerce, "US Trade in Goods with Mongolia," at https://www.census.gov/foreign-trade/balance/c5740.html (accessed 18 January 2014).

14. Alicia Campi (2010), "U.S. Government Policies towards Mongolia in the last 20 years—A Review", *Mongolian & Tibetan Quarterly,* vol. 19, no. 3, p.82.
15. In 1992, the U.S. Pacific Command sponsored Mongolia's first participation in Pacific Armies Management Seminar (PAMS). See the archival material of Ministry of Defence of Mongolia and Official website of Pacific Armies Management Seminar (2010), at http://www.Army.Mil/article/43243/pacific_Armies_Mangement _Seminar-xxxiv (accessed 10 January 2014).
16. Thomas C. Bruneau and Jargalsaikhan Mendee (2013), "Discovering Peacekeeping as a New mission, Mongolia", in Thomas C. Bruneau and Floriana Cristiana Matei, eds., *The Routledge Handbook of Civil-Military Relations,* New York: Routledge, p. 207.
17. Ibid, p. 207.
18. "Fourth Contingent off to Afghanistan", *The UB Post,* 27 January 2005.
19. Brandon Joseph Miliate (2012), *Small power: Mongolia's democratization and foreign policy objectives,* Master of Arts Thesis, submitted to University of British Colombia, Vancouver, at https://circle.ubc.ca/bitstream/handle/2429/43714/ubc_2013_spring_miliate_brandon.pdf?sequence=1(accessed on 16 October 2014).
20. Sharad K. Soni (2009), "India-Mongolia Relations: Implications for Regional Cooperation in North East Asia", Mongolian & Tibetan Quarterly, vol.18, no.2, p.56.
21. Alicia Campi (2010), "U.S. policy towards Mongolia since diplomatic recognition in 1987", in K. Warikoo and Sharad K. Soni, eds., *Mongolia in the 21st Century : Society, Culture and International Relations,* New Delhi: Pentagon Press, p.249.
22. Ankit Panda (2014), "Mongolia Hosts Exercise Khaan Quest 2014", *The Diplomat,* 1 July, at http://thediplomat.com/2014/07/mongolia-hosts-exercise-khaan-quest-2014/ (accessed on 12 November 2014).
23. Ron A. Porter (2012), "*Realpolitik* in Mongolia-US Relations", *Japanese Institutional Repositories* , at http://www.apu.ac.jp/rcaps/uploads/fckeditor/publications/journal/RJAPS_V26_PorterR.pdf (accessed on 16 October 2014).
24. Sharad K. Soni (2006), "Mongolia's Security Thinking and Outside World: A Reappraisal", *Bimonthly Journal of Mongolian and Tibetan Current Situation,* vol. 15, no.6, pp.35-36.
25. P. Stobdan (1998), "Mongolia and the US: Redefining Inner Asia," *Strategic Analysis,* vol. 22, no.1, p. 149.
26. Campi, "U.S. Government Policies towards Mongolia" , p.82.
27. Allan M. Wachman (2009), *Mongolia's Geopolitical Gambit: Preserving a Precarious Independence While Resisting "Soft Colonialism",* EAI Fellows Program Working Paper Series 18, Seoul: The East Asia Institute.
28. Ibid.
29. Porter, "*Realpolitik* in Mongolia-US Relations".
30. Michael D. Rich and Mary E. Morris (1986), *Security Issues in East Asia,* Santa Monica: The Rand Corporation, pp.8-9.
31. Porter, "*Realpolitik* in Mongolia-US Relations".
32. Wei-Fang Wang (2007), "Mongolia's Role in US Strategic Deployment in Central Asia in Post-Color Revolution Era", *Bi-monthly Journal on Mongolian and Tibetan Current Situation,* vol. 17, no. 2, pp.18-19.

CHAPTER 15

Mongolia and China: Evaluating the Growth in Relationship

Sharad K Soni and *Vaishali Krishna*

Today the relationship between Mongolia and China has been growing at a fast pace that raises a key question, i.e., whether the bilateral relationship between the two sides can serve as a "role model for Asia". Given the extent of relationship in the past two decades the Chinese policy makers seem to be quite optimistic as their viewpoints indicate that the two countries can prove it as they have managed to overcome historical tensions. Even the Chinese media strongly favours the way Mongolia-China relationship is shaping much in line with China's neighbourhood policy or what Beijing calls it as its "Periphery" policy. Beijing based *Global Times* goes on saying that "China's neighbours should have a clearer understanding that the closer they get to China, the more benefits they can acquire from its growth".[1] Stressing that good ties between the two countries are important for China's security, an article appeared in the *Beijing News* records that "China and Mongolia share an extensive border. If both countries have good ties, there will not be any security concern for Beijing".[2] Herein the question arises if Mongolia too has similar approach in its thinking. The revised Concepts of Mongolia's National Security (2010) and Foreign Policy (2011) have implicitly identified China as Ulaanbaatar's major security concern. Even so, the bilateral relationship is growing smoothly so much so that the two sides have now upgraded their ties to the level of a 'comprehensive' strategic partnership, which covers political, economic and security cooperation. It is in this context that the thrust of this paper is to examine the extent and pattern of bilateral relationship between Mongolia and China taking into consideration the post-Cold War dynamism that influenced these two neighbouring countries to come closer from both the geostrategic as well as geo-economic points of view.

Background

Ever since Mongolia came under Qing dynasty's rule in 1691 the Chinese dominance remained intact until 1911 when the Chinese revolution offered Mongols an opportunity to liberate themselves,[3] thus began the struggle for independence of Outer Mongolia as it was then known to the world.[4] Soon after Mongolia found that it had a little choice but to associate itself with one of its two geographic neighbours—Russia and China who tried to seek domination of the Mongol steppe due to their own political ambitions.[5] It was, therefore, but natural that it had to serve as a buffer between Russia and China. Although the Outer Mongols declared themselves independent in 1911 under the leadership of the Jebtsundamba Khutukhtu, the head of the Buddhist hierarchy in Mongolia, they could manage to secure just "autonomy," not "independence." This status was ratified in a treaty signed in 1915 after difficult negotiations between the Outer Mongols, the Russians and the newly emerged Republic of China. Finally, Mongolia realised its independence in 1921 after a revolution led by Soviet supported Mongolian revolutionaries and in 1924 it was proclaimed as the Mongolian People's Republic (MPR). Mongolia's status vis-à-vis Soviet Russia and China, however, was far from resolved so much so that Mongolia soon became the most sensitive spot in the Sino-Soviet rivalry, also referred to as "Sino-Soviet Cold War".[6]

For almost seven decades until the end of the Cold War period, the erstwhile Soviet Union dominated Mongolia's internal and external policies which contributed much to further deterioration of relations between Mongolia and China. But the Soviet collapse in 1991 and subsequently the end of the Cold War altered the geopolitical situation of Mongolia. This encouraged both Mongolia and China to pursue their future relations with each other in the framework of new geopolitical realities being witnessed on China's northern borderlands. The overall changes in the Sino-Mongolian relations both in terms of the ground reality as well as policies of the two countries with regard to each other are in no way considered to be the sudden occurrence. It rather was influenced by a series of events in the middle and late 1980s that led to the Sino-Soviet rapprochement following a radical shift in Moscow's China policy.[7] A significant breakthrough in the normalization of Sino-Soviet relations came to the light only after the Soviet leader Mikhail Gorbachev announced his Vladivostok initiative on 28 July 1986, which marked a dynamic shift in Moscow's Asia policy in general and China policy in particular. Improvement in relations with China was the fundamental issue addressed by Gorbachev during his seminal Vladivostok speech, and hence, Mongolia too figured prominently in his overtures.[8] Perhaps Gorbachev was very well aware of the fact that normalization of Sino-Soviet relations to a great extent also depended on improvement in Sino-Mongolian relations.

No wonder then that Gorbachev addressed the issue of Soviet troop withdrawal from the Mongolian territory which continued to be a major Chinese security concern posing obstruction to the normalization of both the Sino-Soviet as well as Sino-Mongolian relations. A Soviet-Mongolian Protocol then followed which was signed in Ulaanbaatar on 2 March 1990. The Protocol declared the complete withdrawal of Soviet troops by 1992, which was actually occurred on 15 September 1992, a few months after the Soviet collapse that made the task easy as it also meant an end to Soviet "encirclement" of China.[9] The withdrawal of Soviet/Russian troops from Mongolia also reduced any major security threat to China from its neighbours to the north and northwest for the foreseeable future, thus paving the way for the full normalization of relations between Mongolia and China. In fact, China recognized the importance of normalizing its relations with Mongolia, even when the latter was still perceived as a Soviet protected "buffer" zone. To begin with, a Consular Treaty between Mongolia and China was concluded on 9 August 1986 that marked an improvement in their relations. But Mongolia's approach towards its relations with China was still cautious. The scenario in 1987, however, was one of improvement particularly after June when a delegation from China's National People's Congress visited Mongolia and restored links between the two parliamentary bodies. In July 1989, the head of Chinese Communist Party's Foreign Relations Department, Zhou Liang led a delegation to Ulaanbaatar which culminated in the signing of an agreement on the restoration and complete normalisation of relations between the Mongolian People's Revolutionary Party and Chinese Communist Party. In 1990, soon after the establishment of a multi-party political system in Mongolia, the new Mongolian President P. Ochirbat visited China for the Sino-Mongolian summit which was described as a historic milestone in Mongolia's difficult relationship with China.

Meanwhile, the emergence of new geopolitical realities surrounding Mongolia provided the best ever opportunity for Mongolia and China to push their relations in the 1990s. What one could find is that with the end of the Soviet era and consequently the Cold War era the global geopolitical power structures went through a sweeping change and so occurred the parallel changes in expectations and attitudes toward international relations.[10] The post-Cold War changes in relations between Mongolia and China too have been a by-product of global geopolitical and regional geostrategic changes.[11] This is more so because until the end of the Cold War Mongolia-China relations had always been influenced by the state of Sino-Russian/Soviet relations in which Mongolia had nothing but a buffer status. In other words, Mongolia was described as "A Puppet Republic" whose destiny was manipulated by its two neighbours-Russia and China for the most part of the twentieth century.[12] The end of the Cold War pushed Mongolia to attain its "real" independence and pursue its own independent foreign policy in matters of its international relations. Therefore, the post-Cold War concepts of a "multi-pillar foreign policy" and a "balanced relationship" with regard to its powerful neighbours emerged from extensive discussions among policy planners to find a suitable option that would take into account Mongolia's new geopolitical reality and the interests of its neighbours without compromising the country's own sovereignty. Such concerns resulted in focussing on Mongolia's search for a "third neighbour", who could act as a balancing power vis-à-vis Russia and China. However, the open door policies of both Mongolia and China coupled with sheer desire to improve their bilateral ties saw a growth in future relations.

Post-Cold War Dynamism

In terms of post-Cold War dynamism it has been seen that Mongolia got a rare historical opportunity to regain its "de-facto independence" but had to suffer an economic imbroglio. The time was ripe for the improvement of Mongolia's relations with China and the two sides left no stone unturned in doing so. China's positive response came so quickly, "as if to fill in the power vacuum left by the Soviet Union".[13] Simultaneously, at the domestic front principles of reforms and restructuring began to take hold in Mongolia with first moves made to rationalise the administration along with the drive for economic efficiency.[14] Following the 1990 visit of the new Mongolian President P. Ochirbat to China, positive signs came from Beijing as well when in 1991 the then Chinese President Yang Shankun visited Mongolia, marking the first such visit by a Chinese head of state in many years. During this visit the two sides concluded several agreements resulting in the establishment of direct ties between two countries' various ministries, organisations, local areas and private firms.[15] An inter-governmental agreement granting Ulaanbaatar overland access to Chinese seaports for trading purposes was also concluded during Yang's visit. Another visit to China was paid by the then Mongolian Prime Minister D. Byambasuren in 1992 with the sole aim of bringing the two countries closer to further development of their relations.

Notwithstanding the developments in bilateral relations it was the year 1994 that marked the restoration of normalised relations when a new Treaty of Friendship and Cooperation was signed relatively on a new basis during Chinese Premier Li Peng's visit to Mongolia. Article 1 of the Treaty clearly mentioned that Mongolia and China made commitments to "develop their good neighbourly relations and cooperation on the basis of mutual respect for each other's independence, sovereignty, and territorial integrity, for the principle of mutual non-attack, non-interference in internal affairs, for equality of rights, for mutual advantages, and for peaceful co-existence."[16] The two sides also agreed to "sustainably develop an equal and mutually advantageous cooperation on a long-term basis in the political, economic, trade, cultural, educational, scientific-technological, health, environmental protection, road and transport, and telecommunications fields."[17] But the most important clause of this Treaty was their understanding that neither of them "will take part in any military-political alliance directed against each other and will not conclude any treaty and agreement with a third country that may adversely affect the state sovereignty and security of the other Party." Mongolia and China also decided that they will not "allow a third country to use its territory which may adversely affect the state sovereignty and security of the other Party."

Since the conclusion of the 1994 treaty there has been significant growth in Mongolia-China bilateral relations albeit expression of security concerns raised by Mongolian leaders time and again. Several high level visits showing commitments towards long-term stable relations between the two countries have also been undertaken. A landmark event in the post-Cold War Mongolia-China relations was marked by a visit of the Chinese President Jiang Zemin to Mongolia in July 1999. It signified China's support to Mongolia's independence and sovereignty in addition to forging mutually beneficial cooperation in political and economic fields. The visit was dominated by discussions on several key bilateral issues including Mongolia's quests for

(a) transit through its territory of the proposed gas pipeline and energy transmission lines between Russia and China; (b) reducing the Chinese tariffs on transit transportation of Mongolian goods through Chinese railway; and (c) establishing a highway transportation link between Ulaanbaatar and the Chinese port of Tianjin.[18]

It was around this time that China's national security interests began to be focussed on maintaining cordial relations with neighbouring countries that resulted in developing a cohesive regional policy, known as "*zhoubianzhengce*" (periphery policy) or "*mulinzhengce*" (good neighbouring policy) to be pursued with regard to China's relations with neighbouring countries.[19] Such a policy was aimed at finding the common ground with Asian countries, particularly the neighbouring ones, in both economic and security fields "by conveying the image of a responsible power [China] willing to contribute to stability and cooperation in the region."[20] Hence, economic diplomacy has been one of the main guiding principles in China's periphery policy,[21] in addition to settling the border disputes peacefully with neighbours. In other words, establishing good relationships with neighbours was intended to provide Beijing "with a more secure environment in its periphery as a leverage to increase its influence in world affairs."[22] What is relevant to be noted here is that all these concerns were summarised as China's security concept in just four key words, i.e., mutual trust, mutual benefit, equality and coordination in a working paper adopted in 1999.[23] Mongolia, obviously, figured prominently in China's periphery policy.

Soon after taking over power the Chinese President Hu Jintao, the successor of Jiang Zemin, visited Mongolia in June 2003 which was an endorsement that the new leadership in China too had adopted a positive attitude towards its northern neighbour. Hu's talks with his Mongolian counterpart focussed mainly on four points:[24] Firstly, the Chinese side desired that on the basis of the existing friendly relations between the two countries, Sino-Mongolian partnership of good-neighbourliness and mutual trust be established, and that the two countries would forever be good neighbours, good friends and good partners; secondly, the frequent exchange of top-level visits between the two countries should be continued in the interest of further expanding bilateral relations; thirdly, efforts should be made to promote mutually beneficial trade and economic links between the two countries and seek cooperation of various channels, fields and types; and lastly, the two sides should strengthen their cooperation in international and regional affairs in joint efforts to maintain peace and stability in the region. As such the exchange of dignitaries at the highest level and information shared between the two countries have been contributing much to the development of their bilateral relations in almost all the key areas.

However, the post-Cold War dynamism was most visible in the growth of Mongolia's economic cooperation with China which can be gauged from the fact that Chinese investment in Mongolia over the years was found to be especially impressive. With bilateral trade already booming, Chinese-backed private sector investment increased dramatically. As of October 2000, a total of 512 Chinese companies made their capital investments in Mongolia with large amount going to animal husbandry, agriculture and service sector. According to the Mongolian News Agency, *Montsame*, out of a total amount of 600 million dollars foreign direct capital investment China's share alone accounted for 140 million dollars.[25] China also became Mongolia's largest trading partner in 2000 when the volume of trade between the two sides reached at 377 million dollars.[26] According to *Xinhua news agency*, in 2003, the trade volume between Mongolia and China further increased to 440 million dollars, a growth of 21 per cent over 2002.[27] So, within ten years since 1990 when there was hardly any trade between Mongolia and China, Beijing has been able to fill in Mongolia's economic vacuum created by the Soviet collapse. Such a growth in Mongolia-China economic cooperation would not have been possible if the two sides had not taken diplomatic initiatives. In 2001, both sides concluded an economic agreement in Beijing which stipulated that China will not only be Mongolia's most important trading partner, but also remain its largest direct foreign investor. Reacting on the agreement, some analysts at that time described it as paving the way for "Beijing's gradual reassimilation of Mongolia",[28] though reality has been far from this observation.

Growth in Relationship beyond Strategic Partnership

Although diplomatic initiatives worked in a systematic manner for enhancing Mongolia's relations with China, the decline in Mongolia's trade with Russia by 80 per cent in early 1990s was also one of the main reasons for bringing Mongolia and China close.[29] Russia, on the other hand, sought to rebuild strong relations with Mongolia, particularly in the late 1990s, to enhance its standing as a regional power. As a result, in 2000, Russian President Vladimir Putin made a landmark visit to Mongolia which was described as "countering China's influence". Russia lowered prices of oil and energy exports to Mongolia and enhanced cross-border trade, apart from writing off 98 per cent of

Mongolia's state debt.[30] Since then there has been growth in Mongolia-Russia relations but China has never been ignored so far as Mongolia's economic and trade ties is concerned. What is important to keep in mind is that Mongolia's economy today is almost entirely dependent on China. For the last 15 years China continues to be the largest trade partner of Mongolia. In 2014, Mongolia's trade with China accounted for 61.7 per cent of Mongolia's total foreign trade with a total trade turnover of around US$ 6.8 billion. While Mongolia's export to China accounted for almost 80 per cent of the country's total export, its import from China accounted for 30 per cent of Mongolia's total import.[31] During the period from 1990 to 2013 the volume of Chinese investments in Mongolia reached US$3.8 billion, which accounts for 26.4 per cent of total foreign direct investments (FDI) in Mongolia in the entire assessment period. Today China is the largest provider of foreign direct investment (FDI) to Mongolia, providing 51 per cent of total FDI. Canada and the Netherlands, the second and third largest providers, accounted for just 8 and 6 per cent respectively, while FDI from the United States to Mongolia remains minimal.[32]

At present, over 5,000 Chinese firms operate in Mongolia, with a combined investment of around US$2.5 billion, with US$1.4 billion invested by PetroChina alone.[33] Chinese workers, both illegal and legal, form the major chunk of foreign workers, and evidently in 2010, their official number was 16,675, though analysts believe the actual number is two or three times higher.[34] Another point of concern is that while Chinese overseas development aid (ODA) to Mongolia remains nominal compared to states like Japan, it is changing the way Mongolia views and uses aid.[35] Chinese aid is 'unconditional' as it does not require accountability to the extent aid from USAID does and it is focused on infrastructure and mining, both on the high priorities for Mongolia.[36] In recent years, Mongolia has been developing intensive cooperation with China in the mining, energy and infrastructure sectors, besides paying significant attention on the importance of expanding cooperation in the fields of road and transportation. In 2014, the two sides renewed the mid-term programme on trade and economic cooperation which was adopted in 2008. All these developments in Mongolia-China relations took place due to the advancement from good neighbourly relations to a strategic partnership that began in 2011. The strategic partnership defined the basic principles and directions of the future bilateral relations between the two countries.

While Mongolia's 2011 revised foreign policy concept obliquely identifies

China as the country's largest security concern which has been reflected in Ulaanbaatar's post-2000 foreign policy concerns, there has been no looking back and the two countries went beyond their strategic partnership. What they did further was upgrading the level of their partnership from Strategic to a 'Comprehensive' Strategic Partnership in 2014, thus making commitments to develop all-round cooperation in political, economic and security fields. Earlier in 2013, the Action Plan for Mid and Long-Term Development of Strategic Partnership was signed during the official visit of the Prime Minister of Mongolia to China. But the Chinese President Xi Jinping's visit to Mongolia on 21-22 August 2014 was a major breakthrough as it was for the first time in 11 years that such a high-ranking dignitary from China paid an official visit to Mongolia with high hopes on both sides. The visit also symbolised the philosophy of "amity, sincerity, mutual benefit and inclusiveness" in China's diplomacy towards its neighbours in the contemporary times. The most important achievement of Xi's visit was the signing of a joint declaration proclaiming the development of a comprehensive strategic partnership that aimed, among other things, at raising the level of mutual trust, consolidating the bilateral cooperation, and reinforcing shared trading and investment activities. The declaration outlined the principles on which Mongolia-China relations would be based: mutual respect for sovereignty, independence, the self-rule and territorial integrity of each other, non-intervention in each other's domestic affairs, peaceful coexistence, equal and mutually beneficial cooperation, and mutual respect for the path chosen by the two sides for their own development.[37]

In addition to the declaration, 26 intergovernmental and interdepartmental agreements as well as eight contracts and agreements between business entities of the two countries in trade, infrastructure, energy and financial cooperation were signed. Following were the main agreements in different areas of mutual concerns:[38]

1. **Policy and Security Realms:** The two countries agreed to establish a permanent exchange programme between their legislatures besides setting up a strategic dialogue mechanism between their foreign ministries. They agreed to continue with their efforts for defence cooperation through bilateral consultations and jointly defend their common interests in areas of defence and security. Both sides decided to broaden their interaction in the UN, the Shanghai Cooperation Organization (SCO) and the Conference on Interaction and

Confidence-building Measures in Asia (CICA). China pledged to help Mongolia join the Asia-Pacific Economic Cooperation mechanism and play an active role in East Asian security cooperation.

2. **Economic and Trade Fields:** The two countries agreed to increase their trade volume to US$10 billion by 2020 and promote both traditional and new areas of cooperation, such as coal gasification and mineral production. They also agreed to work jointly to develop new energy sources and construct gas power plants. The agreement also included electricity exports to China, nature conservation, agricultural and livestock production etc. A long-awaited proposal was approved on raising the volume of freight delivery to 100 million tons annually by 2020. The two sides also agreed to study the potential for creating a cross-border free trade zone along the Chinese and Mongolian border towns of Erenhot/Erlienhot and Zamyn-Uud respectively.[39] Mongolia offered to supply goods to the Chinese market on favourable terms, including tax-free agricultural products in limitless quantities.
3. **Infrastructure and Mining Sectors:** The two countries agreed to work out a programme for the medium-range trade and economic cooperation in the infrastructure and mining sectors which would be instituted by bodies such as the Intergovernmental Commission on Trade, Economic, Scientific and Technical Cooperation and the Cooperation Council.
4. **Cultural Arena**: China agreed to provide 1000 scholarships to Mongolian students, train 500 Mongolian troops and invite 500 young Mongolians as well as 250 journalists to China in the next five years. Both sides also agreed to cooperate in enhancing the tourist inflow in each other's countries.

Upgrading its relationship with China by signing a 'Comprehensive' Strategic Partnership Mongolia is seeking closer ties to take advantage of Chinese investment, while China wants more support from its neighbours at international forums as Beijing pursues increased influence in regional affairs. On 22 August 2014, while delivering his speech at the Mongolian Parliament, President Xi Jinping clearly remarked that "China is willing to offer opportunities and room for common development to Mongolia and other neighbours" at a time when Beijing "promised more shared development and less tension with its neighbours."[40] The two sides appear to be serious in deepening their relationship which is also evident from the fact that they celebrated the 65th Anniversary of the establishment of their diplomatic relations by organizing commemorative events throughout the year in 2014 that was declared as a "Year of Friendly Exchanges between Mongolia and China".

Nevertheless, one may also find that "hungry for Mongolia's coal, metals, and other minerals, China has dominated the Mongolian economy, stoking fears in Ulaanbaatar of even greater Chinese control."[41] This has resulted in imposing strict new laws mandating government oversight of foreign investment, especially from foreign sources. Ulaanbaatar has created a two-tiered system of "China-phobic" resource nationalism that could alter the future trajectory of the mining industry. According to Backes, China "looms large over the Mongolian economy, and fears abound in Ulaanbaatar about the prospects of becoming Beijing's newest natural resource appendage."[42] Despite such tensions, Mongolia is becoming increasingly dependent on China for consumer goods and as a market for its raw materials. This is more so because improbability of a huge inflow of Russian investment into Mongolia's natural resources sector makes it very unlikely that in the near future Russia will provide a viable alternative for Ulaanbaatar either in terms of exports or foreign investment. Even Mongolia finds the Russian petroleum products as "increasingly expensive" which "fail to meet soaring consumer and industrial demand."[43] Campi, thus, stresses that "although Mongolia is sensitive to Chinese activity in the mineral sector, it is willing to let China become a significantly larger supplier of oil products, at least in the short term, to break the back of its dependency on more expensive Russian petroleum products."[44] China also has a vital role in regional economic cooperation projects. Since the early 1990s, the UNDP and the individual governments have been touting the development of Northeast Asia as an integrated unit, with individual countries offering complementary assets. China and North Korea could supply cheap and abundant labour; Mongolia and Asiatic Russia (Siberia), mineral and natural resources; and Japan and South Korea capital and technical expertise. China is, therefore, vital for Mongolia's participation in such regional plans.

Conclusion

While post-Cold War Mongolia pursues its foreign policy of maintaining friendly relations with all nations of the world, the way its relationship has been growing with China point to the fact that the two sides complements each other in matters of bilateral concerns. Several experts view Mongolia's relationship with China through the prism of the re-emergence of China as a great power in the post-Cold War world, though the revised Concepts of Mongolia's National Security (2010) and Foreign Policy (2011) have implicitly identified China as Ulaanbaatar's major security concern. Even so Mongolia cannot afford neglecting China out rightly due to having a 4677 kms common border line that helps the two sides especially to expand their economic and trade cooperation. At the same time, one may find that Mongolia's foreign policy has strongly been affected by its two geographic neighbours-China and Russia. But when geography comes into play, every resource has to go through either China or Russia, and therefore, every deal including in the mining sector signed with one might provoke the other into accusing Mongolia of favouring its rival.[45] However, the fact remains that most of the exports go through China. In addition, the 'third neighbour' approach of Mongolia's foreign policy complicates the trilateral relations between Mongolia, China and Russia, but it also gives Beijing an opportunity to bring Mongolia closer to its pursuit of greater regional clout and gain more support in international affairs. China is supporting some Mongolian endeavours like Ulaanbaatar's dialogue on security issues in Northeast Asia; the convocation of a summit involving Russia, Mongolia and China; and Mongolia's entry into the Asia-Pacific Economic Cooperation.

Today the driving engine of Mongolia-China 'Comprehensive' Strategic Partnership is trade and economic cooperation. Since Mongolia has become an international transportation hub due to its unique geographical advantages, China and Mongolia are planning to jointly promote the construction of a rail road between Asia and Europe. Besides, Mongolia has expressed its willingness to actively participate in the construction of the Silk Road Economic Belt proposed by China, which aims at exerting positive influence on the development of Central and South Asia. On its part, China has already made it clear that it is all set to become "a trustworthy, responsible and good neighbour" as well as "a good friend and a good partner for Mongolia." Therefore, the two sides must reflecton building their 'comprehensive' strategic partnership as an opportunity to take the Sino-Mongolian relations to a higher level in the interests of the people of the two countries and in the interests of establishing peace and security in Northeast Asia. To that end, one must not forget that in the democratic era the most important factor in Mongolia's foreign relationship is tied to economics not politics,[46] and hence China would remain to be a key partner in Mongolia's growth trajectory but not at the cost of latter's national interest.

Notes and References

1. "China media: Mongolia ties", 22 August 2014, http://www.bbc.com/news/world-asia-china-28892457(accessed on 20 November 2014).
2. Ibid.
3. Morris Rossabi (2013), "Sino-Mongol Border: From Conflict to Precarious Resolution", in Bruce A. Elleman, Stephen Kotkin and Clive Schofield, eds., *Beijing's Power and China's Borders: Twenty Neighbors in Asia*, New Delhi: Pentagon Press, p.171.
4. Today's Mongolia was then known as Outer Mongolia to distinguish itself from Inner Mongolia which came under Qing dynasty's direct rule in 1636, earlier than Outer Mongolia. Unlike Outer Mongolia, Inner Mongolia was never able to claim its independence from China. Since 1 May 1947 it became an autonomous region of China, and came to be known as the Inner Mongolia Autonomous Region (IMAR). For more details, see Sharad K Soni (2006), *Mongolia-China Relations: Modern and Contemporary Times*, New Delhi: Pentagon, pp. 116-141.
5. Larry W. Moses (1972), "Inner Asia in International Relations: The Role of Mongolia in Russo-Chinese Relations", *The Mongolia Society Bulletin*, vol. 11, no.2, p.56.
6. O. Edmund Clubb (1971), *China and Russia: The Great Game,* New York and London: Columbia University Press, pp. 466ff.
7. Soni, *Mongolia-China Relations*, p. 183.
8. For more on Gorbachev's Vladivostok Initiative, see Sharad K. Soni (2002), *Mongolia-Russia Relations: Kiakhta to Vladivostok*, New Delhi: Shipra Publications, pp.218-221.
9. Soviet "encirclement" of China was represented by the deployment of a huge number of Soviet forces along all sides of China's borders with Mongolia. Often described in western writings as a Soviet "satellite", Mongolia was perceived to be serving as a "buffer" by protecting critical points along the Chinese and Russian borders.
10. Saul Bernard Cohen (2003), *Geopolitics of the World System*, Lanham: Rowman & Littlefield Publishers, p. 87.
11. Sharad K Soni (2009), "China's Periphery Policy: Implications for Sino-Mongolian Relations", *India Quarterly*, vol.65, no.3, 2009, p.254. The global geopolitical and regional geostrategic changes can be understood in the following manner: Firstly, the collapse of the Soviet Union left the existence of only one superpower—The United States; secondly, although turmoil and conflict continued, it was limited in scope and geostrategic implications; and thirdly, more open borders allowed globalisation and regionalisation to prosper, with both positive and negative consequences (pp.253-254).
12. Bar-Erdene Batbayar (1999), *Twentieth Century Mongolia*, Cambridge: The White Horse Press, p.244. This work is divided into three parts in which "Book Three" is entitled as "A Puppet Republic", see pp.243-413.
13. See *Country Study for Japan's Official Development Assistance to Mongolia: A Committee Report*, Based on the discussions and findings organised by Japan International Cooperation Agency, Tokyo, March 1997, p.40.
14. Alan Sanders (1991),"Restructuring and Openness", in Shirin Akiner, ed., *Mongolia Today*, London & New York: Kegan Paul International, p.74.
15. US Department of State (1993), Bureau of Public Affairs, *Background Notes: Mongolia*, October.
16. For the full text of the China-Mongolia 1994 Treaty, see *Mongolian Defence White Paper, 1997-1998*, Ministry of Defence of Mongolia, Ulaanbaatar, 1988, pp.93-95.

17. Ibid.
18. *Zasgiin Gazriin Medee* (Ulaanbaatar), 15 December 1998.
19. You Ji and Jia Qingguo, "China's Re-emergence and Its Foreign Policy Strategy," in Joseph Y.S. Cheng, ed., *China Review, 1998*, Hong Kong: Chinese University Press, 1998, p.128.
20. Suisheng Zhao, "The Making of China's Periphery Policy", in Suisheng Zhao, ed., *Chinese Foreign Policy: Pragmatism and Strategic Behavior*, Armonk: M.E. Sharpe, 2004, p.258.
21 . The importance of economic diplomacy is being stressed in China's overall foreign policy, see Yang Fuchang, Qin Yaqing and Heng Xiaojun (2002), *Contemporary China and its Foreign Policy*, Beijing, World Affairs Press, p.195.
22. Suisheng Zhao, "The Making of China's Periphery Policy", p.259.
23. "China's Position Paper on the New Security Concept", China's Working Paper submitted to the ARF Foreign Ministers Meeting, 31 July 1999 cited in Pan Zhenqiang (2004), "China's Security Agenda in 2004, *Foreign Affairs Journal*, Chinese People's Institute of Foreign Affairs, Beijing, no.71, March, p.18. For more on a new security concept featuring mutual trust, mutual benefit, equality and cooperation, see *White Paper onChina's National Defence in 2002*, Information Office of the State Council of the PRC, Beijing, 2002, p.5.
24. "President Hu Jintao Holds a Formal Talk with Mongolian President", 4 June 2003 at http:///www.chinaembassy.se/eng/xwdt/t101635.htm
25. "The PRC: Mongolia's Main Investor", *Montsame* (Ulaanbaatar), 23 June 2001, cited in Alexander Tarasov (2004), "The Chinese in the Transbaikal" *Far Eastern Affairs*, vol.32, no.1, January-March, p.113.
26. Ibid.
27. See Ch. Sumya (2004), "Ulaanbaatar: President's China trip secures 'visa-free' status with Macao", *The UB Post* (Ulaanbaatar), 9 July.
28. See, Bruce A. Elleman and Sarah C.M. Paine (2001), "Security Pact with Russia Bolsters China's Power", *International Herald Tribune*, 6 August.
29. Nomin Lhagvasuren (2000), "Russia Seeks to Restore Position in Mongolia as Most Favored Neighbor", 16 November, at http://www.eurasianet.org/departments/insight/articles/eav111700.shtml (accessed on 20 May 2014).
30. Ibid.
31. Ministry of Foreign Affairs, Mongolia (2015), "Mongolia-China Relations", 21 April, at http://www.mfa.gov.mn/en/index.php?option=com_content&view=article&id= 3604%3 Amongolia-china-relations&catid=170%3Aneighboring-states&Itemid=181&lang=en (accessed on 25 May 2015).
32. Jeffrey Reeves (2012), "Response to PacNet No. 43-Ten Things We Get from Mongolia", PacNet No. 43R, 31 July, Pacific Forum CSIS, Honolulu, Hawaii, athttp://csis.org/files/publication/Pac1243R.pdf (accessed on 11 January 2013).
33. Alicia J. Campi (2013), The New Great Game in Northeast Asia: Potential Impact of Energy Mineral Development In Mongolia on China, Russia, Japan, and Korea, Asia-Pacific Policy Papers Series, no. 15, Washington, DC : Edwin O. Reischauer Center for East Asian Studies, Johns Hopkins University-SAIS, p.3.
34. Ibid.
35. Reeves, "Response to PacNet No. 43-Ten Things We Get from Mongolia".
36. Ibid.
37. Mark Goleman (2014), "Mongolia and China: Segue to Comprehensive Strategic Relations", 4 October, at http://journal-neo.org/2014/10/04/rus-mongoliya-i-kitaj-perehod-k-vseob-emlyushhim-strategicheskim-otnosheniyam/ (accessed on 14 November 2014).

38. Ibid.
39. Zamyn Uud border town is located in Dornogobi province of Mongolia and is situated at a distance of 780 kms from the capital Ulaanbaatar and 8 kms from Erlianhot town of People's Republic of China. It is a southern border port town with an area of 47.8 thousand hectares and population of 9000. It is the main hub providing border border-crossing services to Mongolia's major foreign trade and passengers flow and serving as a bridge among Mongolia, China and Asian countries. Zamyn Uud has a beneficial geographical location and convenient transportation services.
40. Wu Jiao and Zhao Shengnan (2014), "Xi pledges to boost ties with neighbors", *China Daily*, 23 August.
41. Oliver Backes (2013), "China at the Gates: China's Impact on Mongolian Natural Resource and Investment Policy" 6 May, at http://csis.org/blog/china-gates-chinas-impact-mongolian-natural-resource-and-investment-policy/ (accessed on 12 December 2013).
42. Ibid.
43. Alicia J Campi (2013), "Sino-Mongolian oil deal undercuts Russian role", Online Asia Times, 15 May at http://www.atimes.com/atimes/China_Business/CBIZ-01-150513.html (accessed 11 July 2013).
44. Ibid
45. Benny Wilbrink (2013), "Mongolia: from Puppet to Puppet Master?", 19 May, at http://www.upflund.se/utrikesperspektiv/2013/5/19/mongolia-from-puppet-to-puppet-master.html#.Ue_KKtIzhGY(accessed 10 July 2013)
46. Alicia J Campi (2012), Mongolia's Strategic Views on the Roles of Russia and China in its Future Development", *Mongolian & Tibetan Quarterly*, vol. 21, no.2, p.92.

CHAPTER 16

Return of Geo-economics: Republic of Korea's 'Resource Diplomacy' towards Mongolia

Jitendra Uttam

The return of geo-economics[1] manifested in the emergence of a distinct trend of economic regionalism has enormously benefited Mongolia, a country endowed with world's 10th largest reserves of natural resources. It is proven that Mongolia has one of the world's largest reserves of radioactive minerals such as uranium and rare-earth elements, copper, molybdenum, gold and coal. Indeed, geological data collected over the period since the 1920s and recent explorations have proven Mongolia's vast mineral reserves, though only 15 per cent of the country's territory has been mapped. There are over 6,000 deposits of around 80 different minerals discovered in Mongolia. Similarly, East Asia's giant manufacturing economies relentless search for mineral resources have found a match in Mongolia's enormous natural resource base. This new match has elevated Mongolia's status in the foreign policy calculus of large manufacturing economies in the region. Moving beyond the geopolitical rules set by two giant neighbours—China in the South and Russia in the North, Mongolia has embarked on a decisively distinct foreign policy based on clear recognition of a 'third neighbour' which allows economic space for countries like Korea. This paradigmatic shift in Mongolia's foreign policy thinking allows recasting of nation's dependent status into an independent, non-aligned, multi-pillar external posture.

Mongolia's changing foreign policy behaviour marked by its 'third neighbour' policy initiative meets with the Republic of Korea's (hereafter Korea or South Korea) explicit 'resource diplomacy' aimed to feed its enormous demand for mineral resources coming from export-oriented mass-manufacturing industries. Giving due recognition to Korea's increasing appetite for mineral resources, government officially promulgated 'resources diplomacy' during Lee Myung Bak administration. In fact, Korea's so-called resource diplomacy was essentially a defensive measure to protect the lines of energy supply necessary to ensure the inputs necessary to continuously promote its rapid economic growth. This brand of diplomacy provided a basis upon which South Korea was able to reach out and involve itself with many countries that in the past could not receive priority in its foreign policy calculus. In this sense, Lee Myung Bak administration's resource diplomacy offered an opportunity for South Korea to develop and deepen relationships with energy producing countries in Central Asia, the Middle East, Africa, Latin America, and Russia.

Though, South Korea and Mongolia have historical ties, however their bilateral relations developed significantly since the two countries launched diplomatic relationship in 1990. Korea has supported Mongolia in its transition to market economy. In turn, by hosting number of Korean companies, Mongolia played an important role in improving inter-Korean relations. Mongolia's trade with South Korea has almost quadrupled over the last decade and the Asia's fourth biggest economy is now the third largest trading partner of the resource rich Mongolia after China and Russia. In addition, South Korea is the largest labour market for Mongolians. Estimates suggest that 38,000 to 40,000 Mongolians work, study and live in South Korea. According to the Foreign Investment and Foreign Trade Agency of Mongolia (FIFTA), South Korea is the 4th largest investor in Mongolia with total foreign direct investment (FDI) of over US$ 255 million since 1990. South Korea is also a key donor providing approximately US $ 137 million since 1990 in committed loans and grants to Mongolia. Major investments from South Korean companies and their other business engagements in Mongolia include: 1) Skytel: a JV with South Korean SK Telecom and Mongolian shareholders; 2) Unitel Corp.: a 50/50 South Korean-Mongolian JV that started providing GSM services from 2006; 3): Korea Telecom bought

40 percent of the Mongolian Telecom for US$ 4.5 mn at privatization; 4) Seoul Group: a property company with the first public luxury residential project in Ulaanbaatar; and 5) Korean Development Bank is expected to be hired as part of the management team to run newly established Mongolian development institution. Other major South Korean companies including state-owned Korea Resources Corp, steelmaker POSCO and Korea Electric Power Corp. (KEPCO) have decided to bid for the Western Tsankhi coalfield, the largest area of the Tavan Tolgoi mine. The South Korean consortium is jointly bidding with Japanese and Russian companies. In March 2011, Lotte E&C-led South Korean consortium has signed a preliminary deal with Mongolian Railways to build a 1,040 Kilometre railway track in Mongolia.

It is in this background that the ideas and arguments in this paper point to the fact that the return of geo-economics has positively affected bilateral economic ties between South Korea and Mongolia, exemplified by the success of Korea's resource diplomacy in Mongolia. It also highlights that the end of Cold War which considerably weakened geo-politics dominated by Russia and China and gave rise to the geo-economic concerns. The success of European Union, ASEAN, and NAFTA in crating regional economic entities provided great impetus to bring back geo-economics in Northeast Asia. This new shift has brought Korea at the centre-stage of Mongolian foreign policy thinking which intends to diversify its dependence away from neighbouring great powers namely China and Russia.

Korea, Mongolia and the Return of Geo-economics

Geo-economics is a relatively new term which has had much more limited academic adoption and is used in popular writings to express ideas ranging from managerial concerns over the competitive economic positioning of states and cities[2] to the basic 'post-Cold War' strategic notion that economic competition has now eclipsed military confrontation at the centre of inter-state relations.[3] The post-World War II rise in regional economic groupings such as European Union, North America Free Trade Agreement, ASEAN, SAARC and so forth brought region over nation as the core economic territory that can have better leverage to reconstruct rules of trade, investment, competition and overall market functions. By contrast, geopolitics is an expression shaped by both academic and popular usages going back to imperial concerns with the links between geography, state territoriality and world power politics. Cold War era dominant paradigm was based on the idea where politics remained in command and geopolitics was driven by ideological contest rather than merely economic factors. In the 1980s, the rise of Japan invited mercantilist responses from Europe and the United States as many experts believed that in fact Japan had risen on the back of mercantilism. Recent crises in North America and European Union have revived dormant mercantilism, with many accusing Germany and the United States of pursuing a mercantilist agenda. Thus, the clear assertion by Daniel Bell (1990) that "economics is the continuation of war by other means" still remains valid.[4]

In the context of globalization, the language and logics of inter-state rivalry are increasingly predicated on "the grammar of commerce".[5] In this way, Luttwak has maintained that state authority could actually be reasserted anew "not in the names of strategy and security this time, but rather to protect 'vital economic interests' by geo-economic defences, geo-economic offensives, geo-economic diplomacy, and geo-economic intelligence".[6] The geopolitical discourse developed by John Agnew (2003), Simon Dalby (1990 & 2003), Derek Gregory (2005), Jennifer Hyndman (2004), Gerard OTuathail (1996 & 2003) and Joanne Sharp (2000) made it possible to explore how geo-economics and geopolitics operate as alternately hopeful and fearful discourses shaping the worldviews.[7] The geo-economic discourse is also being employed in many other parts of the world to imagine, amongst other things, a wide range of post-national and trans-border regional growth strategies.[8] Simply put, the imaginative geographies of geo-economic enframing differ from those of geopolitical scripting because they enable the imagination of an expanding economic flatness rather than the sorts of political partitions and unevenness that Agnew, Dalby, OTuathail, Sharp and others have traced in twentieth century accounts of evil empires, clashing civilizational blocs and American exceptionalism.[9] Geo-economic visionaries tend as a result to anticipate capitalist inclusion rather than the expulsion or containment of evil others. Their focus is on networks not blocs, connections not iron curtains, and trans-border ties instead of national territories.

In this backdrop, it can be argued that the distinctive visions of such geo-economic *gurus* enframes the world in a newly smooth and planed way, an optimistic geo-economic way that replaces closed and fearful visions of competing territories and enemies with an expanding and supposedly level playing field of market-mediated integration. In short, while geopolitical discourses lead to fear-filled fascination with foreign threats ranging from 'peer competitors' to 'rogue regimes' to 'terrorist cells', geo-economic discourses compensate and console by offering a hope of transcending the divisions. This post-Cold War shift from geo-politics to geo-economics has brought new thinking in the foreign policy making. Mongolia and Korea which are part of the single Northeast Asian geo-economic unit, benefited enormously from this new trend, that has been termed as the 'return of geo-economics' in the region. Geopolitics of Northeast Asian region created strategic divergence leading to region's economies seeking procurement of resources in the far-flung areas ignoring resource-rich Mongolia and vast regions of Russian Siberia. On the back of resurgent geo-economics, regional economic integration has become a dominant discourse in the regional interaction. The ongoing paradigmatic shift in Korea's foreign policy towards Mongolia is the part of this increased geo-economic ascendancy.

Practice of Korea's Resource Diplomacy

As a late-late comer in the race to secure resources abroad, large manufacturing economy of Korea feared to be left behind by more powerful economic risers such as China, India and ASEAN etc., and rushed into high-level diplomacy to establish strategic partnerships with resource-rich developing countries.[10] In order to feed the enormous appetite of resources by Korea's giant mass-manufacturing industries ranging from shipbuilding, to steel, automobiles, petro-chemicals and construction, Korea's developmental state always sought uninterrupted access to raw materials. In a great hurry, Korea's large conglomerates are moving swiftly to secure stable supply of resources but they lack coherent strategy to ensure control on resources in foreign lands. In order to firm-up a coherent strategy to tap foreign resources, Korea launched its ambitious 'resource diplomacy'. Before his official visit to Russia and Central Asia in September 2004, Korean president RohMoo Hyun first time used the term 'resource diplomacy'. The concept of resource diplomacy has since been continuously extended and involves a more active strategy that seeks equity stakes in energy exploration in Latin America, Africa, Middle East, Central Asia, South Asia and Far-eastern Russia. Other raw materials as well as agriculture and the issue of food security were added to the targets of Korea's much publicized 'resource diplomacy'. As a consequence, regions that previously received little attention in Korea's foreign policy initiatives suddenly became important. For instance, Mongolia which attracted little attention in Korea during Cold War period came into limelight in the post-Cold War period. Sensing increased competition for resources, Korean state offered generous credit programs and investment funds as well as various tax benefits targeted to overseas resource development projects.[11] State-owned energy corporations took the lead in overseas resource development, often in alliance with private companies that hesitated to invest because of the perceived higher risks involved.

Under President Lee Myung Bak, the concept of 'resource diplomacy' was upgraded in scale and scope. According to the new plan for resource development, the government sought to pull up Korea's self-sufficiency in oil and gas from 4.2 per cent in 2007 to 28 per cent by 2016 by investing 20 trillion won ($17 billion) (Ministry of Knowledge Economy, 2010). In addition to securing energy resources, food security came into consideration. This was because of not only soaring food and grain prices, but also the failure of a Korean company (Daewoo) to acquire about half of Madagascar's arable land in 2008. The deal failed because of public protests over the land grab that drove out the Madagascan government.[12] In 2009, the government established a 10-year basic plan for overseas agricultural development, providing credits to finance 100 per cent of Korean firms' investment in overseas farmland. "Offshore food production" has been considered as an infant industry in Korea which anticipates active state protection. For this purpose, government has provided US $ 197 million budget between 2007-2011 for loans to Korean companies with target to secure 385000 hectares of farmland by 2018 producing 1.8 million tons of wheat, corn and soybean.[13] The strategy was revised in 2011 and 'Overseas Agriculture Development Promotion Act' was enforced in January 2012. At the end of 2011, 85 projects in 20 different countries were being conducted. Important regions where Korean companies invested in securing food grains are mainly in Central Asian and the countries of South East Asia.

Korea's approach to overseas resource development placed an emphasis on a bigger role for the private sector. State-owned corporations in alliance with related ministries and policy banks created 'resource development funds' of 1 trillion won ($860 million) to promote private sector investment in overseas resource development projects.[14] Furthermore, in 2011, Korea's National Pension Service extended its overseas resource development investment program of 20 trillion won ($17 billion) for 10 years, which was approved in 2007. In addition, it announced a plan to set up a private equity fund with Korean business groups to invest in overseas resource development.[15]

It can be argued that the proactive Korean government support for overseas resource development is a revised version of the time-tested mercantilist national growth strategy adjusted to the imperatives of economic globalization. This reflects the ongoing transformation of an inward-looking 'developmental state' into an outward-looking 'mercantilist developmental state' since the

1997/1998 financial crisis. Careful analysis of Korea's Official Development Assistance (ODA) provides further evidences to validate ever closer links between resource diplomacy and industrial policy. Korea's traditional trade policy focus towards Asia is moving towards resource-rich Africa. Korea which joined DAC (Development Assistance Committee) in 2009 mainly followed poverty alleviation which has been the general trend in managing the ODA across countries. However, resource-poor Korea increasingly faces the dilemma—whether to focus on 'poverty alleviation' or focus on 'national resource diplomacy'. There is a growing call that Korea should focus mutually-beneficial ODA strategy that re-aligns ODA not only to alleviate poverty but also to secure natural resources as well. Recently, ODA in Korea has been integrated into high-level resource diplomacy as an effective political vehicle to better facilitate nation's overseas resource development drive in selected developing countries.

Mongolia in the Framework of Korean 'Resource Diplomacy' Calculus

Mongolians and Koreans are ethnically related people cut off by centuries of history. In the 13th century, Mongolians swept across China and came down to the Korean Peninsula, and were on the brink of invading Japan until several naval disasters changed their mind. Between 1231-1259 Mongol Empire launched a series of campaign against the Goryo dynasty causing tremendous loss to civilian lives and eventual transformation of Korea into a vassal state under the over-lordship of Mongol Yuan Dynasty for approximately 80 years. Mongol and Korean rulers were also tied by matrimonial alliance as some of the Mongol princes and aristocrats married Korean princesses and vice versa.[16] Furthermore, Mongolia's occupation of Korea left linguistic affinities, shared genes and wild horse herds, known to this day as Mongolians, on the South Korean island of Cheju. Today's bonds reflect, to some degree, the solidarity of two small nations living on the edges of a rising China. Commercially, Mongolia is an outpost for Korean business. On an ethnic level, Koreans and Mongolians are like fraternal twins.

A new but significant reason for seeing Northeast Asia as a "Third Neighbour" was South Korea, because in the early 1990s, it appeared to be a good model for Mongolian economic development. Mongolia is one of the few countries that maintains full-scale diplomatic relations with both Koreas and careful about maintaining a balanced relationship. Mongols and South Koreans feel a common racial, linguistic and historical bond which explains the high hopes both nations had in the 1990s for the expansion of economic and educational ties. The KOICA (Korean International Cooperation Agency) has had an active, growing grant aid and technical cooperation program in Mongolia since 1991. As of 2011, KOICA had provided about $137 million in committed loans and grants for energy-related projects, long-distance education and human resource development assistance.

Perhaps more importantly, South Korea, in response to its own financial crisis in 1997, welcomed cheap Mongol labour, often illegal, in its factories. Estimates suggest that at least 34,000 to 40,000 Mongolians work in South Korea and send earnings back home. Remittances from Mongolians working in South Korea have become an important source of income. With influx of Mongolian labour in South Korea, the country now has more Mongolians than Japan, Europe and the US combined. Among these workers are a number of Mongolian professional boxers and athletes, who use Korea as a stepping stone to further international recognition. Symbolizing the growing proximity with Mongolia, Korean universities have established Mongolian language departments and scientific expeditions to Mongolia have been sponsored by the Korean Government and NGOs. Korea's prestigious Seoul National University and Dankuk University have set up Mongolian language departments and exchange programmes involving professors and students with Mongolian universities. Adding to this, Korean government has provided hundreds of scholarships to Mongolian students for conducting their studies in Korean universities.

Since 1999, the year Kim Dae Jung, then South Korea's president, flew here, the Ulan Bator-Seoul route has been one of the busiest for Korean Air and Mongolian Airlines. In August 2011 as part of a three-nation tour of Central Asia, Korean President Lee Myung Bak made a three-day state visit to Mongolia. Mongolian President Elbegdorj and President Lee upgraded the bilateral cooperation to the level of "comprehensive partnership" that included a trade pact comprising elimination of restrictions on foreign investment, incorporating a dispute-resolution mechanism, and protection of intellectual property rights. This type of state-to-state relationship signifies mature, comprehensive bilateral cooperation, including multi-directional cooperation in politics, economy, trade, security, culture and other fields. Now, South Korea has become Mongolia's fourth-largest trading partner, with two-way trade volume amounting to US $ 427 million in 2013. According to the Foreign Investment and Foreign Trade Agency of Mongolia (FIFTA), South Korea has emerged as the 4th largest investor in Mongolia with total investment amounting to US$ 255 million since 1990. Also, South Korea has donated close to US$137 million since 1990 in loans and grants to Mongolia.

In the 1990s, bilateral trade turnover increased from $9 million in 1991 to about $60 million in 2000, making South Korea the fifth largest trade partner for Mongolia. In 2011, Korea became Mongolia's third largest trading partner, with bilateral trade volume amounting to $230 million, an 85-fold increase from $2.71 million in 1990. In recent times, number of Korean imports has increased even more, particularly in cars, SUVS, and consumer goods. Korean FDI amounted to about $60 million in 280 joint ventures by the end of 2000. Most of this was connected to Korean textile manufacturers using Mongolia's quota free status with the United States. The major South Korean investments in Mongolia include: Skytel—a JV with SK Telecom; Unitel Corporation—a 50-50 percent Korean-Mongolia JV providing global cell services since 2006; Mongolian Telecom—40 percent Korean-owned since its privatization; Seoul Group—a property company specializing in public luxury residential housing; Samsung mining with Erdenet copper mine and the Korean Development Bank will be part of the management team in Mongolian Development Bank to fund major investment projects.

A nineteen-member South Korean consortium, led by state-run Korea Rail Network Authority and top builders such as Daewoo Engineering & Construction, Hyundai Engineering & Construction, and Lotte Engineering and Construction, signed a preliminary deal in March 2011 with Mongolian Railways to build over the next five years a $3 billion 1,040 Kilometre rail track extending from Tavan Tolgoi mining area to Choibalsan City, which links to the trans-Siberian Railroad. South Korea is already the third largest customer of Mongolian coal. Completion of the rail link would facilitate Mongolia to diversify its customer base for copper, rare earths, and coal away from China to Korea and other countries in the region. Similarly, in order to enhance fuel and civil nuclear cooperation, Director-General of the Mongolian Nuclear Energy Agency, Dr. Enkhbat Sodnom made an official visit to the Korea Nuclear International Cooperation Foundation (KONICOF), and showed interest in obtaining Korean radiation-monitoring equipment, develop joint projects to look for isotopes in the water supply, assistance with cancer diagnosis, and learning about techniques that Korean government employed to educate its public about the usefulness of nuclear energy. Furthermore, officials from Mongolia's Nuclear Energy Authority and academics from the Nuclear Research Center of Mongolian State University attended an international seminar held in Seoul on the infrastructure development of nuclear energy. South Korea's Ministry of Education, Science and Technology organized First Korea-Mongolia Nuclear Power Cooperation Seminar in Ulaanbaatar where twenty nuclear power specialists from the Korea Atomic Energy Research Institute and the Korea Institute of Radiological and Medical Sciences discussed Korean nuclear power development and progress in technology. Areas such as nuclear power safety and training, small and medium-capacity nuclear reactors, nuclear medicine, and radiation technology were examined for mutual cooperation. Training doctors and medical experts and funding new hospitals for Mongolia have emerged as a niche industry in Korea. In July 2012 the foundation for a National Diagnostic Centre was laid within the Second Central Clinical Hospital. The Korean government has provided $55.4 million in a soft loan from the Korea EXIM Bank of the total $65 million required. Mongolian doctors will be trained in Korea and Korean doctors will come to Mongolia.

In sum, it is believed that Mongolia represents a unique investment opportunity for South Korean investors due to strong political support, favourable economic environment and attractive investment projects. An optimistic view is that South Korean investments in Mongolia would increase as investors seek to capitalize on the expected boom in this resource-rich country. Investors are expected to capitalize on significant growth in the Mongolian capital market and pursue private equity deals in both resource and non-resource sectors. Natural resources, infrastructure and property in Mongolia are key areas where we expect South Korean investors, operators and developers to be increasingly active in coming years.

Paradigmatic Shift in Mongolia's Foreign Policy Thinking

Having subsistence economy for centuries as a nation of herders, Mongolia now contemplates a rapid economic revolution brought about by the possibility of extraction of large quantities of mineral resources. Given the proven reserves of mineral wealth, the projections of growth are staggering. As industrialized countries search the globe for increasingly scarce raw materials, Mongolia is seen as a new destination and an eager partner to do business. In fact, Mongolia stands at the cusp of a process that could have a transformative effect on the economy and prosperity of the state. As a result of increased activity in the mining sector, Mongolia's GDP grew by 11.7 percent in 2013.[17] Though, despite substantial increase in mining output, Mongolia's gross domestic product slowed down to 7.8 percent in 2014 but it is still very high.[18] Mongolia is enjoying the attention of Asian businesses as it extends its brand of resource diplomacy in the new emerging geo-economic territory. Mongolians have described their country as a tiny pony stuck between two huge elephants, namely Russia and China. Mongolia became a Soviet satellite after it looked to the victorious Bolsheviks for protection from China. The Chinese government at the time wanted to claim both Inner and Outer Mongolia as Chinese territory. Much of Mongolia's history is, therefore, comprised of being pulled between larger powers. Now, though, the country is using its mineral wealth to carve out an independent global position by reaching to new found geo-economics of the East Asian region but historical odds remain a formidable force.

Mongolia has roll out a legislative framework that enables foreign commercial enterprises to begin exploiting the vast reserves of coal, copper, gold, uranium and other subterranean treasures that have sat, largely untapped.[19] Table: 1 provides estimated reserves of mineral deposits in Mongolia but this estimation is based on the limited mapping of the country.

Table 1: Estimated Reserves of Minerals in Mongolia

Minerals	Estimated reserves/as of January 1, 2012/
Coal (million tons)	18,473.2
Iron (million tons)	1,046.6
Copper (thousand tons)	83,807
Lead (thousand tons)	1,740
Gold (placer) (tons)	221.47
Gold (hard rock deposit) (tons)	2,180.9

Source: Mineral Resources Authority of Mongolia.

This has prompted intense competition between mining ventures from Russia, the PRC, Australia, Canada, Korea, the United States, and elsewhere. Among the many highly-charged, deeply divisive issues arising in contemplation of such swift economic development of Mongolia's mining sector is how to take advantage of China's thirst for natural resources without becoming utterly beholden or vulnerable to Beijing's own aspirations in the region. For instance, the most obvious market for the enormous reserves of coking coal in Mongolia's Tavan Tolgoi mines—the sort of coal used in the production of steel—is China. It appears that Mongolia is deferring the development of improved rail links directly to China in favour of expanding, first, links to the Russian, broad-gauge lines that will enable rapid transportation of goods to and from Russian cities and ports.[20]

There is considerable resistance in Mongolia to allow the China to dominate the development of its resources, even though doing so would most likely lead to the greatest profit—but also greater leverage by Beijing over Mongolia. One political activist in Mongolia, Gombosuren Arslan, states "it's not a question of whether Mongolia will get money or not, but of the very existence of Mongolia as an independent country. . . will Mongolia become a colony of China?"[21] With the China and Chinese enterprises becoming ever-more active investors in Mongolia, these questions—coupled to historical animosity directed at China—seem rather prevalent in Mongolia. As it is, China is Mongolia's greatest source of FDI and greatest market for Mongolian exports.[22] Indeed, the Chinese Ministry of Commerce reports that bilateral trade between the PRC and Mongolia reached "$2.4 billion in 2009, 50 times higher than 1991 and accounted for 47.4 percent of Mongolia's total foreign trade. China has been the largest trade partner of the country for 11 consecutive years." By far China is Mongolia's biggest export destination as in 2013 it took 90 percent of Mongolia's exports.

To ensure that Mongolia is not utterly swallowed by the rising China, Mongolian statesmen have said they are eager to diversify commercial dependencies, seeking investors from among its "third neighbours". Consequently, Ulaanbaatar has actively courted bids from mining enterprises associated with states other than China and Russia.[23] Mongolia's government understands that whichever offer it accepts is laden with geopolitical importance.[24] Some analysts view the eagerness by foreign firms for a stake in the Mongolian market as an element in a new "great game" that encompasses not only Mongolia, but also Central Asia. Igor Torbakov explains "The latest conceptualization sees the Game as being largely driven by the desire of Russia and China to squeeze the United States out of Central Asia and establish their exclusive control over the strategically located and energy-rich region.[25] Of course, while Russia and China may both object to the insinuation of the United States to Central Asia, Moscow and Beijing are themselves engaged in a quiet effort to hold the other in check. With the emergence of competition over mining resources, it is easy to appreciate why Munkh-Ochir Dorjjugder, an analyst associated with Mongolia's National Security Council, writes: "Mongolia's national security—both in theory and in practice—will be defined in terms of perceived success in multi-dimensional, geo-economic balancing rather than the relatively simple geo-political and/or geo-strategic balancing that dominated both scholarly thought and practical actions since Mongolia's Democratic Revolution in 1990."[26]

Mongolia's legacy of dependence on Qing (Manchu) and then Soviet protectors generated an acute sense of independence that led the nation to adopt a posture of gracious defiance, embodied in the "National Security Concept" and the "Concept of Mongolia's Foreign Policy," which clearly articulates what has come to be known as the "third neighbour" policy.[27] In essence, Mongolia has moved beyond geographic constraints to cultivate supportive relationships with powerful states that might counterbalance the inclinations of Russia and China.[28] Mongolia is in the process of shifting from a "satellite" foreign policy of dependence on Moscow to what Ulaanbaatar describes as an "independent, non-aligned, multi-pillar, open" foreign policy. By tying its security to the interests of "third neighbours," Mongolia has made clear its intention to act internationally without being constrained by the predilections of either Moscow or Beijing. However, the unspoken premise is that integration in the world outside its immediate ambit will help assure Mongolia's security should it be undermined by the interests, or actions, of its immediate neighbours.[29]

Indeed, Ulaanbaatar's relationship with "third neighbours" may provoke a security dilemma. This is a geopolitical gambit. In this context, Mongolia has reached out to the European Union, to Japan, to India, and to Korea—where it is among the few states to have unusually close ties to both North and South Korea—and to the United States.[30] It has acted out of a belief that "more partners result in greater balancing opportunities and hence, a more guaranteed external security environment.[31] By effectively playing the "values" card with wealthier and influential democracies, Mongolia has received investment, technical assistance, aid, and collaboration in various developmental projects. Mongolia has demonstrated a clever capacity to cultivate relationships with all the great powers of Asia, as well as other states, in a manner that has thus far restrained potential adversaries from exerting hegemonic influence on it. Mongolia's "multi-pillared" foreign policy illustrates the principle that "weaker states can persist, and often frustrate attempts at subjugation by more powerful states, even if they could never defeat the more powerful state."[32]

Conclusion

Mongolia's 'independent, non-aligned, multi-pillar' foreign policy aims to reach out beyond next door China and Russia and construct deeper engagement with the so-called 'Third Neighbours'. In the 1990s Mongolian thinking about Northeast Asia expanded beyond strategic and political considerations and reach out to economic realities. Yet, hopes for large investment from a diverse group of Northeast Asian countries to counterbalance the influence of

Mongolia's two giant neighbours have only been partially realized. Mongolia hopes that economic integration with other Northeast Asian economies would secure its sovereignty and economic development. Among other Northeast countries, Korea figures prominently in Mongolia's shifting foreign policy thinking. In this context, success of South Korea's resource diplomacy to engage Mongolia offers hope that at the periphery of giants in Northeast Asia, South Korea and Mongolia are in the midst of far-reaching dynamic bilateral engagement that can have impact on the emerging regional strategic posturing. Mongolia-Korea partnership, cemented by demand-supply matrix, has created a new geo-economics in the region that can have impact on emerging regional geo-political and strategic environment. Also, this bilateral partnership matches Korea's aspiration for middle power diplomacy aimed at acquiring meaningful status in the international system. In fact, Mongolia's "Third Neighbour" policy is in response to the return of geo-economics which has fundamentally altered the choices before countries of the region. 'Resource diplomacy' that Korea launched in the post-cold war period matches Mongolia's aspiration to diversify its traditional dependence and reach out to countries like South Korea.

Notes and References

1. In the post-Cold War period inter-state rivalry took a decisive turn from geo-political calculation to what Luttwak (1993) called geo-economic defences, geo-economic offensives, geo-economic diplomacy, and geo-economic intelligence. The re-rise of these geo-economic variables is commonly referred as the 'return of geo-economics. For details, see E. Luttwak (1993), "The coming global war for economic power: there are no nice guys on the battlefield of geo-economics", The International Economy, 7 (5): 18-67.
2. K.A. Schlevogt (2001), "Institutional and Organizational Factors Affecting Effectiveness: Geoeconomic comparison between Shanghai and Beijing", *Asia Pacific Journal of Management* 18 (4): 519-533.
3. R. Cruz de Castro (2000), "Whither geoeconomics? Bureaucratic inertia in U.S. post-cold war foreign policy", *Asian Affairs: An American Review* 26 (4): 201-222.
4. Daniel Bell (1990), "Germany: The Enduring Fear. A New Nationalism or a New Europe", *Dissent*, Vol. 37, No.4 (Fall): 461-468.
5. E. Luttwak (1990), "From geopolitics to geo-economics: logic of conflict, grammar of commerce", *The National Interest* 20:17-23.
6. E. Luttwak (1993), "The coming global war for economic power: there are no nice guys on the battlefield of geo-economics", *The International Economy* 7(5): 19.
7. For details, see J. Agnew (2003),*Geopolitics: re-visioning world politics*, New York: Routledge; S. Dalby (1990), *Creating the Second Cold War: the discourse of politics*, London : Pinter Publishers; S. Dalby (2003), "Calling 911: Geopolitics, security and America's new war", *Geopolitics* 8(3): 61-86; Derek Gregory (2004), *The Colonial Present*, Oxford: Blackwell; J. Hyndman (2004) "Mind the Gap: bridging feminist and political geography through geopolitics", *Political Geography* 23: 307–322; G. O'Tuathail (1996), *Critical Geopolitics: the politics of writing global space*, Minneapolis: University of Minnesota Press; G. O'Tuathail

(2003), "Just Looking for a Fight: American affect and the invasion of Iraq", *Antipode* 35 (5): 856-870; J. P. Sharp (2000), *Condensing the Cold War: reader's digest and American identity*, Minneapolis: University of Minnesota Press.

8. For details, see A. Smith (2002), "Imagining Geographies of the 'New Europe': geo-economic power and the new European architecture of integration", *Political Geography* 21: 647–670; M. Sparke (2002), "Not a state, but more than a state of mind: cascading Cascadias and the geoeconomics of cross-border regionalism", in *Globalization, Regionalization and Cross Border Regions*, ed. Perkmann, M. and N.L. Sum, 212-240, London: Palgrave; M. Sparke and V. Lawson (2003), "Entrepreneurial political geographies of the global-local nexus", in *A Companion to Political Geography*, ed. Agnew, J., K. Mitchell and G. OTuathail,315-334. Oxford: Blackwell; N. L. Sum (2002), "Globalization, regionalization and Cross-border modes of growth in East Asia: The (re-)constitution of 'time-space governance', in *Globalization, Regionalization and Cross-border Regions*, ed. Perkmann, M. and N.L. Sum, 50-76. London: Palgrave.

9. For more details, see M. Sparke (2003), "American empire and globalization: postcolonial speculations on neo-colonial enframing", *Singapore Journal of Tropical Geography* 24 (3): 373-389; and M. Sparke (2005), *In the space of theory: post-foundational geographies of the nation-state*, Minneapolis: University of Minnesota Press.

10. For details, see Ian Taylor (2006), "China's oil diplomacy in Africa", *International Affairs* 82(5): 937–959; R. Kaplinsky and M. Morris (2009), "Chinese FDI in Sub-Saharan Africa: Engaging with large dragons", *European Journal of Development Research* 21(4): 551–569.

11. Funding support for long-term resource development in Korea includes bilateral ODA credit program provided by the Export–Import Bank and credit programs by related ministries. In case of investment failure, repayment of principal loans is exempted. If Korean firm investing in overseas resource development is exempted from tax for dividend income in host country, then the same amount of tax is also exempted in Korea.

12. As the prominent food insecure nation, Korea's name figured at the fore front of what is now being described as 'global land grab'. Many of these land purchases happened in South East Asia and Africa. Korea's Rural Land Development Corporation directly owned and operated some of these farms. The prominent land deal was announced in 2008 when Daewoo Logistics proposed to lease 1.3 million hectare of farmland in Madagascar for 99-years of lease. This proposal created widespread unrest and caused the fall of the government in Madagascar. For further details, see J. Borger (2008), "Rich countries launch great land grab to safeguard food supply", *Guardian* 22 November; J. Parker (2009), "The Madagascar Model", *The Economist* , 13 November.

13. Sungwoo Park (2011), South Korea to increase overseas farming on record food cost, Bloomberg; accessed at http://www.bloomberg.com/news/articles/2013-03-27/south-koreans-in-farm-u-turn-as-chaebol-era-s-rapid-growth-ends

14. Ministry of Knowledge Economy (2010), "Energy policies: Promote overseas energy development projects", http://www.mke.go.kr/info/resource/resource_05.jsp, accessed 20 November 2011.

15. A. Nomura (2011), "Korean public pension fund's investment in overseas energy resources", *Nomura Journal of Capital Markets* 2(4): 1–4.

16. William E. Henthorn (1963), *Korea: the Mongol invasion*, Leiden: E J Brill.

17. World Bank (2015), data retrieved on Feb. 8, 2015, at http://data.worldbank.org/country/mongolia

18. Asian Development Bank (2015), *Asian Development Outlook: Financing Asia's Future Growth*, Manila: ADB.

19. Uradyn E. Bulag (2009), "Mongolia in 2009: From Landlocked to Land-linked Cosmopolitan", *Asian Survey*, 50 (1): 97-103.
20. Ganbat Namjilsangarav (2010), "Mongolia coal railway to link with Russia," *Bloomberg Business Week*, 25 June, at http://www.businessweek.com/ap/financialnews/D9GI5O182.htm.
21. Peter Stein (2009), "China casts its shadow on Mongolia," *The Wall Street Journal Asia* (December 15), accessed at http://online.wsj.com/article/SB30001424052748703954904574595651461527632.html
22. David Stanway (2010), "FRONTIERS-Doing business in Mongolia a tightrope walk," *Reuters* (May 27), accessed at http://www.reuters.com/article/idUSSGE64B04P20100527?type=marketsNews. Regarding anti-Chinese sentiments in Mongolia, see Alicia Campi, "Mongolia's Uneasy Relationship With China: Fast-growing economic ties are contributing to a new interest in things Chinese among Mongolians— and to manifestations of hatred," Transitions Online (May 26, 2010), accessed at http://www.tol.org/client/article/21485-mongolias-uneasy-relationship-with-china.html; and Mitch Moxley (2009), "The Neo-Nazis of Mongolia: Swastikas Against China," *Time* (July 27), at http://www.time.com/time/magazine/article/0,9171,1910893,00.html?iid=digg_share#ixzz0p8RvPGNZ
23. Of the eleven initial offers, Mongolia has settled on a short list that includes "BHP Billiton (Australia), Jindal (India), Vale (Brazil), Peabody (USA), Shenhua (China) and three consortiums from South Korea, Japan and Russia," *Eurasia Capital*, "TAVAN TOLGOI: At the Crossroad", Research Note, February 8, 2010, accessed at http://www.eurasiac.com/files/Tavan_Tolgoi_Feb08_10.pdf
24. Belgravia Mining, "Exporting the Tavan Tolgoi Coal: Choosing the Best Way Out", accessed at http://www.mining-mongolia.com/index.php?option=com_content&view=category&layout=blog&id=14&Itemid=13; *Eurasia Capital*, "TAVAN TOLGOI: At the Crossroad," Research Note, February 8, 2010, pp. 8–9. accessed at http://www.eurasiac.com/files/Tavan_Tolgoi_Feb08_10.pdf
25. Igor Torbakov (2007), "The West, Russia, and China in Central Asia: What Kind of Game is Being Played in the Region?," *Transition Studies Review* 14 (1): 152–162.
26. Munkh-Ochir Dorjjugder (2009), "Same Rules, New Dimensions for Mongolia's National Security: Adapting to the New Geo-Economic Environment, Opinion, October, accessed on August 6, 2015 at http://www.brookings.edu/research/opinions/2009/10/mongolia-dorjjugder
27. "The Concept of National Security," accessed at http://www.mongolianembassy.us/eng_foreign_policy/the_concept_of_national_security.php; Ministry of Foreign Affairs, "Concept of Mongolia's Foreign Policy," *Diplomatic Bluebook 2006* (Ulaanbaatar: Ministry of Foreign Affairs, 2006), pp. 225–230.
28. N. Altantsegtseg (2003), "Russian-Mongolian and Sino-Mongolian Relations since [the] 1990s," *World Affairs* (Ulaanbaatar) 2:231(08), pp.59–74.
29. Dorjjugder, "Same Rules, New Dimensions for Mongolia's National Security".
30. Rahul Bedi, "Defense ties with Mongolia expanded: Bid to monitor China's military activities," *The Tribune* (August 10, 2007), accessed at http://www.tribuneindia.com/2007/20070810/main5.htm;HisaneMisake (2009), "The great Japan-Mongolia love affair," *Asia Times*, Online (February 28), accessed at http://www.atimes.com/atimes/Japan/IB28Dh01.html.
31. Dorjjugder, "Same Rules, New Dimensions for Mongolia's National Security".
32. Brantly Womack (2006), *China and Vietnam: The Politics of Asymmetry*, New York: Cambridge University Press, p. 20.

CHAPTER 17

Mongolia and the European Union: Cooperative Partnership

Madan Yadav

In the changing dynamics of international order after the collapse of the Soviet Union and the end of the Cold War, Mongolia introduced itself from a Soviet satellite to an independent, sovereign, young democratic state in the world community. Popularly known as 'Outer Mongolia' to the outside world it has critical geo-strategic location which is locked with resource hungry China in the south and Russia in the north. Not only this strategic location with abundance of natural resources but also the robust democratic credential attracts several countries or a group of countries to make friendly relations with Mongolia. The relationship between Mongolia and the European Union (EU) is a case in point. Both Mongolia and the European Union share a growing and cooperative partnership based on shared values, commitment to liberal democracy and market economy in the era of globalization. The emergence of diplomatic and political cooperation has dynamically developed since 1989. In 2001, the European Union drafted the first Mongolia-EU Strategy Paper (2002-2006), which was a policy framework for the bilateral and multilateral initiatives. This was followed by the second Mongolia-EU Strategy Paper (2007-2013).[1] EU's cooperation with Mongolia continued to focus on poverty alleviation through sustainable rural development. The Strategy responded to the need to improve living conditions and sustainable employment in the Mongolian countryside and to slow down the rural exodus. Continued work in rural development built on the satisfactory results of the preceding Mongolia-EU Strategy Paper (2002-2006) that also focused on this sector.

The EU is an influential economic and political global actor in the world politics in the era of multi-polar world. In other words, the EU can be defined as a global economic superpower, world's largest and richest trade bloc and has capability to influence the international economic order and political system of international relations. On the other side, Mongolia's foreign policy has adopted a new approach of global strategic alliance for extensive and successful cooperation in the post-1991 period. Within its long term strategy, Mongolia has shown a keen interest to achieve optimum cooperation with EU and its member states in the multi-polar global politics. In this regard, Mongolia's quest for "Third Neighbours" is best suited the framework of comprehensive cooperation with the EU and its member states. The EU and its member states have lauded Mongolia's efforts for dynamic development of liberal democracy in comparison to the authoritarian regime in Central Asia and its neighbours. The EU also considers Mongolia to be a trusted ally to shape the North East Asian security policy, Korean peace process, NATO partnership for peace, economic integration, promoting multilateral cooperation, regional institutional building, use of energy resources, protection of environment and prevention of transnational crimes etc. in this region. It is in this background that this paper examines the state of relations in terms of cooperative partnership between Mongolia and the EU in today's situation.

Political and Diplomatic Relations

Mongolia and the EU have dynamically been developing their relations since early 1990s. The European Union has been assisting humanitarian assistance and support to Mongolia through various programmes since 1991. Like the U.S. and Russia, the EU and its member states also consider Mongolia as an important factor of stability in Central Asia. Mongolia was the OSCE Asian partner for cooperation since 2004, before becoming the 57th member of Organization for Security and Co-operation for Europe (OSCE) in 2012. It was a landmark achievement of "concept of third neighbour foreign policy" shift towards European cooperation and building partnership with EU. Mongolia also engages with NATO's Individual Partnership and Cooperation Program besides holding the Chairmanship of 'Community of Democracies' in 2011-13.[2] The EU launched 'Country Strategy Papers (CSP)' for assistance to Mongolia for 2002-06 and 2007-13 period, and also a follow up for 2014-20 period. All these strategy papers are aimed at enhancement of comprehensive bilateral trade, business cooperation, export, institutional reforms for poverty reduction and promotion of democratic values in society, humanitarian aid, agriculture and development cooperation, environment and education initiatives in Mongolia.

Both Mongolia and the EU have signed the Partnership Cooperation Agreement (PCA) on 30 April 2013. This historical agreement, the first high level agreement between the two sides since 1991, was signed by the EU Representative of Foreign Policy, Catherine Ashton on behalf of the EU. This legal framework is considered to be a significant step for enhancing cooperation in the field of political, economic and cultural ties at regional and international level. Within the framework of PCA, the European Parliament is exchanging inter-parliamentary delegations with Mongolia to discuss their mutual concerns over political and diplomatic developments with European Parliament Cooperation Committee. The common issues of their concerns include economic, energy security, human rights, fundamental freedom, promotion of non-proliferation of weapons of mass destruction, environmental protection, poverty and health issues, technology transfer, regional security cooperation, democratic institution building process, medical research etc. Since Mongolia is an emerging reliable, democratic and commercial partner of EU in North East Asia, the EU Agriculture and Rural Development Commissioner, Dacian Ciolos, visited Mongolia on 18-21 July 2013 for bilateral talks on sustainable agriculture, food Security, rural development, and agro-environmental measures etc.[3] The EU has budgeted EUR 15 million for development cooperation with Mongolia for the period 2011-13.[4] The programme for 2014-20 is expected to be announced soon.

The EU President Jose Manuel Barroso visited Mongolia in November 2013 and fixed the agenda of political, diplomatic and economic development including agriculture, trade, research and innovations etc. He also delivered a lecture on "EU-Mongolia: Third Neighbour and First Class Partner" at National University of Mongolia. He said that "Mongolia and EU have been much closer than you would think from looking at map. Our destines have been tied together in the 13th and 14th centuries when the Pax Mongolica enabled East and West to meet for the first time in history and to travel freely along the silk route which the Yuan dynasty secured as free trade route. The EU-Mongolia project is for the modernization of Mongolia's standardization system, which is closer to European standards".[5] Later, he also inaugurated the EU Film Festivals at 'Black Box Theatre' in Ulaanbaatar where he remarked that "Cinema speaks the universal language. European Cinema is the image of Europe—an image worth cherishing, developing and promoting". He hoped that Mongolian movies events will be organized on the eve of 25th anniversary of EU-Mongolian diplomatic relations in Brussels in 2014.[6] At the same time, the European Commissioner for Education, Culture, Multilingualism and Youth Affairs officially inaugurated "History of Europe" Art Exhibition on 9 September 2014 in Ulaanbaatar.[7] Four EU member countries which have embassies in Mongolia include the Czech Republic, France, Germany and the United Kingdom. The others are accredited from Beijing including the EU's delegation which has a liaison officer based in the Mongolian Ulaanbaatar.

Mongolia's Third Neighbour Policy and its European Framework

Mongolia shifted its legacy of satellite foreign policy of dependence on Moscow to an independent, non-aligned, multi-pillar and open foreign policy after the Soviet collapse.[8] The framework of national security and new approach of foreign policy laid the foundation of third neighbor policy in Mongolia's international relations. It is Mongolia's virtual notion of neighbour than real neighbour for multi-alignment along the idea of realism in international relations. The third neighbour policy is part of the 'preventive diplomacy' for the projected solution of the future disputes with its two powerful neighbours. It is in the framework of Mongolia's geopolitical realities with the spirit of original definition of 'preventive diplomacy' that was given by former UN Secretary General Boutros Boutros Ghali in his 'Agenda for Peace' in 1992.[9] The third neighbour framework of Mongolia's foreign policy favours stronger bilateral relations for building blocks for effective regional and global multilateralism in international relations. This is a new path of search for alternatives in the democratic world and is based on the lessons learned from the Chinese and Russian authoritarian influences in the past. This is the paradigm shift in the liberal democratic Mongolia in the post-Cold War era. The former Mongolian President Enkhbayar once remarked that Mongolia's multi-pillar foreign policy, particularly the third neighbour policy, is the outcome of its strategic concerns that it should not be isolated.[10]

In addition, Mongolia adopted the third neighbour policy in a bid to escape the hard geographical reality as it is surrounded by the two great powers—China and Russia. This geographical position has some constraints also. It is economically still isolated from the international economic cooperation because of its landlocked position which makes it dependent on the two neighbours for its development. Economic security requires the fast economic cooperation with global economy. In search of new allies Mongolia seeks a comprehensive bilateral cooperation with the third neighbours, mainly the EU and its member states, US, Japan, and India among others. The strategic condition of Mongolia in the Eurasian continent presents the security dilemma with no easy solution in the age of globalization of global politics. The Mongolian government prefers third neighbour policy framework to attract more foreign direct investments (FDI) from the U.S., Japan, South Korea and EU in large mineral deposits, energy sector and other sectors of economy. On its part, Mongolia can be the gateway to the North East economy for the EU as it is the land locked bridge between North East Asia and Central Asia. Mongolia's importance also lies into the fact that it is close to the fertile Tumen River Delta and has links with Korean Peninsula. Obviously, Mongolia's third neighbour diplomacy tilts towards trademark of liberal democracy and neo liberalism in the age of economic globalization of the 21st century.

Economic Cooperation

Economic security has become one of the important determinants of the Mongolian foreign policy after 2008. The new coalition government replaced the 'Ministry of Foreign Affairs' with a new 'Ministry of Foreign Affairs and Trade' in 2008. This was an indication of a new paradigm shift in the existing foreign economic policy which turned into a growth-oriented economic policy with a focus on attracting foreign investments in the mineral sector. Mongolian economy is one of the fast emerging economies in the North East Asia. It represents the 'transitional economies' in the world economy. Mongolia and the EU signed a "Trade and Cooperation Agreement" in 1993 to be renewed regularly. The main objectives of this treaty was the enhancement of trade and economic relations including protection of human rights and high level meetings between Brussels and Ulaanbaatar each and every year since its ratification. Mongolia has a vast deposit of natural resources—silver, copper, coal, molybdenum, tin, lead, zinc, molybdenum, tungsten iron, phosphate, gold, uranium, zeolite, rare earth metals, ferrous metals, precious and semi-precious stones etc. for industrial productions.

The natural resources of Mongolia constitute an important factor to attract the EU's FDI investments. Mining accounted for 20 percent of Mongolia's GDP in April 2014, which is twice the ratio of what used to be a decade ago.[11] The economic growth rate was 12.5 percent in 2013 as compared to 6.4 percent in 2010, and it is expected to grow at a double digit growth rate over the period 2013-17.[12] Though the Mongolian economy is still dominated by its two neighbours—Russia and China, the European Union is the third largest trading partner of Mongolia. The total trade between Mongolia and the EU was EUR 184.3 million in 2009 including Mongolian exports to the EU of EUR 44.9 million and EU exports to Mongolia of EUR 139.4 million. Today the EU has a share of 8.1 per cent of the total foreign trade of Mongolia (China—43.3 per cent and Russia—23.2 per cent) with a total volume of 446 million euros. In 2012, Mongolia's export to EU was 28 million while import from EU was 418 million euro. The EU is also one of the largest investors in Mongolia since 1990. Till first half of 2012 there were registered 3.9 billion US dollars worth investment of 738 companies from 25 member states of the EU.[13] Earlier, Mongolia was also eligible for the Specific General Preferential Scheme (GSP+) for sustainable development in order to increase export volume to the EU since 2006.[14] While the main exports from Mongolia to EU are consisted of cashmere, wool and related products, the EU exports to Mongolia mainly include machinery and transport equipment, chemicals and related products.

Mongolia joined WTO in 1997 for the greater global economic cooperation, and it is credited with becoming the first among the TACIS countries, who integrated with the global trade. Mongolia also signed the "Most Favoured Nation" (MFN) Status Agreement with the European Union,[15] which in 2011included Mongolia in the list of beneficiaries of EU's Generalized Scheme of Preferences (GSP).[16] This is as per the recommendation of UNCTAD for the developing countries' products to enter easily in the European market. Today Mongolia has an ambitious trade agenda with the goal of diversifying and enhancing its exports. The EU gives its support to Mongolia's efforts of creating a sustainable environment for business, policies targeting at product diversification, and the improvement of product quality. This would help increase Mongolian exports, increase the value added of its goods, and at the same time would make Mongolian products more competitive in the domestic market.[17]

Globalisation has become a bridge for regional and global economic integration through trade, foreign direct investment etc. The positive, critical and negative attitudes of globalization have vital impact on Mongolia's agriculture and food economic policy and its cooperation with global players specially the EU and its member states. Mongolia has adopted the path of global strategic alliance with EU's corporate world in the field of food security and agriculture cooperation. This is the extensive cooperation within a long term strategy in order to achieve optimum cooperation. The European Union and Mongolia have taken greater initiatives for mutual benefits by cooperating in the fields of sustainable agriculture, food security and rural development. The two sides have inked a bilateral agreement for agriculture and rural development under "EU-Mongolia Partnership and Cooperation Agreement" signed in April 2013.[18]

Mutual Understanding on Energy and Environmental Issues

Energy conservation, sustainable development and environmental protection are the principal agendas of Mongolian strategy for economic development. Therefore, Mongolia has developed the institutional framework for foreign investment and finances for clean development mechanism under many international obligations and ratifications. It ratified the Energy Charter Treaty (ECT) and the Protocol for Energy Efficiency and Related Environmental Aspects (PEEREA) in 1999. Mongolia has also stake in regional economic cooperation. Development of energy infrastructure system and construction of expanded crude oil pipeline in the East, Far East and Mongolia is the primary component of the Tumen River Economic Zone. This will be an effective market for Mongolia's untapped natural and energy resources. In addition, Mongolia also seeks to use North Korea's port of Rajin as conduit to export its energy resources to European market. Mongolia has initiated an energy efficiency programme with international support and multilateral cooperation from the EU and its member states especially Germany and Norway as well as UNDP, World Bank, ADB, USAID, Japan International Cooperation Agency (JICA) and other financial co-partners.

Development of North East Asian Railway and Energy network projects is being considered by Mongolia as a milestone for the future integrated growth and development in the region. Mongolia also pursues possibility of sea access on the Korean Peninsula via China's north eastern provinces. Strategically, the most important factor in Mongolia-EU relations is the development of regional and international highway and railway links between Korean Peninsula and Europe, which will be a direct link between the two sides. Presently, Mongolia is totally depending on China's major northeastern port of Tianjin. Mongolia has also the potential to become a land bridge between European and Asian markets through transportation links. A strong transportation link system in the region can connect North East Asia to natural resources rich

Central Asia and Russia, fast emerging economy China and India to the developed countries like Japan and Republic of Korea.

The EU is a global leader in the sustainable development, promotion of democracy, climate change, non proliferation, energy security, biodiversity and other influential aspects of liberal model of governance around the world. Mongolia has learnt a lot from the experiences of the EU. Till date the parliament of Mongolia has ratified several programmes regarding climate change, bio-diversity, protection of ozone layer, safety of environment and its related concerns. It implemented National Environment Action Plan since 1995 besides accepting the United Nations Framework Convention on Climate Change (UNFCC) in 1996, Kyoto Protocol in 1999, Copenhagen Accord in 2010. The EU is providing administrative and financial support for implementation of environmental protection programmes in Mongolia and North East Asia. All multilateral comprehensive and strategic cooperation of environmental concerns may, in the future, be a reason for comprehensive partnership between Mongolia and the EU as well as North East Asia and the EU where EU's Baltic Sea Region Initiatives will be a model.[19]

Mongolia-NATO Partnership

Mongolia has become a reliable ally in NATO led global war against terrorism and global peace keeping operations. This was for the first time that Mongolia thought of global cooperation beyond Russia and China in international crisis. Mongolia's revised Concept of National Security (2010) and Concept of Foreign Policy (2011) framed guidelines for more active support in international peace keeping operations and military exercises with the US, NATO, EU and individual European states as well as with the countries of Asia Pacific region. The National Security Concept also expresses the similar strategic views on Mongolian national security interests including active and responsible player in North East Asia regional security and Korean Peace process.

Mongolia is part of the NATO's 'partner across the globe'.[20] It is the product of the NATO led International Security Assistance Force (ISAF) in Afghanistan. Mongolia signed the Individual Partnership and Cooperation Agreement (IPCP) with NATO in March 2012. This was the substantial change in the NATO's policy framework for partnership because Mongolia had been seeking partnership with NATO since 1992. It became possible as Mongolia began its military and defence interaction with NATO's European allies including Belgium, Britain, Netherland, Luxemburg, Turkey, Poland

and Bulgaria since 2000 onwards. It has also institutionalized its relations with the EU member states like Germany, Belgium, France, Poland, Turkey and Luxemburg. Mongolia has also enhanced its peacekeeping cooperation with NATO in Afghanistan, Kosovo and Iraq. In all 1200 Mongolian peacekeeping forces have been working as part of Polish Contingent in Iraq since 2003. More than 1100 Mongolian forces plus 400 civil personnel are actively engaged with US, Germany and Belgium along with NATO forces in Afghanistan since 2001. In the past decade, exchanges of high level defence personnel between NATO headquarters and Ulaanbaatar have also increased. Mongolia has now started cooperation with NATO in new areas like consultation, training, military modernization and reforms.

Conclusion

Mongolia pursues an open, non-aligned and independent foreign policy along with national interests in the era of globalization. The EU holds significant place in Mongolia's foreign policy today. Significantly, Mongolia and the EU have celebrated '2014' as special year of 25th anniversary of their diplomatic relations. Although the EU is the third largest trade partner of Mongolia, the mineral sector still constitutes the potential source of economic and trade cooperation between the two sides. Pursuing the third neighbour policy towards the EU and its member states is paying dividend for enhancement of Mongolia's bilateral and multilateral economic, security and defence cooperation. Since North East Asia has become a fertile ground of multilateral security mechanism in the global politics now, the EU needs Mongolia's cooperation to have its active presence in this region.

Moreover, in 2001, the EU drafted its first Mongolia-EU Strategy Paper (2002-2006), which was a policy framework for bilateral and multilateral initiatives. Another Mongolia-EU Strategy Paper (2007-2013) was launched in 2007 which worked properly in strengthening the relations between the two sides. Besides, Mongolia joined the Asia Europe meeting (ASEM) process in 2006, which was another milestone for further enhancement of Mongolia-EU cooperation. Mongolia and the EU are also committed to the global initiatives for non-proliferation of weapons of mass destruction and global peace cooperation in the 21st century. In this regard, Mongolia-NATO partnership has potential to develop cooperation between Mongolia and the European Union and its member states. Since Mongolia has constantly expressed its interest in promoting its relations with the EU and in going beyond the current focus on traditional development cooperation, the EU has responded positively. However, systematic dialogue within the framework of the EU-Mongolia Joint Committee and a stronger involvement of civil society can contribute to the creation of positive conditions for development and growth of cooperative partnership between Mongolia and the European Union.

Notes and References

1. See *Mongolia-European Community Strategy Paper (2007-2013)*, 23 February 2007, at https://ec.europa.eu/europeaid/sites/devco/files/csp-mongolia-2007-2013_en.pdf (accessed on 24 May 2014).
2. The Community of Democracies is a global intergovernmental coalition of states, founded in 2000 to bring together governments, civil society and the private sector in the pursuit of a common goal of supporting democratic rules and strengthening democratic norms and institutions around the world. See Sharad K Soni (2013),"Evaluating Mongolia's Experience of Democratization: The Post-Soviet Scenario", *The Mongol Journal of International Affairs* (Ulaanbaatar), vol.18, 2013, p.30.
3. European Commission (2013), "Building EU-Mongolia Relations on Agriculture and Rural Development", Press Release, Brussels, 18 July, at http://europa.eu/rapid/press-release_IP-13-714_en.htm (accessed on 16 December 2013).
4. "EU Relations with Mongolia", at http://eeas.europa.eu/mongolia/index_en.htm (accessed on 18 January 2014).
5. European Commission (2013), "EU-Mongolia. Third neighbour and first class partner", Speech by José Manuel Durão Barroso, President of the European Commission, 17 November, at http://europa.eu/rapid/press-release_SPEECH-13-937_en.htm (accessed on 18 January 2014).
6. Ibid.
7. "EU to host 'History of Europe' Art Exhibition in Ulan Bator, September 9-27", 3 November 2014, at http://ec.europa.eu/commission_2010-2014/vassiliou/headlines/news/2014/09/20140809-history_en.htm (accessed on 19 December 2014).
8. Sharad K Soni (2015), "The 'Third Neighbour' Approach of Mongolia's Diplomacy of External Relations: Effects on Relations between India and Mongolia", India Quarterly, vol. 71, no.1, p.38.
9. Li Narangoa (2009), "Mongolia and Preventive Diplomacy, Haunted by History and Becoming Cosmopolitan," *Asian Survey*, vol. 49, no. 2,.
10. Ibid.
11. The World Bank, "Mongolia: Overview", at http://www.worldbank.org/en/country/mongolia/overview (accessed on 24 September 2014).
12. Soni, "Evaluating Mongolia's Experience of Democratization", p.31.
13. "Mongolia and the European Union: Hand in Hand to a New Heights", Posted by Khishigdelger Davaadorj, Ambassador of Mongolia to the EU, 1 November 2013, at http://eptoday.com/mongolia-and-the-eropean-union-hand-in-hand-to-a-new-heights/ (accessed on 24 June 2014).
14. "EU-Mongolia Trade", at http://www.eeas.europa.eu/delegations/mongolia/eu_mongolia/trade_relation/index_en.htm (accessed on 24 June 2014).

15. World Bank, "Mongolia Trade Brief", at http://info.worldbank.org/etools/wti/docs/wti2008/brief129.pdf (accessed at 6 June 2014).
16. European Commission, "The EU's New Generalised Scheme of Preferences (GSP)", at http://trade.ec.europa.eu/doclib/docs/2012/december/tradoc_150164.pdf (accessed on 6 June 2014).
17. See "EU-Mongolia Trade".
18. European Commission, "Building EU-Mongolia Relations on Agriculture and Rural Development".
19. Sangsoo lee and Silivia Pastorelli (2013), "Promoting North East Asia Environmental cooperation: Reflection from EU", 30 June, at http://www.e-ir.info/2013/06/30/promoting-northeast-asian-environmental-cooperation-reflections-from-the-eu/ (accessed 7 June 2014).
20. The term 'global partner' and 'global partnership' are referred to as 'Contact Countries'. See Trine Flockhart (2014), "Cooperative Security: NATO Partnership Policy in Changing World", Copenhagen: DIIS Report.

CHAPTER 18

Mongolia-Xinjiang Linkages

Mahesh Ranjan Debata

Geographically, Mongolia's 4,674 km southern border with the People's Republic of China (PRC) parallels the Mongol Altai mountains south-eastwards and then slopes into the Junggarian basin and south of the Gobi Altai range before winding its way through the Gobi semi-desert towards the country's lowest-lying areas around Lake Buir. At its nearest point, the Zamyn-Uud/Erlien rail and road crossing, Mongolia's border is at a distance of about 675 km from the Chinese port of Tianjin on the Yellow Sea coast. In the west, Mongolia is separated from China's northwestern province of Xinjiang Uyghur Autonomous Region (XUAR) by the Altai Mountains and the Junggarian desert. The boundary line between Xinjiang and Mongolia is 1,416 km long, which was delimited in 1982-84. Three Mongolian provinces of Gobi Altai, Hovd and Bayan-Uul border on Xinjiang. Between China and Mongolia there are nine border crossings: five in Inner Mongolia Autonomous Region and four in Xinjiang. While the largest, and most utilised, is the Erlian/Zamin Uud crossing on the Beijing-Ulaanbaatar rail line, the other eight are equally important in view of small-scale trade and business.[1] In June 1991, Mongolia and China opened border crossing points for local traffic.[2] Earlier, in October 1989, the "Treaty on Border System and the Solution to Border Problems" between the two neighbours was approved by both the sides. This is the first border system treaty China signed with a neighbouring country.

In 1993, after both countries agreed, four land ports along the Xinjiang-

Mongolia border such as Laoyemiao of Hami Administrative Offices, Ulastay of Changji Hui Autonomous Prefecture, Takeshiken and Hongshanzui of Altay Administrative Offices were opened.[3] Laoyemiaois some 308 km north of Hami/Burgastai in Gobi-Altay province and the closest major city in Mongolia is Altay. Takeshikenis at a distance of 90 km from Qinghe, 380 km from Aertai/Bulgan, and in Khovd, the nearest city is Dund-Us. Ulastay/Baidag is near Bulgan district in Khovd. Hongshanzui is 240 km from Fuhai, 192 km from Aertai/Dayan, Zengel district in Bayan Olgii, 180 km from the capital city of Olgii. Of the above four border crossings, the port of Bulgan-Tarkshken is the most active, perhaps one of the most important trade conduits between Mongolia and China. This port, opened in July 1989, has an annual handling capacity of 50,000 tons of cargo and 30,000 passengers. A seasonal port, it remains opened from April to December each year. However, Mongolia and China are planning to make the Bulgan-Tarkshken port open for transportation all year around. The border crossing at Bulgansumin Mongolia's Hovd province links China's Qinghe County and Xinjiang's capital Urumqi by an international bus service. The port is located at the top of the western part of the Mongolian transport network, covering the nearby provinces of Bayan Olgii, Khovd, Uvs, Govi-Altai and Zavkhan in Mongolia, and reaching the farther central and western part of Mongolia, in particular the ancient city of Khovd, an important economic and cultural center of western Mongolia.[4] With this Mongolia-Xinjiang linkages have been witnessing warmth in terms of exchanges of people as well as goods.

Against this backdrop, this paper discusses the historical, cultural, trade and border linkages between Mongolia and China's Xinjiang region. While making a historical outline of the relations between the two regions, this paper delineates how the exchanges between western Mongolia and Xinjiang have become more frequent in recent years with increasingly close cooperation in the economic, cultural and non-governmental sectors. Even high profile visits by the political leadership of both the sides have been a common phenomenon, which aims at boosting the relationship between the two regions now and in the near future, the paper adds.

Historical Linkages

The historic-cultural linkage between Mongolia and Xinjiang is age old. According to famous sinologist Owen Lattimore, "there is a great historical similarity between Mongolia and Xinjiang."[5] The Mongols seem to have enjoyed a much more glorious past in comparison to the Uyghurs, who originated in the steppes of modern-day Mongolia and then migrated to the oasis regions in the Tarim Basin between seventh and ninth centuries. In the 7th century AD, Uyghur empire was set up in Mongolia and continued until the end of 9th century AD. After Chinggis Khan had unified Mongolia and began his westward expansion, the Uyghur kingdom in the Turpan-Urumqi area offered its allegiance to the Mongols in 1209 AD, contributing taxes and troops to the Mongol ruler through the tribute system.[6] In return, the Uyghur rulers retained control of their kingdom.

Chinggis Khan's grandson Kublai Khan established the Yuan Dynasty in China in the thirteenth century. During the Mongol rule under the Yuan dynasty, Xinjiang became a part of the Chagatai Khanate. After the break-up of the Chagatai Khanate into smaller khanates in the mid-14th century, the region was ruled by various Persianized Mongol Khans simultaneously, including the ones of Mogholistan (with the assistance of the local Dughlat Emirs), Uygurstan (later Turpan) and Kashgaria. Later, in the 17th century, the Mongolian Junggars established an empire in the region. The Mongolian Junggar is the collective identity of several Oirat tribes that formed and maintained one of the last nomadic empires. The Junggar Khanate covered the area called Junggaria and stretched from the west end of the Great Wall of China to present-day eastern Kazakhstan, and from present-day northern Kyrgyzstan to southern Siberia. Most of this area was renamed as Xinjiang after the fall of the Junggar empire in the 18th century.

During the Qing rule (1644–1911), the Mongols were also in close alliance with the ruling Manchu Court. The other part of historical Mongolia, Outer Mongolia, seized the opportunity of the Qing dynasty's collapse in the year 1911 to proclaim itself an independent country, later named as the Mongolian People's Republic, and now simply Mongolia. Also, in the 1930s and 1940s, Mongol Prince Demchugdungrub (Prince De) set up a series of Inner Mongolian autonomous governments with support from Japan.[7] In the 1940s, uprisings took place in three districts of Xinjiang. Usman Batur, the leader of the uprising in the Altai district, established communications with Outer Mongolia (the present day Mongolia), exchanging livestock for weapons. Outer Mongolia provided Usman Batur with military consultants, weapons, ammunition, training and guerrillas. The uprising occurred in the areas of the Qinghe and Bulgan rivers along the Xinjiang-Mongolia border. Supported by the former Soviet Union, the uprising eventually led to the establishment of the Provisional Government of East Turkistan or otherwise known as Turkic Islamic Republic of East Turkestan (TIRET) on 12 November 1944. The

Republic of China recognized Mongolia on 6 January 1946 and established diplomatic relations the very next month in February 1946.

Mongols on both sides of the Border

The Mongols in Xinjiang are descendants of the ancient Oirat Mongols.[8] They moved to the north of the Tianshan Mountains as a consequence of Chinggis Khan's western expedition in the early 13th century. In the early 15th century, the Mongolian community fell into the Woyela and Eastern Tartar groups. The Woyelas living north to the Gobi Desert included the tribes of Turgut, Durbet, Heshuot and Dzungar. These tribes were called Oleuth or Oirad by the Qing Dynasty (1644-1911). They were nomadic herds-people living in the area from northern Xinjiang to southeast of Lake Balkhash. The Qing dynasty put down the rebellions of Junggar Mongol ruling groups in Ili and arranged the local Oirats on the basis of the Manchu Eight-Banner system, a unique Manchu system of social and military organization that was instrumental in the conquest of the Mings.[9] In 1771, the Turgut tribes, who had moved centuries before into the lower reaches of the Volga River and had a population of over 100,000, returned to China. In 1764 and 1813, the Qing government moved part of the Chahar Mongolian community to Xinjiang and now their descendants mainly live in Bole and Wenquan counties in Bortala Mongolian Autonomous prefecture.[10]

Kharakhoto, the great Mongol city in the middle of the Gobi desert, was abandoned forever when the Yuan dynasty collapsed at the end of the 14th century. There was also the evidence from further west, where the traces of export porcelain have been found in the city of Samarkand in Uzbekistan and also in Kyrgyzstan. It seemed it only remained to fill in the gap-a mere thousand miles from Kharakhoto along the northernmost branch of the fabled Silk Route, through Hami, Turfan and Urumqi to Almalik, which was the ancient capital of the Chagatai khanate known today as Huocheng.[11] Almalik has so far proved elusive, though there is no doubt of its historical importance. Chaghatai, one of Ghengis Khan's four sons, established the khanate bearing his name, covering most of western Xinjiang and reaching as far as Khorosan.[12] The largest non-Mongol ethnic group in Mongolia is formed by the Kazakhs, a Turkic tribe which accounted for some six per cent of the population as per the last census. About 100,000 Kazakhs live in Bayan-Olgii province *(aymag)* in western Mongolia, forming 80 per cent of the local population, and another 30,000 in neighbouring Hovd province. The Kazakhs migrated into Mongolia from Xinjiang towards the end of the 20th century.[13]

Mongols in Xinjiang

In the PRC, there are some 5.5 million Mongols, including 3.4 million in Inner Mongolia AR, where they account for only 14 per cent of the overwhelmingly Han population. Mongolian minority tribes are to be found in Xinjiang Uyghur Autonomous Region—in Bayangolin and Bortala Mongolian autonomous prefectures and Hoboksar Mongolian autonomous county as well as Mongolian autonomous counties in the provinces of Jilin (Qian Gorlos), Heilongjiang (Durbet), Liaoning (Fuxin and Harqin Left Wing), Gansu (Subei) and Qinghai (Henan and Haixi), and in five more provinces.[14] Some Mongolians also live in Ili, Changji, Hami and Urumqi. After the communist takeover of China in 1949, the Mongols were enlisted as one of the 55 minority groups living in China and have been concentrated in the northern part of Xinjiang. According to Chinese census 2010, population of Mongol people in Xinjiang stands at 200,000, roughly 0.85 per cent of Xinjiang's total population.[15] They are divided into three main tribes: The Junggar tribe who has been living in Xinjiang for many centuries, the Turgut who came back from the Volga River or Kalmykia at the end of the eighteenth century, and the Chahar tribe who moved from Inner Mongolia and Hebei province. The languages used by Mongolians in Xinjiang belong to the Mongolian Altaic family, which is similar to the language used in Inner Mongolia. They use Todo Mongolian as their written language which is different from quduma Mongolian used by Inner Mongols as their written language.[16]

Mongols in Xinjiang

Year	Number of Mongols	Percentage
1982	117,510	3.44 %
1990	137,740	2.87 %
2000	149,857	0.8%
2010	179,615	0.8%

Uyghurs in Mongolia

As per the 2010 census, the total number of Uyghurs in Mongolia stands at 300, who are settled in the Hovsgol *Aimag* in the northern region of Mongolia. There has been a language affinity between the people of Xinjiang and Mongolia. Xinjiang's Mongolians speak the Oirat dialect of the Mongolian language, which belongs to the Altaic language family. Both the Tuote and Hangul scripts are accepted as its written forms, with the latter more commonly used in Xinjiang. The Mongolian script used presently comes from the Uyghur script of the 13th century, which has been reoriented by the Mongolians many times and became the modern Mongolian script. As regards religious affinity, Mongols in Xinjiang believed in Shamanism in ancient times. The red sect of Lamaism began to find its followers among the Mongol rulers in the 13th century. In the 16th century, many feudal tribe heads as well as herdsmen shifted to the yellow sect, but Shamanism still finds its traces in Mongolian tradition.[17]

Cooperation in Modern and Contemporary Times

The cooperation between Mongolia and Xinjiang has developed in modern and contemporary times as a result of ever growing relations between Mongolia and China. Exchanges between western Mongolia and China's Xinjiang Uyghur Autonomous Region have become more frequent in recent years with increasingly close cooperation in the political economic, energy, cultural and non-governmental sectors.

Political

High profile visits of leaders of both the sides have been a common phenomenon, which aim at boosting the relationship between the two regions. For example, Mongolian Prime Minister Miegombyn Enkhbold visited Urumqi, the capital city of Xinjiang as part of his tour to China from 22 to 27 November 2006.[18] In September 2007, the first session of talks attended by Mongolia and the working group of Xinjiang Uyghur Autonomous Region was held in Urumqi. Agreements were reached on constructing a cooperation mechanism to promote local cooperation, develop fraternal links at county level and directly cooperate on local offices of the Exit-Entry Administration and legal institutions, etc.

The most recent visit to Xinjiang has been undertaken by Mongolia's Foreign Minister L. Bold on 18-19 January 2014. He visited the new free trade zone at Khorgos[19] and discussed feasibility for increasing regional economic and trade turnover and promoting people-to-people contact. Officials from Khovd province of Mongolia have also accompanied him and put forward proposals on the stimulation of bilateral activities at border checkpoints and relaxing strict rules and regulations. Bold also visited a coal-gasification plant in Yining city where Qinghua group has invested in addition to the Urumqi based Tian Run Company which has investment from Mongolia's Khas Bank (Xac Bank).[20]

Economic

Both the countries understand that developing cooperation at the border areas of the two countries plays an important role in widening bilateral trade and economic cooperation. Mongolia has been paying great attention to strengthen its relations with the border areas and autonomous regions of China. Keeping this in mind, Mongolian Prime Minister Batbold Sukhbaataraired Ulan Baatar's intention in 2010 to develop ties with China's Xinjiang Uygur Autonomous Region, which borders Mongolia.[21] He said this during talks with a Chinese delegation led by Arken Imirbaki, Chairman of the Standing Committee of the Xinjiang Regional People's Congress. Mongolia aims to resolve the questions concerning infrastructure, industry and services at the ports in order to boost ties with Xinjiang in developing agriculture, animal husbandry, ancillary sectors and working industries. Expressing satisfaction over strengthening of bilateral ties, Imirbaki said that the Xinjiang region is ready to develop together with Mongolia.[22]

For China, Mongolia is one of the main destination countries for its exports and an important source country for imports. Since 2004, the Chinese government has identified Mongolia as a priority nation for investment and trade in its "Guidance Catalogue on Countries and Industries for Overseas Development".[23] This classification makes Mongolia a target state in China's "go out policy".[24] Over the past two decades, Beijing has seriously pushed for closer relations with Mongolia. Since 1994, Beijing has pledged non-interference in Mongolia's internal affairs, respect for Mongolian sovereignty and territorial integrity, and willingness for Mongolia to engage with other states.[25] Beijing has offered foreign direct investment (FDI) and unconditional aid to Mongolia, provided a market for Mongolian goods in China, invested in Mongolia's infrastructure, and increased Chinese exports to Mongolia.[26] Cross Border Trade has been the mainstay of cooperation between the two regions. In this process, Xinjiang has played a very significant role. While in 1998 the total value of Xinjiang's trade with Mongolia remained merely as 5.98 million US dollars in 2005, roughly 1/17th of Xinjiang's total international border trade of around 85 million US dollar, it increased sharply almost five times to 28.33 million US dollars in 2006.[27] The trade between the two regions further increased in 2008 to 36.6 million US dollars (out of Xinjiang's total trade of 12 billion US dollars with Mongolia).[28] In recent years, not only the volume of Mongolia-Xinjiang trade increased, but also the visit of Mongolian leaders to Xinjiang became a regular feature. Mongolian entrepreneurs are often present at the Urumqi Trade Fair held in Xinjiang, and are successful in securing many substantial cooperation projects. Extensive cooperation has been conducted in infrastructure construction, energy exploitation, and tourism. The importance of Xinjiang has increased as a significant region in terms of China's border trade with Mongolia.[29]

Energy

It is to be noted that China has a huge demand for energy sources which is evident from the fact that in 2009 the demand for coal reached 3 billion tons. In 2010, 146 million tons of coal were imported, a 40.9 percent increase over the previous year. According to the official statistics, Xinjiang, one of China's key energy and heavy industry bases, is estimated to be short of 1.6 million tons of charred coal required for industrial use every year.[30] In this context, China believes Mongolia as a savior and has thus worked towards currying Mongolia's favour. As a result, import of coal from Mongolia was increased and for this purpose, a six-km long track, specially built for coal transport, was completed in northwest Takeshiken, the second largest port at the China-Mongolia border.[31] The project was first proposed by Mongolia in April 2011 over fears that increased truck hauling of coal might damage trade routes. Mongolia Energy Corporation Limited undertook the project and completed it by the end of July 2011. The Takeshiken port, located in the town of Takeshiken in Xinjiang Uygur Autonomous Region, imported 5,000 tons of raw coal from Mongolia in the first three months of 2011.[32]

Mongolian Energy Commission (MEC) has acquired 19 per cent of a wholly foreign-owned Xinjiang corporation with business scope to invest in coal, copper and iron resources and through which it is working towards the setting up of joint ventures with two Chinese geological bureaus for coal resources.[33] In September 2009, Baosteel Bayi visited the site of our Khushuut coking coal mine via the Khushuut Road. This visit led to around 200 tonnes of bulk samples of coal being transported from the Khushuut site to the customers through the Yarant/Takeshenken border into Xinjiang, PRC. The local customs at Xinjiang made special arrangement for this historical first delivery of coal from Mongolia to Xinjiang through this border.[34]

Border Tourism

As far as cooperation in tourism is concerned, in April 2006 a seminar on tourism development and cooperation was held at the Tarkshken Port in Qinghe County of Altai in China. Several letters of intent on border tourism were signed with Bulgan County in Mongolia. These included "Programs on

Border Tourism of the Government of Qinghe County in China and the Government of Bulgan County in Mongolia", "Letter of Intent for Tourism Cooperation between the Government of Qinghe County in China and the Government of Monkhkhairkhan County in Mongolia".

The year 2009 was an important year for both the regions, which witnessed a number of agreements between the two regions. On April 19, 2009, the Altai Economic and Trade Commission and the Altai Tourism Bureau and other departments jointly pledged to develop tourism between China's Altai and western Mongolia in order to promote the import and export trade. The aim was, through the development of tourism, to create a better understanding between the two countries in the fields of the economy, politics and culture and to enhance cooperation in many other aspects. In June 2009, the Altai administrative office signed cooperation agreements on border tourism with the governments of Khovd and Bayan Olgii provinces in Mongolia. The tourism bureaus and tourist enterprises of both countries also signed detailed cooperation agreements and began to arrange one-day and two-day tours of the Xinjiang-Mongolian borders.

In September 2009, the first international border tourism festival of the Sino-Mongolian Tarkshken Yarantai port was held in Qinghe County of Xinjiang. A Memorandum of Understanding (MoU) on tourism cooperation was signed between Qinghe County of Xinjiang and Uyench County of Mongolia. Xinjiang Kanas International Travel Service Limited signed Letters of Intent with the Mongolia Bulgan Earth Travel Corporation for further cooperation on tourism. As a follow-up action, China and Mongolia collaborated on an exchange between a group of 45 people from Xinjiang Kanas International Travel Service Limited and a group of 40 people from Mongolia. The Aken Aites Culture and Art Festival involved more than ten thousand people. The tourism sector in Xinjiang was hit hard in 2014 because of terrorist attacks, but has started recovering in 2015 as the situation has improved and become more stable.[35] Xinjiang Tourism Bureau's plans to develop cooperation with neighbouring countries including Mongolia will boost employment and bring extra income to the locals in Xinjiang as the regional government believes employment is key to keep Xinjiang stabilize.[36]

Cultural and Academic Cooperation

In addition to trade and tourism, there have also been great developments in cultural and academic cooperation between Xinjiang and Mongolia. In 2006, the Academia Turpanica sent professionals to Mongolia, thus opening up a new chapter in joint studies on Uyghur heritage. In November 2006, a photographic exhibition of Mongolian scenery and customs was held in the Xinjiang International Museum. The 47 photographic works exhibited not only showed Mongolia's picturesque natural landscape, its splendid cultural tradition, streets, pastures and markets, but also showed the lives of the hard-working Mongolian people. This exhibition presented a picture of a prosperous Mongolia, which greatly impressed people of all ethnic groups in Xinjiang and played a positive role in promoting the mutual understanding and friendship of the Chinese and Mongolian people. In 2007, the Academia Turpanica once again sent professionals to Mongolia and reached an agreement on an annual exchange of visiting scholars. From 2007, China and Mongolia would exchange one scholar each year to facilitate the joint exploration of archaeological sites and artifacts. As part of Xinjiang-Mongolian cooperation, International Institute for the Study of Nomadic Civilizations in Mongolia signed an agreement in March 2008 at Turpanto do research on Uyghur cultural heritage for a period of 3 years. The aim of this agreement is to conduct initial research into archaeological discoveries relating to Uyghur heritage by selecting archeological sites in Mongolia and Xinjiang for investigation, inspection, excavation and research using agreed methods of archaeological research. Academic exchange of such type will contribute to clearing up differences of opinion and misunderstandings between academic circles in the two countries.[37] Owing to the increasingly frequent exchange and cooperation in recent years, Mongolia wishes to establish a Mongolian consulate in Urumqi, something which is still under discussion. Mongolia has also suggested setting up a Mongolian trading agency or local trading office in Urumqi.

Conclusion

Despite all the above information about Mongolia-Xinjiang cooperation, cross border trade between the two regions is much below than Xinjiang's border trade with Central Asian countries. It is, therefore, imperative that the two countries promote more meaningful cooperation between local governments and exchange information between legislative institutions in order to establish a workable and efficient mechanism for cooperation in trade and economy. Despite there being four crossings between Xinjiang and western Mongolia, there is not a consulate in Xinjiang to issue visas to Chinese who want to travel to Mongolia for business. Nor is there a consulate in western Mongolia able to issue Chinese visas to Mongolians.[38]

Other issue which bears immense significance is the present and future security situation in the Xinjiang region, which will be a focal point in the relationship between Xinjiang and Mongolia in particular and China and Mongolia in general. Mongolia is not a target for terrorists and no terrorist attacks to date have taken place on Mongolian territory. Even the Mongolian border with Xinjiang is relatively peaceful of all the borders of the eight countries neighbouring Xinjiang. However, given the terrorist situation in Central Asia and China's Xinjiang Uyghur Autonomous Region, Mongolia may not be free from the terrorist threat. Though terrorist activities in Xinjiang have been effectively controlled by the Chinese government, half a dozen of violent terrorist attacks in Xinjiang in the recent past are a clear warning to Mongolia. It is very important for provinces in western Mongolia and China's Xinjiang Uyghur Autonomous Region to cooperate in the security field and intensify border inspection, supervision and exchange of information.

Notes and References

1. Jeffrey Reeves (2011), "Resources, Sovereignty, and Governance: Can Mongolia Avoid the 'Resource Curse'?", *Asian Journal of Political Science*, vol. 19, no. 2, p.176.
2. Alan Sanders (1997), "Mongolia: Looking to the Sea", *Geopolitics and International Boundaries*, vol. 2, no.1, pp. 134 & 148.
3. "The Facts and Figures on Xinjiang, China 2013", China Continental Press, 2013, p.19.
4. Mongolia Energy Cooperation, "Energy Resource Developer", at http://www.mongolia-energy.com/website/MEC/web/coal.php 2014 (accessed on 11 January 2015)
5. Owen Lattimore (1930), "Political Conditions in Mongolia and Chinese Turkestan", *The Annals of the American Academy of Political and Social Science,* vol. 152, p. 318.
6. Tribute system was a mission bearing gifts from China's less powerful neighbour to the Chinese capital, which the Chinese emperor chose to regard as a symbol of a subject-ruler relationship. For more details, see Mahesh Ranjan Debata (2007), *China's Minorities: Ethnic-Religious Separatism in Xinjiang*, New Delhi: Pentagon, pp. 47 & 71.
7. Enze Han (2011),"From Domestic to International: The Politics of Ethnic Identity in Xinjiang and Inner Mongolia", *Nationalities Papers: The Journal of Nationalism and Ethnicity*, vol. 39, no. 6, p. 94.
8. Sharad K Soni (2014), The Mongols of Xinjiang: A Retrospective Overview", *Mongolica*, vol. 47, p.141.
9. For more details, see Mark C. Elliot (2002), *The Manchu Way: The Eight Banners and Ethnic Identity in Late Imperial China*, Stanford: Stanford University Press, pp. 1-10.
10. Ding Xiaolun, ed. (2006), "Entering Xinjiang", Silk Road Book Series, Youlin Tourism Publishing House of China & Xinjiang Fine Arts and Photography Publishing House, p. 162; Soni, "The Mongols of Xinjiang", p.142.
11. John Carswell (2001),"Westward from Mongolia: new research in the Taklamakan", *Asian Affairs*, vol. 32, no. 2, p. 157.
12. Ibid, p. 171.
13. Alan Sanders, "Mongolia: Looking to the Sea", p. 137.

14. Ibid, pp.137-138.
15. "The Facts and Figures on Xinjiang, China 2013", p. 31.
16. Ibid, p. 35.
17. Xiaolun, *Entering Xinjiang*, pp. 162-163.
18. "China-Mongolia trade hits 1.13 billion USD in first Nine Months", at http://english.people.com.cn//200611/22/eng20061122_323936.html (accessed on 3 November 2014)
19. The 528-hectare Khorgos International Center for Boundary Cooperation (ICBC) officially opened on a windswept patch of the Chinese-Kazakh border in December 2011. It was designed as a visa-free zone where citizens of the two countries could trade and enjoy local entertainment. For details, see David Trilling, "On China-Kazakhstan Border Lies a Lopsided Free-Trade Zone", 5 September 2014, http://www.eurasianet.org/node/69856 (accessed on 10 October 2014)
20. "Foreign Minister L. Bold visits the Xinjiang Uyghur Autonomous Region, China", at http://www.infomongolia.com/ct/ci/7317 (accessed on 30 October 2014)
21. "Mongolia, China's Xinjiang region vow to boost ties", 16 July 2010, at http://en.people.cn/90001/90776/90883/7069889.html(accessed on 21 June 2014)
22. Ibid.
23. See Chinese Ministry of Commerce and Foreign Affairs, 2011.
24. For details, see Karl P. Sauvant & Victor Zitian Chen (2014), "China's Regulatory Framework for Outward Foreign Direct Investment", *China Economic Journal*, vol. 7, no. 1, pp. 141-163
25. Sharad K Soni (2007), "Towards Confidence Building: Sino-Mongolian Relations in the Post-Cold War Era", Asian Scholar, E-Journal, Issue No. 3, p.3, at http://www.asianscholarship.org/asf/ejourn/articles/Sharad%20K%20Soni2.pdf (accessed on 10 June 2015).
26. Jeffrey Reeves, *Central Asian Survey*, pp. 175-176.
27. Soni, "Towards Confidence Building", p.11.
28. *People's Daily Online*, "Xinjiang imports coal from Mongolia", 21 October 2009, at http://en.people.cn/90001/90778/90861/6790090.html (accessed on 1 June 2015)
29. Sharad K Soni (2009), "China's Periphery Policy: Implications for Sino-Mongolian Relations", *India Quarterly*, vol.65, no.3, p.258.
30. Ibid.
31. "Xinjiang port upgrades facility to transport Mongolian coal", 4 August 2011, at http://www.Chinadaily.com.cn/bizChina/2011-08/04/content_13049620.htm (accessed on 10 June 2014).
32. Ibid.
33. Mongolia Energy Cooperation, "Energy Resource Developer".
34. Ibid.
35. Cui Jia (2015), "Tourism in Xinjiang is bouncing back", 15 May 2015, at http://usa.Chinadaily.com.cn/epaper/2015-05/15/content_20725538.htm (accessed on 1 June 2015)
36. Ibid.
37. For more details, see International Institute for the Study of Nomadic Civilizations in Mongolia's homepage http://www.nomadic.mn/ (accessed on 31 December 2014)
38. Reeves, "Resources, Sovereignty, and Governance", p. 176.

CHAPTER 19

Mongolia and Kazakhstan: Developing Relations

Mukesh Kumar Mishra

The sixth meeting of Mongolia-Kazakhstan intergovernmental commission for trade, economic, scientific, cultural and technical cooperation which was held in Ulaanbaatar on May 25, 2014, discussed the prospects of cooperation between the two countries for the next two years. Both sides determined a list of actions to be executed in the investment, business, agricultural, transportation, mining, cultural and education sectors. A memorandum of understanding (MoU) between the civil aviation organizations of the two countries was also established during this intergovernmental commission meeting. As part of this MoU, it was decided to start a direct flight between Ulaanbaatar and Astana.[1] This is encouraging in terms of their growing relations in recent years, especially after Mongolia occupied an important place in Kazakhstan's foreign policy after the two sides marked the 20th anniversary of their diplomatic relations in 2012.

It may be recalled that Mongolia was one of the first countries of the world to recognize Kazakhstan's independence and sovereignty and the two countries established their diplomatic relations on January 22, 1992. The vast territory of Kazakhstan, the multi-ethnicity of population, the challenge of building communications and transport infrastructure, problem of accessibility to seas, typical in case of a landlocked country, the dangerous proximity to

Russia, China and the Islamic world and the strategic location in the centre of Eurasia are the determining factors in foreign policy of Kazakhstan. Moreover, Kazakhstan's geographical position of being at the centre of Eurasia puts her into an advantageous position for becoming a link between the East and West of Eurasia.[2] Therefore, to find its place in international community and to play the desired role in world affairs, Kazakhstan had to take into account the changing geopolitical environment in formulating its national security strategy as well as developing its foreign policy doctrine. It is in this background that this paper examines Mongolia's place in Kazakhstan's foreign policy and the state of Mongolia-Kazakhstan relations.

Foreign Policy Initiatives of Kazakhstan and Mongolia

The foreign policy initiatives taken by Kazakhstan have been aimed at creating the atmosphere of mutual confidence, regional and international cooperation and development of relations with all the countries and international organizations on the basis of equality.[3] As Such, Kazakhstan's foreign policy priorities can be identified as following:

a) Maintenance of economic, cultural and humanitarian commonness within the CIS.
b) Integration into the contemporary system of international relations and joining the UN, OSCE and other international organizations.
c) Abandoning the nuclear status of Kazakhstan, which now looked for the traditional nuclear powers the United States, Russia, Great Britain, China, and France to extend security guarantees to Kazakhstan.
d) Cooperation with the major international financial institutions-International Monetary Fund, World Bank, European Bank for Reconstruction and Development in order to attract funds for the economic reforms. .
e) Establishing the system of bilateral relations with other countries, such as the USA, EU, Islamic nations as well as with the neighbouring states of Russia, China, Uzbekistan, Kyrgyzstan, Turkmenistan, Tajikistan, and Mongolia.

Kazakhstan wanted to accomplish a delicate geopolitical balance to stand free from dependent relationships with Central Asia's main players—China, Russia and the United States. It, therefore, proclaimed a "multi-vectored" foreign policy. The "multi-vectored" foreign policy provided for "activist, multifaceted, and balanced" foreign policy to defend Kazakhstan's independence and national interests. In fact, priority was accorded to relations with Russia, China, the United States and the European Union with reiteration of Kazakhstan's commitment to the Shanghai Cooperation Organization (SCO) and the single Eurasian Economic Community (EEC). On December 26, 2014, while delivering an official briefing on the Ministry of Foreign Affairs' 2014 activities Kazakhstan's Foreign Minister Erlan Idrissov gave a broad overview of Kazakhstan's main foreign policy achievements during the past year.[4] He said that "Kazakhstan is attempting to position itself as a "Dialogue Bridge between the West and the East." This development is the result of the adoption of a new foreign policy concept for the period 2014-2020 which has been approved by Kazakhstan's President Nursultan Nazarbayev on January 29, 2014.[5] This new foreign policy concept was developed in line with the "Kazakhstan 2050" strategy announced by Nazarbayev in December 2012. One of the major goals of this strategic initiative is to ensure Kazakhstan's entry into the elite club of the world's 30 most developed countries by the turn of this century.[6]

The new foreign policy concept covers a number of fundamental objectives that include ensuring comprehensive national security, sovereignty and territorial integrity; strengthening world and regional peace and stability; supporting the central role of the United Nations in the existing global order; and diversifying Kazakhstan's economic development. Other priorities focus on the legal protection of Kazakhstani citizens abroad and the active popularization of the Kazakh culture, language and traditions through Kazakh-speaking communities in Europe, America and East Asia. As the Kazakhstani government is preparing to sign the founding treaty of the Eurasian Economic Union (EEU) to become fully operational by January 2015, Eurasian integration is increasingly viewed from Astana as a priority focus area of its diplomacy. Astana has also confirmed its attachment to the principles of multilateralism, as embodied in its active involvement in multiple regional and international organizations. At various times, Kazakhstan occupied the rotating presidency of such entities as the Commonwealth of Independent States (CIS), the Shanghai Cooperation Organization (SCO), the Organization for Security and Cooperation in Europe (OSCE) and the Islamic Cooperation Organization (ICO).

However, it should be kept in mind that although the new foreign policy concept affirms the need to adjust Kazakhstan's external act to its revised priorities for the 21st century, the country still remains committed to its traditional "multi-vector" strategy. This strategy suggests Kazakhstan's pursuit of well-balanced and mutually advantageous relations with Russia, China, the U.S. and the EU. These countries continue to be Kazakhstan's primary partners in such fields as trade, military cooperation or cultural exchanges. At the same time, Kazakhstan keeps on expanding its ties with other countries like South Korea, Japan, India and Pakistan as well as the Arab states of the Persian Gulf. In the past years, Kazakhstan's efforts to diversify its foreign policy partnerships have already resulted in the attraction of new investments and the implementation of many joint projects. Finally, Kazakhstan seeks to enhance its diplomatic relations with such countries where its presence has been limited so far, and Mongolia obviously falls into this category.

Looking at Mongolia, in terms of its state structure it is a unitary State upholding rights, freedoms and free economy. In political and geographical respects, it is a developing country in Asia, landlocked between two great powers China and Russia. Since Mongolia's foreign policy is based on its national interests as defined in its Constitution, the country's specific external and internal situation constitutes the basis for determining its foreign policy objectives, principles and priorities.[7] Mongolia's foreign policy in the political field is an important instrument for ensuring and strengthening its security. Thus its results are "measured first and foremost by how the country's security and independence interests are met and to what extent its international position has been strengthened and its prestige enhanced."[8] In developing its relations with other countries, Mongolia is "guided by universally recognized principles and norms of international law as defined in the Charter of the United Nations, including mutual respect for each other's sovereignty, territorial integrity and inviolability of frontiers, right to self-determination, non-interference in internal affairs, non-use of force, settlement of disputes by peaceful means, respect for human rights and freedoms, and equal and mutually beneficial cooperation."[9]

In its foreign policy Mongolia has committed to uphold peace, strive to avoid confrontation with other countries and pursue a multi-base policy.[10] While always championing its national interests, it respects the legitimate interests of other countries and its partners. Mongolia also stresses on not interfering in the disputes between its two neighboring countries unless the disputes affect Mongolia's national interests. It is also committed to pursue a policy of refraining from joining any military alliance or grouping, allowing the use of its territory or air space against any other country, and the stationing of foreign troops or weapons, including nuclear or any other type of mass destruction weapons in its territory. As a member of the world community Mongolia strives to make active contribution to the common cause of settling pressing regional and international issues. In doing so, it is guided primarily by its national interests, values and fundamental principles. The Concept of Mongolia's Foreign Policy clearly states that maintaining friendly relations with the neighbouring countries like Russian Federation and People's Republic of China shall be priority directions of Mongolia's foreign policy activity. The Concept paper further clarifies that Mongolia's foreign policy activity will be to develop friendly relations with countries of the former socialist community, as well as the newly independent states.[11] When developing relations with these countries, Mongolia will adopt a flexible approach, reinforcing the positive legacy of its past relations while at the same time taking into account the potential of promoting relations in conformity with the new circumstances. Mongolia essentially has the potential of promoting relations with Kazakhstan in conformity with the new circumstances.

Mongolia-Kazakhstan Bilateral Relations

Like other neighbouring countries Mongolia too has an important place in Kazakhstan's foreign policy. And there are reasons for it. The Kazakh leadership has soft attitude towards Mongolia due to the fact that ethnic Kazakhs form the single largest minority in Mongolia. According to the 2010 Census of Mongolia, they form about 4 per cent of Mongolia's total population, and live mostly in the western part of Mongolia.[12] And the western part of Mongolia is at the border of Kazakhstan, though it is not the direct border. So, one can consider the two countries as neighbours. The unique feature of the coexistence of Buddhist Mongols and Muslim Kazakhs in Mongolia is that they have never faced any ethnic related fight among themselves.

Political Relations

After the establishment of the diplomatic relations between Mongolia and Kazakhstan on January 22, 1992, the Diplomatic Mission of the Republic of Kazakhstan to Mongolia opened in May 1997 which was later converted into the full-fledged Embassy in January 2007.[13] The current Kazakh Ambassador K. Koblandin to Mongolia was appointed by the decree of the President Nazarbayev issued on April 1, 2013. On the other side, the Embassy of Mongolia to the Republic of Kazakhstan was opened in Almaty in September 1992 but it was shifted to Astana in 2010. The current Mongolian Ambassador to Kazakhstan Zh. Sukhee was appointed in July 2013. However, the formal relationship between Mongolia and Kazakhstan started when President of Kazakhstan Nursultan Nazarbayev visited Mongolia in 1993. During the visit, the two countries signed the "Agreement on Friendship and Cooperation between the Republic of Kazakhstan and Mongolia." High-level visits between Mongolia and Kazakhstan have been taking on a regular basis. Kazakhstan's deputy Prime Minister I.N. Tasmagametov visited Mongolia in July 1997 and signed several agreements on science, education and cultural cooperation with Kazakhstan.[14] In 1998, a return visit by the President of Mongolia N. Bagabandi to Kazakhstan took place. During this visit, both sides discussed the issue of those citizens of Mongolia who voluntarily went to Kazakhstan.[15] After a long gap, in 2007, Mongolian President Nambaryn Enkhbayar paid an official visit to Kazakhstan.

The very next year, on August 6-7, 2008, during an official visit of Kazakh President Nazarbayev to Mongolia he was awarded with the Order of "Erdene Ochi" ("The Precious rod"), the highest honor of Mongolia for his contribution to the development of bilateral relations.[16] In addition, the visits paid by the Prime Minister, the State Secretary, and the Minister of Foreign Affairs of the Kazakhstan to Mongolia (1992-2006) and visits by the Prime Minister, the Deputy Prime Minister, the Head of the Administration of the President of Mongolia (1994-2007) to Kazakhstan played significant role in the development of political relations between the two countries. The parliamentary relations between Mongolia and Kazakhstan are also developing. In 2002, when Deputy Chairman of the *Majilis* of the Parliament of the Republic of Kazakhstan visited Mongolia a Protocol on cooperation between the two parliaments were signed. Similar protocol was signed in 2003 also when Mongolian Parliament Speaker visited Kazakhstan.[17]

Bilateral political relationship was further strengthened by the participation of a Mongolian delegation at the General Assembly of the International Conference of Asian Political Parties held in Kazakhstan's capital Astana on 24-25 September 2009. On 1-2 December 2010, the Vice-Speaker of the Parliament of Mongolia, G. Batkhuu, participated at the OSCE Summit in Astana. Kazakhstan and Mongolia conduct a favorable cooperation in the international arena which is evident from the fact that Mongolia is a full member of the CICA. Mongolia also supported the Kazakh initiative of declaring August 29 as an International Day against Nuclear Tests as per the resolution of the UN General Assembly. Since 1991, more than 40 bilateral treaties and agreements between the two counties have been signed.

Recently in May 2015, the ministries of foreign affairs of Kazakhstan and

Mongolia held political consultations for the first time during the visit of First Prime Minister of Kazakhstan Bakytzhan Sagintayev to Ulaanbaatar. The talks culminated in the signing of the bilateral cooperation plan for 2015-2016 by the First Deputy Minister of Foreign Affairs of Kazakhstan Rapil Zhoshybayev and Deputy Minister of Foreign Affairs of Mongolia Navaan-Yunden Oyundari.[18] On this occasion Oyundari stated the following:

> The relations with Kazakhstan are very important for the foreign policy of Mongolia. Our presidents recently met in Moscow on the occasion of the 70th anniversary of the Victory in the Great Patriotic War. The inter-parliamentary relations are developing. I express gratitude for the warm reception of the parliamentary group from Mongolia in Kazakhstan in February of this year. We also invite Kazakhstani parliamentarians to take part in the autumn session of the OSCE parliamentary Assembly in Ulaanbaatar on September 15-19.

The Mongolian minister also noted of having a great potential of cooperation between the two countries within the framework of multilateral structures and projects such as the SCO and building of developed infrastructure along the Silk Road. The Mongolian side also proposed to hold regular inter-ministerial seminars and roundtables on matters concerning regional and multilateral cooperation, exchange of specialists and starting of cooperation between diplomatic academies of the two countries. Thus the bilateral political relations between Mongolia and Kazakhstan are developing in a well planned manner.

Economic and Trade Cooperation

Beginning 1991 Kazakhstan has become one of the world's expanding petro-states. It has been estimated that if current development plans are implemented, Kazakhstan's existing 1.3 million barrels per day (BPD) output will rise to 2.7 million by 2020.[19] While the most of Kazakhstan's output is today shipped to the world market via the Caspian Pipeline Consortium line ending at Russia's Novorossiisk Black Sea port, Astana is also looking east for exports and trade, most notably with China, to which it currently exports about 400,000 BPD via a pipeline.[20] However, according to Day (2008), Kazakhstan is not limiting its eastward foreign and economic policies to China but has been expanding its ties with Mongolia.[21] The relations between Kazakhstan and Mongolia have not developed in a vacuum as the two nations already share their platform in the Shanghai Cooperation Organization (SCO).

Kazakhstan has been described as a "magnet" for foreign investment since 1991, attracting nearly US$40 billion, mainly in the energy sector.[22] Since 2000 it has been discreetly investing some of its surplus petroleum revenue in Mongolia in which a number of Kazakh companies are involved. Majority of these companies are involved in the production, service, geology and mining sectors of Mongolia.[23] In 2007, a delegation of Kazakh government officials led by E. Nigmatulin, the Chairman of Kazakhstan's Ministry of Industry and Trade Investment attended the opening of the Mongolian-Kazakh Business Forum in Ulaanbaatar. The two sides discussed the improvement of bilateral cooperation in the mining, banking and financial sectors as the existing bilateral trade volume remained low at about US$20 million per annum. The same year when Mongolian President Enkhbayar visited Kazakhstan the countries reportedly decided to work "on the possibility of drawing up a joint programme of investments by Kazakh investors in Mongolia's economy as well as on the supply of crude oil to Mongolia".[24]

Mongolia has always been interested in Kazakh investment in such sectors as mining, infrastructure, agriculture, housing construction and town planning in addition to working on the possibility of increasing the supply of wheat from Kazakhstan to Mongolia. During Enkhbayar's visit, the two countries also discussed the prospect of improving the level of the Mongolian exports of meat and agricultural products to Kazakhstan. The Kazakh President Nazarbayev expressed his willingness to import Mongolian ore for its metallurgical industrial unit.[25] Mongolia has also pursued Kazakhstan for its assistance in developing Mongolian oil and energy sector. Both sides are also involved in discussing Kazakh investment in constructing an electric power station to utilize Mongolia's Shivee Ovoo's coal deposits and a fifth thermo-electric power station in Ulaanbaatar.[26] The Mongolian government is optimistic that if it is successful in attracting Kazakh and foreign investment in its hydrocarbon industries, the country could fulfill its domestic demands for oil products in near future. Since 2007 Mongolia's energy sector has been able to raise foreign investment worth almost US$640 million. As of now Russia is the main supplier of oil products to Mongolia, accounting for about 90 per cent of total imports, while imports from Kazakhstan and China amount to only eight and two per cent respectively.[27]

Today, there are two main issues which are high on Mongolia's list of priorities that include establishing a joint investment fund and concluding an agreement on Kazakh wheat exports. However, despite the good intentions of Kazakhstan and Mongolia about increasing their trade ties, global influences outside their control are affecting their relations. Nevertheless, it seems likely that Mongolia will conclude its wheat agreement, as Kazakhstan is Central Asia's only grain exporter. Wheat is essential for Mongolia as for most of the last decade the country had suffered from drought, which had caused wheat shortages. As regards the trade between the two countries, in 2011 it amounted to US$ 19.2 million (imports of Mongolia was US$ 2.3 million, while exports to Kazakhstan was US$ 16.9 million). The turnover in 2012 further increased to US$ 21.7 million (imports to Mongolia was US$ 2.5 million, while exports to Kazakhstan was US$ 19.2 million). As of 2014, the volume of trade turnover between the two countries increased sharply to reach at US$ 58.9 million.[28] However, in order to expand their trade cooperation further both countries could prepare a list of goods and services that might be delivered. Moreover, Kazakhstan is going to host an International Exhibition "Expo-2017" in Astana, where Mongolia is willing to present itself at the highest level.

Cultural Ties

The cultural ties between Mongolia and Kazakhstan have been developing on the basis of a number of agreements signed between the two sides in the last 20 years. In accordance with the intergovernmental agreements in the field of education, annual student exchange programme between universities of the two countries is running successfully. A branch of the East Kazakhstan's State University was opened in Ulgii City, the administrative center of Bayan-Ulgii province, as per the joint decision of the Ministries of Education of Kazakhstan and Mongolia during 2001-2002. In order to study the monuments of ancient Turkic culture, history and culture of the Kazakh Diaspora in Mongolia, the Kazakh-Mongolian joint ethno-archaeological research expedition is also operational. Agreements on cooperation in education and a programme for cooperation in other areas of cultural field were also signed for the years 2009-2012.

Today, over 230 Mongolian youth study in different institutions in Kazakhstan.[29] Kazakhstan has agreed to continue these traditions as part of strengthening cultural and educational cooperation between the two countries. The most noteworthy agreement in the educational field has been on receiving in Kazakhstan 120 people of Mongolia's Bayan-Ölgii province annually to undertake study in construction, agricultural, farming, veterinary and service sectors. According to the intergovernmental agreement in the sphere of education, there is an annual exchange of students between of higher education institutions of the two countries.

The Kazakh diaspora in Mongolia is one of the major factors in the smooth conduct of Mongolia-Kazakhstan cultural ties. Besides, participation by the representatives of the two countries at various scientific conferences, symposia, art competitions and sports competitions in Kazakhstan and Mongolia on a permanent basis has become a regular feature.[30] Earlier, on 30-31 May 2012, Ch. Dambazhav, the head of the Monastery "Dashchoilin", Vice-President of the World Council of Buddhists and the President of the Conference of "Asian Buddhists for Peace", participated at the 4th Conference on "The World and Traditional Religions" held in Astana.[31] He was elected as a member of the Council of Religious Leaders as well.

Conclusion

Despite historically short and bad timing of transition to market-based economy, Mongolia-Kazakhstan relations have developed significantly for the last two decades. Mongolia regards Kazakhstan as a traditional partner and the people of the two countries are fraternal. They are inherits of nomadic civilizations. The two countries believe in preserving their national traditions and cultural heritage, and pay respect to human values in developing modern economy and culture. Both have sustainable conditions for further development of bilateral relations and collaboration as they follow similar positions to ensure regional and global security, regional integration and international cooperation on the basis of their respective foreign policy.

Today the two sides are cooperating each other in various areas of political economic and cultural fields including mining of Mongolian minerals and oil exploration. They are also cooperating each other at multilateral forums such as SCO. Mongolia is an observer at the SCO and Kazakhstan is supporting Mongolia to become a full member. The fact that Kazakh President Nursultan Nazarbayev visited Mongolia twice—first in 1993 and then in 2008 and more recently the First Prime Minister of Kazakhstan Bakytzhan Sagintayev visited Mongolia in May 2015 only point to Mongolia remaining as one of the important countries in Kazakhstan's foreign policy.

Notes and References

1. "Perspectives of Mongolia-Kazakhstan relations and cooperation until 2016 were considered", 28 May 2014, at http://vom.mn/d/5420 (accessed on 28 September 2014).

2. Adel E. Abbishev (2002), *Kazakhstan in Focus: Ten Years of Independence*, Almaty: Center for Foreign Policy and Analysis, p.129.
3. Ibid.
4. Zhulduz Baizakova (2015), "Kazakhstan's Foreign Policy: One for All, or All for One?", Eurasia Daily Monitor, vol. 12, Issue 18, 29 January, at http://www.jamestown.org/programs/edm/single/?tx_ttnews%5Btt_news%5D=43470&cHash=58815b454125efa5a316a132ab4f393b#.Vc-a6_mqqko (accessed on 12 March 2015).
5. Georgiy Voloshin (2014), "Kazakhstan Adopts New Foreign Policy Concept", The CACI Analyst, 5 February, at http://www.cacianalyst.org/publications/field-reports/item/12904-kazakhstan-adopts-new-foreign-policy-concept.html (accessed on 1o October 2014).
6. Ibid.
7. Sharad K Soni (2001), "Mongolia's Foreign Policy Priorities", *Himalayan and Central Asian Studies*, vol.1, no.1, January-March, p.61.
8. *Concept of Mongolia's Foreign Policy*, point 7, 21 February 2011, at http://www.mfa.gov.mn/en/index.php?option=com_content&view=article&id=80%3Aii-&catid=36%3A2009-12-20-21-52-14&Itemid=55&lang=en (accessed on 15 December 2014).
9. Ibid, point 8.
10. For a detailed analysis of Mongolia's foreign policy, see Sharad K Soni (2015), "The 'Third Neighbour' Approach of Mongolia's Diplomacy of External Relations: Effects on Relations between India and Mongolia", *India Quarterly*, vol. 71, no.1, January-March, pp.39-41.
11. See *Concept of Mongolia's Foreign Policy*.
12. National Statistical Office of Mongolia (2011), "Mongolia Population and Housing Census 2010: Main Findings", http://www.slideshare.net/Ochiro/mongolia-2010-population-census-main-findings (25 December 2014). For more detailed information on the main areas of Kazakh concentration in Mongolia, see Sharad K Soni (2010), "Post-Soviet Migration of Mongolian Kazakhs to Kazakhstan", in Anita Sengupta and Suchandana Chatterjee (eds.), *Eurasian Perspectives: In Search of Alternatives*, Delhi: Shipra Publications, pp.212-217.
13. See Kazakhstan Embassy in Mongolia, "Kazakhstan and Mongolia", at http://www.kazembassy.mn/en/content.php?id=20 (25 December 2014).
14. Ts. Baatar (2002), "Present Situation of Kazakh-Mongolian Community", The Mongolian Journal of International Affairs, nos. 8-9, p.95.
15. Ibid.
16. "President awarded highest Kazakhstan state award of Mongolia", *Kazakhstan Today*, 7 August 2008, at http://www.kt.kz/eng/president/kazakhstan_president_awarded_highest_state_award_of_mongolia_1153457183.html (28 December 2014).
17. Kazakhstan Embassy in Mongolia, "Kazakhstan and Mongolia".
18. Kazinform (2015), "Ministries of Foreign Affairs of Kazakhstan and Mongolia signed cooperation plan for 2015-2016", 26 May, at http://www.inform.kz/eng/article/2780245 (accessed on 30 May 2015).
19. John C.K. Daly (2008), "Kazakhstan and Mongolia Broaden Relations", *Eurasia Daily Monitor*, vol.5, Issue 74, 18 April, at http://www.jamestown.org/single/?tx_ttnews%5Btt_news%5D=33562#.VdDsSPmqqko (accessed on 28 December 2014).
20. Ibid.
21. Ibid.
22. Sharad K Soni (2013), "Kazakhstan-Mongolia Relations: Issues and Trends", in G. M.

Mir (ed.), *Globalizing Eurasia: Potentials and Challenges*, Srinagar: University of Kashmir, p.121.

23. *Montsame*, 15 April 2007.
24. See Daly, "Kazakhstan and Mongolia Broaden Relations".
25. *Interfax-Kazakhstan*, 14 August 2007.
26. Soni, "Kazakhstan-Mongolia Relations: Issues and Trends", p.121.
27. Wu Kang, Usukh Batsaikhan and Tsevegjav Bulganmurun, "Energy Cooperation in Northeast Asia: The Role of Mongolia", p.93, at http://www.apu.ac.jp/rcaps/uploads/fckeditor/publications/journal/RJAPS_V26_Wu_Usukh_Tsevegjav.pdf (accessed on 26 September 2014).
28. Kazinform, "Ministries of Foreign Affairs of Kazakhstan and Mongolia signed cooperation plan for 2015-2016".
29. Soni, "Kazakhstan-Mongolia Relations: Issues and Trends", p.122. For a detail analysis of Mongolia-Kazakhstan relations covering different aspects, see pp.113-132.
30. Kazakhstan Embassy in Mongolia, "Kazakhstan and Mongolia".
31. Ibid.

CHAPTER 20

Mongolia and India: A Strategic Partnership in the Making

Sharad K Soni

As Mongolia and India are going to celebrate 60 years of the establishment of their diplomatic relations on 24 December 2015, indications are high that the strategic partnership between the two countries is moving forward against a backdrop of growing Chinese influence in the Northeast Asian region. It was during the Indian Prime Minister Narendra Modi's May 2015 visit to Ulaanbaatar that both sides decided to elevate their ties to the level of strategic partnership.[1] Though such an elevation of bilateral ties from comprehensive partnership to a strategic partnership is influenced by several factors, India's willingness to have its presence felt in Northeast Asia is also a key aspect. This is more so because Northeast Asia is becoming a major factor in India's strategic vision in the East Asian region, especially after the 'Look East' policy was upgraded into a more action-oriented 'Act East' policy in November 2014.[2] On the other side, in the past few years there have been behavioural changes in the post-Soviet Mongolia's foreign policy that was adopted in 1994 when this young democratic country embarked on all kinds of reforms in its internal and external affairs. Since then it continued to pursue a policy of balancing the two giant geographic neighbours-Russia and China until the Mongolian Parliament approved an updated National Security Concept in June 2010 and a revised Foreign Policy Concept in February 2011. Both the documents redefined the new strategic direction of Mongolia's security and foreign policy. In particular, the new foreign policy strategy marked a clear shift from the existing policy that is now aimed at balancing China's growing influence, both in terms of strategic as well as economic, and thus China has covertly been identified as Mongolia's principal security concern.

Though the original concept of Mongolia's foreign policy known as a 'Multi-Pillar' foreign policy is still working at its full strength, it is presently laden with balance of influence behaviour aimed at China. Herein the "third neighbour" policy of Mongolia's diplomacy of external relations, particularly with the United States, Japan, South Korea and India holds its importance. In such a scenario, the equation that is emerging between Mongolia and India points to Ulaanbaatar's growing reliance on New Delhi to balance Chinese influence not only in Mongolia but also in the Northeast Asia as a whole. Counting on the "third neighbour" policy Mongolian strategic thinkers and policy makers consider India as an important country for developing a partnership that could include strategic elements and help work together in regional and sub-regional groupings. Similarly, Mongolia too is required in India's strategic imagination as a valuable balancer against China's increasing influence in South Asia. The two sides complement each other for being traditionally close due to cultural bonding based on Buddhism which is the biggest asset for building up their strategic partnership. It is in this context that this paper deals with the extent and pattern of relationship between Mongolia and India with a focus on the transition the two sides have made in their bilateral ties to reach the level of a strategic partnership. Besides, it also explores the prospects of strategic partnership between the two countries on the basis of developments taking place in the bilateral ties since Modi's visit to Mongolia.

Background

Despite geographical aloofness Mongolia and India have been in close contact due to their civilizational linkages spanning over a period of over 2500 years.[3] It was due to the advent of Buddhism that India was well known in the Mongolian steppe of Inner Asia long before the appearance of the Mongols into the historical arena. Buddhism that reached there through Central Asia from its original homeland in India played a significant role in the pre-Mongol period in bringing the ancient nomadic tribes that ruled the Mongol land to become familiar with the Indian culture. These linkages have not only been fascinating, intense and inseparable but have also gone beyond all human activities from language, literature, religion, medicine and folklore to culture and traditions. Such a legacy of traditional linkages based on Buddhism has provided room for regular interaction, assimilation and exchanges between the two countries. This resulted in establishing a very close and friendly relationship in contemporary times so much so that they are today known as "spiritual" neighbours. However, having identified itself more as a country belonging to the Northeast Asian region,[4] Mongolia has been in close contact with India not only on the basis of their traditional relationship but also on the basis of post-Cold War realities that have altered the geostrategic situation of Mongolia in particular and Northeast Asia in general. Yet, looking back in the past on the developments in the bilateral ties, especially since the establishment of diplomatic relations, one can gauge the level of "Trust" the two countries have for mutual benefits in diverse areas.

Prior to the establishment of diplomatic relations the first direct political contact between Mongolia and India came about a few months before India's independence, when a three-member Mongolian delegation participated in the First Asian Relations Conference held in New Delhi in March 1947. The main objective of holding this conference was to bring Asian nations together at a common platform and to understand their social, economic and political problems and also to promote cooperation among the people of Asia.[5] Since then the leadership of the two countries have been in constant contact with each other that led to the establishment of diplomatic relations between the two countries on 24 December 1955. India was not only the first country outside the then Socialist bloc to establish full diplomatic ties with Mongolia but also lent unwavering support to Ulaanbaatar's efforts of becoming a full-fledged member of the United Nations in 1961. Influenced by the historico-cultural bonds the political relationship between the two countries have always given due importance to their Buddhist connection. It is more so because Buddhism helped the nomadic Mongols become united and civilized so much so that it served the Mongols as a prime source of common identity. During the nineteenth and early twentieth centuries Buddhism also served as an effective instrument for whipping up the Mongol nationalism against more than 200 years of Manchu-Chinese domination. This resulted in the proclamation of Mongolia's independence in 1911 with Jebtsundamba Khutagt, the head of Mongolian Buddhist Church ascending the throne as Bogdo Khagan (Holy Emperor).[6] But Mongolia fell victim to Sino-Russian negotiations over its political status until 1921 when it was finally declared as an independent country following a revolution, though it existed as a "constitutional monarchy" till the demise of the Bogdo Khagan in 1924.[7] Since then it came to be known as the Mongolian People's Republic that was renamed as Republic of Mongolia after the new constitution came into force in 1992.

Irrespective of its political status in different span of time Mongolia's Buddhist identity has been the most obvious phenomenon in the history of Indo-Mongolian spiritual intercourse. One may ask as to why India is known as Mongolia's "spiritual neighbour." First of all the fact that India is the birthplace of Buddha provides enough reason for the Buddhist Mongolia to call India as its "spiritual neighbour." India is venerated in Mongolia not only as a "land of Buddha" and a "land of Dharma" but also as a country to which the Mongolian people attribute all that have been considered the highest attainments of wisdom and learning.[8] India is seen as such a divine place, where emphasis is given on Buddhist principles of denouncing anger and hatred, violence and rancor, apart from promoting universal peace and harmony through individual attainment of compassion and serenity.[9] The Mongolians call India by a special name, *Enetheg*.[10] The Mongolian translation of the two great collections of Indo-Buddhist works known as *Kanjur* (108 volumes) and *Tanjur* (226 volumes) is yet another evidence of spiritual linkages between India and Mongolia.

Secondly, the River Ganga is revered as sacred by the Mongolians in the same way as Indians do. For example, in Mongolia, anybody who keeps '*Gangajal*' (the holy water from River Ganga) at home is considered as the luckiest one. In fact, there is a group of lakes known as 'Ganga Lake', which is located in the eastern part of Mongolia, about 12 kms. from Dariganga *Sum* (county or district), in Sukhbaatar *aimag* (province). The legend has it that a long time back a man who was a native of Dariganga visited India. While returning back he brought with him holy water from the River Ganga, which he placed in the sand, thus the formation of Ganga Lake took place. This is the only group of lakes, which is located in desert and is considered as sacred by the people of Mongolia. And thirdly, Mongolian language has traditionally been enriched by a vast terminology and rich phraseology borrowed from Sanskrit. This is evident from the Mongolian script of *Soyombo* and Quadratic which were invented by Undur Gegen Zanabazar (1636-1723), the first Jebtsundamba Khutagt, to study Buddhism. The very word *Soyombo* is of Sanskrit origin, i.e., *svayambhu* which in a more precise term meaning 'self-being' (*svayam* means 'self' and *bhu* means 'being') or 'freedom'.[11] Though the script perished after a while, the first alphabet *Soyombo* to which the script owes its name became the national symbol of Mongolia signifying its independence and sovereignty even today.[12]

While Mongolia was embarking on a democratic transition after a peaceful revolution in 1989-90, a major development took place to strengthen not only Mongolia-India diplomatic relations but also their Buddhist linkages. This was the arrival of Ven. Kushok Bakula Rimpoche in Mongolia who became instrumental in the revival of Buddhism in this small country apart from deepening the cultural and spiritual ties between the two countries. In 1990, he was appointed as the Indian ambassador to Mongolia which lasted for more than 10 years until he retired in 2000. When he arrived, Mongolia was still a communist country but shortly afterwards he witnessed the transition to a democratic society where he could travel freely and work for the revival of Buddhism. He was credited with establishing monasteries and nunneries besides granting ordination to a number of Mongolians. He was often called "*Elchin Bagsha*", the teacher ambassador.[13] Such evidences of Mongolia-India spiritual linkages make it imperative for the two sides to cooperate each other in varied areas of mutual concerns in this era of globalization.

Post-Cold War Progress in Bilateral Ties

The progress in Mongolia-India bilateral ties in the post-Cold War period has largely been the result of the emergence of a democratic Mongolia which saw fresh developments in Ulaanbaatar's relations with the outside world. Basically, it was the new Mongolian constitution adopted in 1992 that brought to an end of Mongolia's legacy of dependence on Moscow, besides providing an opportunity to reach beyond geographic constraints to nurture relationships with countries far away. Consequently, in 1994, in order to refurbish its internal and external policies Mongolia adopted two foundational documents—Concept of National Security and Concept of Foreign Policy which articulated a policy of balance that is known as the 'third neighbour' policy. Even an updated Concept of National Security approved in July 2010 and a revised Concept of Foreign Policy ratified in February 2011 continued with giving much emphasis on 'third neighbour' policy, though a new element has been added, i.e., the balance of influence approach in Mongolia's diplomacy of external relations. Pursuing such a policy provided an impetus to the existing relations between Mongolia and India following the signing of a post-Cold War Treaty of Friendly Relations and Cooperation in 1994. A solid foundation was, thus, laid down for the development of bilateral relations as well as cooperation on mutually beneficial issues at the regional level.

Moreover, the beginning of 2001 set the tone for all round development in bilateral ties when the then Mongolian President N. Bagabandi visited India. The visit marked the signing of new agreements in areas of information technology, defence and legal matters. However, it was the issue of rise of international terrorism and religious fundamentalism that concerned the two sides most. In a joint declaration the two sides "condemned terrorism in all its forms, irrespective of political, philosophical, ideological, religious, ethnic, racial or any other consideration that may be invoked to justify them."[14] Even in 2004, when the then Prime Minister of Mongolia N. Enkhbayar paid an official visit to India, both the countries "strongly condemned the menace of international terrorism and its devastating effect on democratic societies, development and on human civilization itself."[15] Commonality of views on several regional and international issues resulted in the two countries' involvement in numerous activities in political, economic and cultural fields including the expansion of their existing defence ties. In December 2005, when Mongolia's Minister for Foreign Affairs, Ts. Munkh-Orgil, visited the two sides agreeing in principle to launch a new joint project for the establishment of a satellite-based e-network for tele-education and tele-medicine in Mongolia. It was stipulated that under this project, not only Mongolian educational institutions would be connected to Indian educational institutions through a dedicated satellite but also one or two Mongolian hospitals would be connected to Indian medical institutions. The project was initiated in order to "enable Mongolia to have direct access to quality education and medical services through use of modern technology."[16]

At the same time, both sides also agreed to strengthen cooperation in the field of agriculture by signing a MoU for the establishment of an India-Mongolia Friendship Agropark in Darkhan Uul *Aimag* (province) of Mongolia for Research and Demonstration. India decided to provide agricultural equipment, tractors and trucks, sprinkler irrigation system etc. to be used at this Agropark.[17] Other agreements included cooperation in the areas of solar electrification in rural areas of Mongolia as well as digitalization of precious Buddhist manuscripts preserved at Mongolian State Library. In order to reinforce cultural links between the two sides a Chair of Buddhist and Sanskrit Studies in the National University of Mongolia was also established in accordance with the bilateral agreement concluded in April 2006. As regards defence ties the two countries since 2001 have moved forward in the fields of training, bilateral visits and joint military exercises. India has been providing training facilities to Mongolian defence personnel in English language, peace keeping and military operations. The first joint military exercise was held in Mongolia in October 2004, while the second one took place in December 2005 at the Counter-Insurgency Jungle Warfare School at Vairangte, in India's north eastern state of Mizoram bordering Myanmar. Since 2010, this joint exercise began to be called 'Nomadic Elephant' which aims at sharpening their counter insurgency skills and enhancing their training infrastructure for UN peace keeping missions. The latest tenth joint exercise took place at Gwalior Military Cantonment from 23 January to 6 February 2015, which according to Brig SC Panwar of Indian Army, "has enhanced mutual interoperability for counter terrorism/ insurgency assignments under the United Nations mandate".[18] Since 2006 India has also been participating in the multinational peace keeping annual exercises in Mongolia called 'Khaan Quest' which has now become one of the signature training events for the participating nations. The latest Khaan Quest 2014 exercise has been the twelfth annual rehearsal that involved such segments as "Command Post Exercise, Field Training Exercise, Engineering Civil Action Program projects and a Cooperative Health Exchange.[19]

However, it was the visit of Mongolian President Ts. Elbegdorj to India in 2009 that Delhi found itself on the right track in the strategic imagination of Ulaanbaatar to emerge as Mongolia's "third neighbour" in the true sense. This is more so because Mongolia began to be considered as critical for India's Asian strategy that resulted in the two countries upgrading their bilateral ties to comprehensive partnership. Such a change in the extent and pattern of relationship between the two countries opened a new era in the contemporary history of their bilateral ties. Elbegdorj's visit, indeed, marked the signing of the first comprehensive partnership treaty to cooperate in developing Mongolian uranium mining by India with a MoU on the peaceful use of radioactive minerals and nuclear energy. Remarkably, mining has now become the backbone of the Mongolian economy by taking over animal husbandry of the 1990s, which offers enormous business opportunities to the outside world.[20] Given that India's own demand for imported natural resources multiplies manifold, Mongolia has been visualized as a natural and long-term economic partner. In 2010, while addressing members of the Southern India Chamber of Commerce and Industry (SICCI) in a bid to promote bilateral trade, the then Mongolian Ambassador to India, Voroshilov Enkhbold invited Indian businessmen to invest in priority sectors such as mining, healthcare,

ICT, tourism, entertainment, agriculture, oil and infrastructure that has not been tapped fully. Highlighting that the Mongolian government encourages investment in priority sectors and grants tax incentives to foreign direct investment, he said that "Indian businessmen investing in infrastructure will get income tax exemption for the first 10 years and 50 per cent tax relief for subsequent five years."[21]

Such an offer of incentives for Indian businessmen received further boost by a three-day state visit of the then Indian President Pratibha Devisingh Patil to Mongolia in 2011 which was hailed as one of the most significant developments in the existing state of relationship between the two countries. The visit was all the more important as Indian President toured this geostrategically important country after a gap of 23 years. During her visit to Mongolia the two sides recognised that due to joint efforts India-Mongolia bilateral relations intensified in political, security and defence fields and a good start of cooperation has been made in areas such as mining, minerals, business and investment. Both sides also agreed to encourage cooperation in the fields of nuclear energy, mining, agriculture, culture, education, health and science, in particular information technology and promote ties in social welfare, natural environment and between local governments. The three key documents then signed between the two sides included Defence Cooperation Agreement, MoU on Cooperation between Mongolia's Committee for National Development and Reforms and India's Planning Commission and MoU on Media Exchanges.[22] In 2013, another progress was made in the ever-growing relationship when India offered to cooperate with Mongolia in developing its renewable energy sector as well as in human resources development.

Quest for Developing Strategic Partnership

Recently, Mongolia's freedom of strategic choice has drawn attention to the commonality of interests with India, and hence the two countries have clearly defined their geostrategic interests.[23] India is being visualized as the fourth alternative for providing security and development in Mongolia, the first and second are the two geographical neighbours—Russia and China, while the third is believed to be the U.S. As China has been continuing as the largest trade partner of Mongolia it appears that to a large extent it has been able to fill the economic vacuum in Mongolia created due to the collapse of the former Soviet Union. Yet, as some analysts believe, Mongolia will have to keep a watch on the two geographical neighbours in order to ensure that it no longer faces the Cold War like situation. Chinese leadership, though, has been repeatedly saying that "China will never be a military threat to any nation".[24] Russia, on the other hand, seems to be not in a position to provide the protective shield similar to that it had earlier in Mongolia.[25] Japanese and western interests are limited mainly to economic interests due to Mongolia's rich natural resources. But interestingly, as mentioned above the U.S. is being treated as Mongolia's principal "third neighbour" country.[26] Nevertheless, Mongolia appears to be in a serious dilemma of how to continue forging value based relations with the United States without jeopardizing its increasingly important economic ties with China. In such a scenario, what Mongolia and India need to do is to develop their strategic partnership that the two sides agreed to obligate during Modi's visit to Mongolia in May 2015.

Evidently, in a joint statement issued on 17 May 2015 during Modi's visit, the Prime Ministers of both India and Mongolia confirmed that developing a strategic partnership, which is guided by the universally recognized principles of sovereign equality of states, the principles of the United Nations Charter, collective interests of the two peoples and the fundamental ideals of the 1994 Treaty of Friendly Relations and Cooperation and other bilateral documents, would be their common yet a new objective of their respective foreign policies.[27] India also announced a US $1 billion credit line to Mongolia for infrastructure development as part of its quest for developing strategic partnership with Mongolia. The two sides further agreed to deepen defence cooperation besides exploring potential for tie-ups in areas like the civil nuclear sector. Lack of technical knowhow for the exploitation of Mongolia's vast uranium reserves (68,000 tons) is a major concern for Ulaanbaatar, and that is where India could be an important partner in view of its experience with nuclear energy.[28]

In order to develop a strategic partnership the two sides also put forward frameworks for future cooperation during Modi's visit to Mongolia and signed the following bilateral documents:[29]

1. Air Services Agreement;
2. Treaty on the Transfer of Sentenced Persons;
3. Agreement on Cooperation in the Field of Animal Health and Dairy;
4. Memorandum of Understanding on Cooperation in the field of Traditional Systems of Medicine and Homeopathy;
5. Memorandum of Understanding on the establishment of Cyber Security Training Centre in the Ministry of Defence of Mongolia;

6. Memorandum of Understanding on the establishment of India-Mongolia Joint Friendship School in Mongolia;
7. Programme on cooperation in the field of Culture for the period 2015-2018;
8. Memorandum of Understanding for cooperation between the National Security Council of India and National Security Council of Mongolia;
9. Memorandum of Understanding on cooperation between Ministry of External Affairs of India and Ministry of Foreign Affairs of Mongolia;
10. Memorandum of Understanding between Ministry of New and Renewable Energy of India and Ministry of Energy of Mongolia;
11. Memorandum of Understanding between Ministry of Home Affairs of India and Ministry of Justice of Mongolia for enhancing cooperation in Border Guarding, Policing and Surveillance;
12. Memorandum of Understanding between Tata Memorial Centre of India and National Cancer Center of Mongolia for gifting of Bhabhatron-II Tele-therapy Unit along with a Radiotherapy Simulator; and
13. Memorandum of Understanding between Foreign Service Institute of Ministry of External Affairs of India and Diplomatic Academy of Ministry of Foreign Affairs of Mongolia.

While these agreements and MoUs will help build confidence for a more convenient relationship, the two countries can ponder over various alternatives to expand their economic and trade ties as well, especially when India has made commitments to continue supporting Mongolia's endeavour to create a business friendly foreign investment regime. But it will also be kept in mind that Mongolia is landlocked between China and Russia, and so goods have to be shipped through ports in China or Russia which increases freight rates and also delay in delivery schedule. This has been the prime reason for India and Mongolia not being able to develop their bilateral trade to the desired extent. Even so Mongolia's rich mineral deposits, including radioactive minerals, could help power India's low-carbon growth, while India could help Mongolia in developing indigenous capabilities and economic opportunities in the mining sector.[30] Given the huge potential to collaborate in the agriculture sector, the two sides can foster deeper and closer cooperation in animal husbandry, production of dairy products, sharing of expertise and know-how, technology transfer and other forms of cooperation in an effort of developing their strategic partnership.

Conclusion

Today India being the "spiritual home" in the eyes of the Mongolians and over 80 per cent of them following Buddhism offer a unique opportunity for both sides to further strengthen their civilizational bonds. India has come a long way since 1955 when it became the first country outside the Soviet bloc to establish diplomatic relations with Mongolia. In the post-Cold War period, Mongolia is considered to be critical for what several analysts describe "a rising India's Asian strategy". This Asian strategy has now been focussing on India's extended neighbourhood policy, particularly in East Asia and Central Asia. Indeed, the recent push to boost India-Mongolia relations owes much to Ulaanbaatar's 'third neighbour' policy and is driven by strategic concerns. Since Mongolia has been described by the Indian Prime Minister Narendra Modi as "an integral part of India's Act East Policy",[31] New Delhi has been patiently expanding its defence and security links with Ulaanbaatar as part of an effort to build strategic ties with China's neighbours. The Northeast Asian identity of Mongolia together with socio-economic and political ties with other countries particularly in Asia generates much scope for further expansion and concretization of Indo-Mongolian cooperation in various sectors.

Evidently, there is a commonality of views between the two countries on several regional and multilateral issues. They are committed to enhance their cooperation on these issues, particularly those related to peace and stability in the Asia-Pacific region, including through enhanced interaction at multilateral forums such as the ASEAN Regional Forum (ARF) and the Asia Europe Meeting (ASEM). India's ongoing role in East Asia, which includes both the Southeast Asia as well as Northeast Asia may have far reaching consequences to the extent of benefiting Mongolia so far as issue of regional cooperation is concerned. Obviously, Mongolia could seek India's support and certainly in view of the recent developments in their relations due to the upgradation of bilateral ties to strategic partnership, it seems possible in all sense. There is ample space for the strategic partnership to further consolidate. This is more so because the strategic partnership between the two countries is certainly part of the current transformation of the East Asian order, and India will not let loose opportunity to make its vibrant presence in the region with one more reliable partner like Mongolia.

Notes and References

1. The significance of Narendra Modi's visit to Ulaanbaatar lies in the fact that he has been the first Indian Prime Minister to undertake a trip to Mongolia and also the first Indian leader to address the Mongol Great *Khural* (Parliament) on 17 May 2015. Even after sharing stronger ties no Indian Prime Minister before him has ever visited the mineral rich Mongolia.
2. On 12 November 2014, in his opening statement at the 12th ASEAN summit held in Myanmar's capital Naypyidaw, Prime Minister Narendra Modi unveiled India's plan to scale up its 'Look East' policy to an upgraded 'Act East Policy'. He said that "... the intensity and (the) momentum with which we have enhanced our engagement in the East, is a reflection of the priority that we give to this region... A new era of economic development, industrialization and trade has begun in India. Externally, India's 'Look East Policy' has become 'Act East Policy'." See Anil Sasi (2014), "'Look East' has become 'Act East Policy', says PM Modi at ASEAN summit", *The Indian Express,* 13 November, at http:// indianexpress.com/article/india/india-others/look-east-has-become-act-east-policy-pm-modi-at-asean/ (accessed on 15 January 2015).
3. More detailed explanation of this aspect can be found in author's own article appeared earlier in June 2009 Issue of *Mongolian & Tibetan Quarterly*. Some of the portions in this paper have also been taken from the same article. See Sharad K Soni (2009), "India-Mongolia Relations: Implications for Regional Cooperation in North East Asia", *Mongolian & Tibetan Quarterly* (Taipei), vol.18, no.2, pp.50-65.
4. For more on identity issues of Mongolia, see Tsedendamba Batbayar (2002), "Mongolia's New Identity and Security Dilemmas", *The Mongolian Journal of International Affairs* (Ulaanbaatar), nos.8-9, pp.3-11.
5. Sharad K. Soni (1990), *Mongolia-India Relations (1955-1989),* Unpublished Dissertation, Submitted to Jawaharlal Nehru University for the award of M.Phil degree, New Delhi, p.5.
6. Tsedendambyn Batbayar and Sharad K Soni (2007), *Modern Mongolia: A Concise History,* New Delhi: Pentagon Press, p.15. The new State came to be known as "Empire of Mongolia" but soon the independence of Mongolia was replaced by the autonomy under Chinese suzerainty in accordance with the Sino-Russian-Mongolian treaty of Kiakhta (1915). After it declared its independence in 1921 a new era began in Mongolia's history with communist party ruling the country until the Soviet collapse in 1991 which paved the way for the country's transition to democracy. For more details, see Sharad K Soni (2002), *Mongolia-Russia Relations: Kiakhta to Vladivostok,* Delhi: Shipra, pp. 12-38; 46-57; 217-231.
7. Buyantyn Dashtseren (1997), *The History and Culture of Mongolia*, Calcutta: The Asiatic Society, p.32.
8. Vasanta Iyer, "Cultural Perspectives in Modern Mongolia," in K. Warikoo and Dawa Norbu, eds. (1992), *Ethnicity and Politics in Central Asia*, New Delhi: South Asian Publishers, p.268.
9. *Ibid*, p. 267.
10. Dashtseren, *The History and Culture of Mongolia*, p.68.
11. Lokesh Chandra (2000), "Soyombo and Svayambhu: Evidence of Ancient Ties between India and Mongolia", in O Nyamdavaa and Gurdeep Singh (eds.), *Mongolia and India: Spiritual Neighbours*, New Delhi: Himala Publishers, p.2. According to Lokesh Chandra,

"the Mongolian flag *soyombo* is the Buddhist *svayambhu* with its extraordinary array of mystic symbols arranged vertically."

12. A few scholars are also of the opinion that the symbol of *Soyombo* is based on Vedic thoughts. During his period the Mongolian language and literature borrowed heavily from Indo-Tibetan literature including the Vedic philosophy. See Gauri Shankar Gupta, "India and Mongolia", in K. Warikoo and Sharad K. Soni, eds. (2010), *Mongolia in the 21st Century: Society, Culture and International Relations,* New Delhi and London: Pentagon, pp.108-109.
13. Amitava Dutta (2003), "The Venerable Kushok Bakula", *Bharat Rakshak Monitor*, vol. 6, no. 3, November-December.
14. Sharad K Soni (2001), "Editor's Page", *Himalayan and Central Asian Studies*, vol. 4, no.1, p. 2.
15. See "Visit of Prime Minister of Mongolia, January 14-20, 2004", at http://www.meaindia.nic.in/pressrelease/2004/01/16pr01.htm (accessed on 25 June 2013).
16. Yogeshwar Varma (2007), "India-Mongolia Relations," *Indian Studies in Mongolia* (Ulaanbaatar), no.1, p.18.
17. *Ibid.*
18. Press Information Bureau, Government of India, Ministry of Defence, "Tenth India-Mongolia Joint Exercise Culminates", 6 February 2015, at http://pib.nic.in/newsite/PrintRelease.aspx?relid=115231 (accessed on 28 April 2015).
19. In addition to the U.S., Mongolia and India the other nations participated in "Khaan Quest 2014" included Australia, Bangladesh, Belarus, Canada, China, Czech Republic, France, Germany, Hungary, India, Indonesia, Japan, Mongolia, Nepal, Pakistan, Poland, Republic of Korea, Russia, Singapore, Tajikistan, Thailand, Turkey, and the United Kingdom. In terms of importance the Khaan Quest "enables opportunity for international peacekeepers to share their knowledge and experience in peacekeeping operations, execution techniques, learned lessons, and real-life practices among the Soldiers." See Ankit Panda (2014), "Mongolia Hosts Exercise Khaan Quest 2014", *The Diplomat*, 1 July, at http://thediplomat.com/2014/07/mongolia-hosts-exercise-khaan-quest-2014/ (accessed on 28 April 2015).
20. Sharad K. Soni (2015), "The 'Third Neighbour' Approach of Mongolia's Diplomacy of External Relations: Effects on Relations between India and Mongolia", *India Quarterly*, vol. 71, no. 1, p. 45.
21. *The Hindu*, 8 October 2010.
22. The Office of the President of Mongolia, Public Relations & Communications Division, 'President Elbegdorj and President Patil participate in signing documents on bilateral ties and cooperation', 28 July 2011, at http://www.president.mn/eng/newscenter/viewnews.php?newsid=577 (accessed on 11 August 2013).
23. Back in 1999, an analyst was of the opinion that Mongolia and India could define their geostrategic interests. See Ranjan Gupta (1999), "India and Mongolia: A Geostrategic Perspective", *Regional Security Issues and Mongolia* (Ulaanbaatar), no.6, p.30.
24. In 2008, during a speech delivered at Tokyo's Waseda University, the then Chinese President Hu Jintao ruled out any possibility of China becoming a "military threat to any country." He said, "China will never seek hegemony or territorial expansion", adding that "peaceful development is the strategic choice of the Chinese government and its people." See Chong Zi and Qin Jize, "President Hu Pledges Peaceful Development," at http://www.chinadaily.com.cn//china/2008-5/09/content_6672143.htm (17 April 2013).

25. Gupta, "India and Mongolia", p. 30.
26. A well-known analyst, however, believes that no American official today will declare that the US is willing to protect Mongolia from any enemies, see Alicia Campi, "Mongolia in North East Asia—The New Realities", *The Mongolian Journal of International Affairs* (Ulaanbaatar), no.12, 2005, p.51.
27. Ministry of External Affairs, Government of India, "Joint Statement for India-Mongolia Strategic Partnership (May 17, 2015)", 17 May 2015, http://mea.gov.in/bilateral-documents.htm?dtl/25253/Joint+Statement+for+IndiaMongolia+Strategic+Partnership+May+17+2015 (accessed on 22 July 2015).
28. Soni, "The 'Third Neighbour' Approach of Mongolia's Diplomacy of External Relations", p.47.
29. See Ministry of External Affairs, Government of India, "Joint Statement for India-Mongolia Strategic Partnership (May 17, 2015)".
30. "PM Narendra Modi asks Mongolia to partner in India's economic transformation," *The Economic Times*, 17 May 2015, http://articles.economictimes.indiatimes.com/2015-05-17/news/62276881_1_chimed-saikhanbileg-ulan-bator-mongolian (accessed on 22 July 2015).
31. "India grants $1 billion credit to Mongolia; deepens defence ties", 18 May 2015, at http://www.business-standard.com/article/pti-stories/india-grants-usd-1-bln-credit-to-mongolia-deepens-defence-ties-115051700274_1.html (accessed on 22 July 2015).

Index